D1158396

PERSONALITIES AND EVENTS

IN JEWISH HISTORY

PERSONALITIES
AND EVENTS
IN JEWISH HISTORY

by

CECIL ROTH

PHILADELPHIA

The Jewish Publication Society of America

1961 — 5721

PHILLIPS MEMORIAL
LIBRARY
PROVIDENCE COLLEGE

DS
119
R78

Copyright, 1953, by

The Jewish Publication Society of America

All rights reserved — no part of this book may be reproduced in any form without permission in writing from
the publisher except by a reviewer who wishes to
quote brief passages in connection with a review
written for inclusion in magazine or newspaper.

Second Impression, 1961

 1

Library of Congress Catalog Card Number: 53-7602

Manufactured in the United States of America

PREFACE

THIS volume contains a selection of the articles and essays on historical subjects which I have published in the course of the past quarter of a century. Some of them were contributed to the so-called "scientific" periodicals and deal with unexplored paths of study; others were "popular" surveys or revaluations; a few were prepared for public delivery and in spite of pruning may still show a rhetorical tendency. Ideas which I first developed in certain of the papers helped me when in due course I tried to understand and to present Jewish history from a wider perspective; while others were in due course summarized in a few lines, or even a few words, in my later writing. These are, in fact, selections of the raw material ("Chips from an historical workshop," one might call them) used in my subsequent books and monographs.

A number of the essays have been selected without any ulterior motive, simply for the sake of picturesqueness. A good many of the most colorful deal with Italy, my first love; none with Anglo-Judaica, to which I hope to devote one day a similar volume. I am dealing with some of these topics afresh, and on the basis of a fuller study of the source material, in a forthcoming book on the Jews and the Renaissance.

Owing to the long period of time over which these essays were composed, and the different purposes and publics for which they were written, differences of style and outlook are inevitable. I have modified these to some extent in preparing the volume for the press. If my writing has meanwhile lost some of its vivacity, that must be reckoned the penalty, not only of years, but also of University teaching.

On the other hand, in revising these essays for the press, I have become acutely conscious that a good many of them show clearly that they were written in a different age from the present—perhaps only a decade back, but separate from today by an aeon of change. Apart from the world-cataclysm, the ultimate results of which it is impossible yet to evaluate, two tremendous events in Jewish history have happened during the past ten years. One is the annihilation of the great mass of European Jewry. Not only six million human beings, but an entire historical epoch came to an agonizing end in the gas-chambers of Auschwitz and Birkenau. On the other hand, when I wrote, Zionism was a theory, and Jewish Palestine an experiment; today, the theory has justified itself (it is not I think wrong to say, has been compelled by events to justify itself) and Jewish Palestine is a reality. Everything in Jewish writing that bears the slightest relation to actuality must necessarily reflect this utter revolution in Jewish life and thinking and being; and the reader is begged to make allowance for this.

He must, moreover, realize that the implications, direct or indirect, are far wider than might appear at the first glance. I have repeatedly referred, for example, to European civilization: is it proper to think in such terms after what was permitted to happen in Europe between 1939 and 1945? I have spoken of potential services of European Jewry in the future: but in much of Europe, Jewish life is now nothing more than a charnel-house memory. I alluded with horror to the excesses in Italy in 1797, when perhaps a couple of dozen persons were killed; but, on a single day in 1943, over one thousand Jews were deported by the Nazis from Rome alone to a horrible fate in the gas-chambers of Poland. This is not a mere matter of detail. In a couple of essays which I published in the nineteen-thirties—*Persecution or Economics? The True Cause of Jewish Migration;* and *The*

Most Persecuted People?—I initiated I think the wider reaction against what has been termed the "lachrymose" interpretation of Jewish history. I still think that I was right at the time when I wrote. But I could not republish these articles now, after massacres a hundred times greater in magnitude than any recorded in the past have been perpetrated before our eyes, the balance of the Jewish population in the world has been catastrophically changed in consequence, and the numerically greatest as well as the most cultured of all Jewish communities have been wiped out by that human brutality which I had deliberately previously discounted. I could not have imagined, when I wrote my somewhat nostalgic picture of the burning of the ghetto gates, with which this volume closes, that I would myself see the renewal of the ghetto—not as a mere social institution, but as an antechamber to the extermination camps.

Even in lands which escaped the Nazi devastation, conditions have altered during the past twenty years. It is absurd for us to imagine that, since Hitler set up anti-semitism as a major political and social issue, on the national and international stage, our position in any land is precisely the same as it was. An incidental result is that the loss of Jewish identity is, to say the least, not so easy (or in the case of many persons so desirable) a process as it was a generation ago. This change of atmosphere has been reinforced by the emergence of the State of Israel, which has had a powerful influence on Jews everywhere. It was I thought obvious when I carried out a lecture tour in the United States in 1949, after an absence of some twelve years, that since my last visit the Jewish consciousness, especially among the younger generation, had become far stronger and more healthy than it had been formerly. At the time when I wrote most of these essays, conditions were different.

All these alterations in atmosphere and circumstances cannot fail to become apparent from time to time to the reader; and it may perhaps be salutary for him to be reminded of the reason.

In re-editing the "scientific" essays, a majority of the footnotes and references have been omitted; any person therefore who wishes to find the authority for statements made, or to obtain guidance for further information, or to ascertain the structure of my hypotheses, must have recourse to the original sources. If this results in introducing some students to the superb collections of the *Jewish Quarterly Review* or the *Revue des Etudes Juives*, the publication of this volume will have been doubly justified.

It remains for me to express my thanks to the various periodicals in which these essays were originally published for their generous permission to republish them in the present volume.

Cecil Roth.

Many of these essays—especially those of a more popular type—were republished (occasionally without the author's knowledge) in periodicals, Trans- or Cis-Atlantic, other than those in which they first appeared, and no record was kept. Hence the bibliographical references given are not complete. Some of the material now appears in English for the first time. There has been a fair amount of revision throughout, in points both of fact and of style, but no attempt has been made to carry this out exhaustively. In a few cases, the titles have been changed.

CONTENTS

PERSONALITIES AND EVENTS

IN JEWISH HISTORY

1. PARALLEL AND PARADOX IN JEWISH HISTORY[1]

i

IN MY study in London, before I left to collaborate in
the Menorah School held in New York one summer,
some years ago, I was preparing my inaugural address. I
phrased the exordium in the style which I felt to be properly
indicated for such an occasion. I drew attention, with the
platitudinous pomposity pardonable (or at least pardoned)
in a transatlantic visitor, to the vastness of the Jewish
population of New York—greater by far than that of any
other city of the modern world and exceeding by many
times any agglomeration of Jews that has ever been found
in one single spot of the earth's surface since Jewish history
began. I dilated upon the new conditions which had been
brought about by this vast concentration and by the un-
paralleled migration which had brought it about. I called
attention to the decay of old prejudices, to the establishment
of more intimate relations between the Christian and the
Jew, and to the new tolerance in which the rising generation
can participate. I expatiated upon the problems of the new
age, faced with new conditions and new questionings, and
no longer trammeled by the tradition of the past. I spoke
of the new developments—religious, social and cultural—
which recent years had witnessed and of the inevitable call
for adjustment. I touched upon the novel type of spiritual
leader which the New World had produced. I enlarged, in

---

[1] Revised form of the opening address delivered before the Menorah
Summer School in New York in July 1930, and published in the *Menorah
Journal*, vol. XVIII, pp. 15-26.

a word, with a careful marshaling of all of the providential commonplaces which seemed adapted to the circumstances, upon the utter uniqueness of the present situation in the New World, preparatory to launching out on my main theme.

As I arrived at this point, I felt a still, small voice disturbing my complacency. Whenever I embark in the course of my writing upon an unusually specious generalization, or conclude a passage with some trite rhetorical peroration, I find this uncomfortable companion disturbing me, urging me to tear it up and write something sensible for a change. It is my Historical Conscience.

"Oh, do go away," said I, with some annoyance. "I am engaged upon a very important piece of work."

My uncomfortable companion persisted.

"What is the matter now?" I inquired.

"Everything," replied my Historical Conscience, concisely.

"What do you mean?" said I. "Can you deny the facts that I have stated? I have compiled this survey of conditions in New York with the utmost care. I have consulted for my data the *American Hebraite,* various *Jewish Year Books,* and the published sermons of a popular rabbi—a cumulative value, as you know very well, considerably superior in these enlightened days to that of the Bible. What authority have you got to challenge their statements?"

"Oh, nothing much," said my Historical Conscience. "Only that of a good-for-nothing pseudo-historian named Cecil Roth." And I felt myself impelled to go to my file and take out of it the manuscript of a newly completed work upon the history of the Jews in Venice. There, in the chapter entitled "Life in the Ghetto," I found the following passage:[2]

---

2 Slightly modified in the version actually published.

[In the Venetian Ghetto] relations with the outside world, whether amatory, social or literary, were close and constant. Rabbis had begun to speak of Jesus as one of the Jewish prophets, while Gentiles on their side flocked to hear the sermons in the synagogues. Pietists complained how Hebrew culture was neglected in favor of Italian. Ignorance of the sacred tongue was so far spread that there was a movement for prayers in the vernacular. The spirit of reform was rife. There was a strong current of opposition to the Talmud and talmudic literature. Works were written attacking Jewish tradition, evoking a whole literature in Hebrew, Italian and Spanish in its defence. The ceremonial laws were not infrequently neglected. Ingenious arguments were put forward in favor of going in a gondola, or even riding, upon the Sabbath day. Mystical tendencies, and the miraculous stories attached to them, were openly scoffed at. The nineteenth century was anticipated in the disputes concerning the introduction of instrumental music in the synagogues. We even find the phenomenon of the card-playing rabbi, more concerned with explaining Judaism to the Christian than with teaching it to the Jew. Literary and intellectual life, though centered in Hebrew studies, was by no means confined to them. We find vernacular playwrights, apologists, astronomers, mathematicians and economists vying in activity. From that day to this, it is doubtful whether so surprisingly modern an atmosphere has ever at any other time prevailed in Jewish life.

ii

My perusal of this passage set me meditating. From seventeenth-century Italy I was carried back in imagination five or six centuries further, to Cordova in the age of the Caliphs. There I found an essential similarity to conditions of today which was in many ways more striking still than that which the Venetian ghetto had provided. The Moslem Empire was, at that time, the center of the world's civilization. A traveler who went from Paris to Cordova made the acquaintance of a higher civilization, just as one does who goes from Cairo to Paris today. There was a world-language and a world-culture quite as specious and as compelling as the Anglo-Saxon culture of the twentieth century. Every man who had the slightest pretension to education knew Arabic, which was more necessary by far than, say, English is under similar circumstances at the present time. Accordingly, Jewish authors who wished to reach the enlightened world wrote their works in that language, utterly neglecting Hebrew. Even the minority who remained faithful to their ancestral tongue were influenced by the models and inspiration of their environment to an extent far greater than is the case with Hebraists in any part of the world today. Arabic had indeed become a semi-sacred medium. Its position was fully comparable to Yiddish of half a century ago, with the significant difference that it was used to some extent even in religious worship, and trespassed upon Hebrew as the medium for so characteristic a function as the composition of rabbinic *responsa*.

As for the Jewish observances, they were on the downward grade. Eminent rabbinical authorities in France of the period of the Second Crusade give evidence that, fifty years before, the practice of affixing the *mezuzah* on the doorposts had been virtually unknown; while in Spain a visiting scholar found to his horror that the most complete ignorance prevailed with regard to the custom of wearing phylacteries. It is true that Darwin and Darwinism were not yet thought of. However, their place was anticipated by Averroës and the Aristotelian philosophy which he taught. Just as our spiritual leaders of today and yesterday apologetically attempted to find Evolution indicated, or at least indicable, in the Bible, so Maimonides and his generation succeeded in proving, to their perfect satisfaction, that the

Bible harmonized admirably with Philosophy, as then conceived. The perfect balance between Judaism and secular culture seemed at last to have been established.

This ideal state of affairs lasted for only a very short period—short, at least, in comparison with the enormous antiquity of the Jewish people. Before long it became manifest that the glittering culture of the Moslems was not destined to prevail. Aristotle, as Averroes had interpreted him, had after all not said the last word in human knowledge. Arabic was not always to remain the medium of polished intercourse throughout the world. This epoch passed entirely away; and those who had pinned themselves to it found themselves in a backwater, neglected by the tide of progress in Jewish life. The theories and reconciliations which seemed so apt and so durable in their day have joined so many of their precursors in the limbo where such things finally come to rest. Those works written in the polished vernacular of the age in order to reach the widest circle of readers and to ensure their durability have been lost, except in those cases where their immortality was ensured by a providential translation into Hebrew, however inelegant. It was fortunate that there had been a residuum of the Jewish people, long despised as obscurantist, which had been left untouched by the specious tide of progress and which continued its life almost unaffected by the rise and fall of Arab culture. Thus Judaism overrode the disaster, and the Jew pursued his way.

iii

This, however, is by no means the closest parallel in our history to problems and conditions of today. For that, we must go back ten centuries further still, to the age of Hellenism. If a New York Jew of today could be miraculously transported back into the Alexandria of nineteen or twenty centuries ago, he would find the general atmosphere familiar down to almost the last detail. The city contained perhaps some one hundred thousand Jews at this period—not so many, of course, as New York does now, but approximately in the same proportion to the general population, of which they formed (it is believed) about one third. Indeed, the number definitely exceeded the Jewish population of any city of Europe or America until perhaps half a century ago, and that of all but perhaps twelve places (half of which are in the United States of America) today.

Alexandria was, like New York, a comparatively new city. It was an artificial creation: a colony originally erected in foreign, "barbaric" territory, which had rapidly developed into the greatest seaport and one of the greatest cultural centers of its day. If straight streets and town-planning on the rectangular style lead to any intellectual reaction, that must have been common to the lot of the ancient Alexandrian and the modern New Yorker.

In this setting, a life indistinguishable in essentials from that of this most modern city of the modern world was evolved. It was an age when Hebraic culture was in utter decadence. The last word in human knowledge seemed at this time to have been expressed in the current Greek philosophy, with which Hebraism had to be reconciled if it were to retain any permanent value. The use of Greek alone was fashionable. In order to have a chance in the world, Jewish literature had to be produced in the vernacular. Modern phenomena, such as religious reform, social climbing, assimilation and scientific antisemitism, were rampant. When spirituality sought its material expression, it was in much the same way as today. The synagogues were huge. I cannot help thinking that the trustees of certain recent structures in New York must feel a little envious when they read of that extraordinary Alexandrian place of worship so vast that the beadles had to signal with flags in order to indicate to the worshipers that the time had come to say Amen (unless the hum of conversation and not the size of the edifice was responsible for this need). The congregants were Jews of a sort with whom we of today would have much in common. We are informed that there were many who forgot their Judaism from one year's end to the other, recollecting it only on the occasion of the Day of Atonement, when they crowded the synagogues and sought pardon for their sins. The time-honored Palestinian names were replaced by flashy Greek equivalents. Ignorance of Hebrew was general. The Bible was familiar only in a faulty Greek translation, the errors in which occasionally caused some perplexity to earnest inquirers. The New Translation of the Holy Scriptures recently produced in the United States in order to oust the venerable Authorized Version from Jewish homes was anticipated long before by Aquila, whose deliberately harsh Greek rendering was intended to perform the same unkind office for the Septuagint. So far had Hebrew become forgotten that it did not figure even on the tombstones, with the exception, sometimes, of the ancient greeting *Shalom*—"Peace." And, if you visit some of our modern cemeteries, you will find that it is precisely this familiar word that is seized upon for the identical purpose by Jews ignorant of Hebrew today.

The literature which was produced—without exception, in Greek—was incredibly modern in tone. A whole library of works—expository, apologetic and belletristic, without counting translations—was offered to the attention of the cultured world. There were anticipations of Graetz, of Mendelssohn, of Zangwill, of Houston Stewart Chamberlain; and all imagined that, by writing in Greek and not in Hebrew, they were assured of immortality. There were historians, nationalist and assimilationist. There were philosophers who endeavored to prove that Judaism was rational, and antiquarians who discovered that it anticipated all that was best in Hellenic lore. There were dramatists who elaborated biblical themes for their plots—the precursors of the historical novelists of today. There were nationalists who attacked Judaism, and apologists who defended it. It would hardly surprise me to find that there was an Alexandrian Jewish Publication Society to foster Jewish literature, or a journal to present it in periodical form.

Communal organization was no less familiar. There were Ethnarchs and Councillors and Elders and Fathers of the Synagogue. There was (if we may assume that the analogy of Rome was valid for Egypt too) a feminist movement, which resulted in the appointment of the female counterparts of this last office at least, who were perhaps the heads of the ladies' organizations attached to the synagogues. There were separate congregations established for those who hailed from different places in the "old country," with intense rivalries between them. There was, probably, an Alexandrian Jewish Committee which was prepared on occasion to send delegations abroad for the defense of Jewish rights. Since there were Jews, there were, inevitably, antisemites. Need I add, to complete the picture, that the latter were recruited sometimes from the Jewish ranks? A notorious case was Tiberius Alexander, nephew to the great Philo, whose father was Alabarch of Alexandrian Jewry, and who acted as Chief of Staff to Titus during the siege of Jerusalem.

The brand of Judaism which was practiced was one which would be more familiar to us than to any generation that has intervened. Reform was rampant. Even the spiritual leaders, if we may take Philo for an example, were entirely

ignorant of Hebrew. They had only a slight acquaintance
with the living Jewish tradition as developed in Palestine,
close at hand though it was. They made up for it, however,
by a minute acquaintance with Greek literature, especially
with the contemporary drama; and they were familiar figures
at the theater. If they were conversant with the Bible, it
was in the Greek version: and this constituted it seems the
whole of their knowledge of the basic Jewish literature.
This did not, to be sure, narrow their outlook. It served
them mainly as the text about which to group their ethical
discourses. The fashionable doctrines of the time were
those of Plato. Just as ten centuries later the sages of Cordova
could harmonize the Bible with Aristotle, and as the spiritual lights of our modern world can prove that it maintains
its value in spite of the march of modern science, so the
Jewish philosophers of ancient Alexandria were able to
show that it anticipated, or supported, or in any case did not
necessarily oppose, the Platonic craze of the moment. The
Law was read mystically, spiritually, symbolically, allegori-
cally—anything but literally. "In that case," said the Younger
Generation of that day, "why continue to observe the precepts of the Law?" And the sages answered, just as many
traditionalists do today, that observance at any rate does no
harm, whereas neglect causes needless offense to those who
view the matter in a different light; and, above all, that a
man should avoid weakening the solidarity of Judaism by
isolating himself from the community in these matters. Two
thousand years have passed since then, and as far as essentials
go we are just where Philo and his contemporaries left us.

This too, however passed away: passed away so completely
that, but for recent archaeological discoveries and the good
fortune of the foremost of the writers of the age to qualify
for inclusion amongst the Fathers of the Church, we would
today know nothing whatsoever of its existence. The only
permanent trace left in the Jewish life of subsequent ages

is perhaps in the philosophical interests of Saadiah of Fayyum and in some doctrines of the Zohar, which may conceivably (it is hazardous to say more) be traced back to an Alexandrian origin. Otherwise, Hellenistic Jewry has completely disappeared —notwithstanding its vast numbers, its elaborate organizations, its stately synagogues, its wealth, its culture, its intellectual champions. Hillel, the Palestinian contemporary of this age, is a living force in Jewish life even today. Philo, though his intellect was perhaps more keen and though the volume of his extant work is immeasurably greater, has become an antiquarian diversion, familiar only to assimilated Jews like ourselves.

iv

How the phenomenon took place is another question. It is one of the mysteries of Jewish history. One thing may however be said with a considerable degree of certainty. It was not the result of any great cataclysm. There was no deadly persecution nor vast political upheaval. The whole culture, long before the Arabs came, simply melted into nothingness. Perhaps this resulted in part from altered economic circumstances, in part from growing enmity of the environment, in part (perhaps the most important factor) from the growth and presence of Christianity. But above all, as it seems, it was the absence of Jewish backbone which rendered it unable to stand up against a hostile, or even less a friendly world. And this happened (it is a point which Zionists will do well to note) in spite of the inspiration of a living Jewish tradition close at hand in Palestine—nearer and easier of access than it can be for a good part of the Jewish world today, despite the improved communications.

With an example such as this before our eyes, it is difficult to continue to speak so glibly, so confidently, about

the future of any of the great Jewish agglomerations of the
modern world, facing conditions precisely analogous to those
which I have endeavored to delineate and reacting to them
in a manner so similar that the account sounds more like
the fantasy of a political satirist than a sober historical
description.

Already, indeed, there are signs that our modern synthesis
is being dethroned in just the same way as that of Arabized
Jewry in the twelfth century and Hellenistic Jewry in the
first. Darwin, the fashionable idol of yesterday, who formerly
occupied the place which Plato and Aristotle held in earlier
ages, has been ousted from the unquestioned supremacy
which he once held. The shallow rationalism of the Victorian era is gone. The eleemosynary epoch in Jewish history
has fortunately seen its best day. The attack on tradition,
on the basis of the Bible, has been triumphantly repulsed,
and the war has been carried back into the opposite camp.
Higher Criticism itself does not stand where it did twenty
years ago; and there is an increasing recognition that the
date and composition of the Scriptures need not necessarily
affect their validity in modern life. The unquestioned
supremacy of the German language and German method
in Jewish scholarship had waned even before its final catastrophe. Mysticism, so decried by Graetz and his school, is
coming back into its own. The fathers of Reform Judaism—
Holdheim, Geiger or Wise—would feel perhaps more uncomfortable spiritually among us today than the Vilna Gaon.
The nineteenth-century synthesis at which our fathers arrived is passing away before our eyes. Is that the presage of
a profounder decay which will carry us away with it? And
is our Anglo-Saxon culture as a whole necessarily more
durable than the Arabic or the Greek of their day? It is
not easy to answer the question with any degree of confidence.

Personally, I have a deep-rooted belief (and here I am
at one, I believe, with the vast majority of Jews, even in

this unregenerate age) in the eternity and indestructibility of Israel. "The Jews," asserted Disraeli in the House of Commons, in a famous speech, "have outlived Assyrian Kings, Egyptian Pharaohs, Roman Caesars and Arabian Caliphs"; and he went on to insinuate that they would in all probability outlive the gibes of the Right Honorable gentleman who had just sat down. We all, with very few exceptions, feel in very much the same way. There is, however, no logical ground nor historical support for this belief. Around us, we witness assimilation going on to a depressing degree. The losses to Judaism by intermarriage, by ignorance, by indifference, by actual conversion, are reaching proportions which are thoroughly intimidating; if we were to go by the actual conditions and indications of the present time, there would seem to be very good ground for believing that in America and Western Europe (except in the largest centers where the process is more difficult) Judaism and the Jews will have disappeared entirely within a century or two at the utmost.

In the average Jewish family of today, the line of the graph is unmistakable. The old generation in Eastern Europe observed in gladness all of the six hundred and thirteen precepts of the Law, and many others, and lived a life which was essentially Jewish. Their children, in England or America, began to find it a little irksome. To discover members of the third generation vitally interested in their ancestral tradition is nowadays almost exceptional. The fourth remain Jews in anything more than name only by accident. The same phenomenon is being repeated throughout the world. It seems impossible to escape the conclusion that, within a few generations, the whole body of the Jews of our Western countries will have gone the same way, and will be wallowing in the slough of assimilation. Ultimately, the time may come when nothing will be left except the merest recollection of the ultimate origin of a few scattered groups of families.[3]

There is only one possible reply to make. The Jewish people has withstood the action of thirty centuries and it is not to be imagined that it will suddenly collapse at the thirty-first. However, as a historian, I cannot but recognize that historical precedent does not permit the application of this belief to any one particular branch of the Jewish people, however numerous, however deep-rooted, however long settled. The human body, I am informed by physiologists, reconstitutes itself entirely within a short space of years, at the end of which no particle of its original components is left. The Jewish people, throughout its past, has been in much the same case. The whole of our history presents one constant procession of communities which have sprung up and withered away entirely after a brief period of florescence. There is no guarantee that we in England, or you in America, will not follow in the same path.

v

Permit me to draw your attention to a couple of characteristic precedents for decay. I will not speak of the Samaritans, once a powerful rival of Israel, but now reduced to a pious handful whose main function in existence seems to be the provision of an annual spectacle for Palestinian tourists. Let us approach closer to ourselves, in place and time. When the Jews were chased out of France, a few survivors were permitted by the tolerant policy of the Popes to remain in Avignon and the surrounding territories in the south of

---

[3] This was written in 1930. Since then, the renewal of organized antisemitism, the catastrophe in Central and Eastern Europe and the birth of the State of Israel have done a good deal to change the attitude and perhaps the prospects of Diaspora Jewry.

the country which were then under their rule, known as
the Comtat Venaissin. To this exiguous area the ancient
glories of French Jewry were henceforth restricted. Here,
for many centuries, the tradition of Rashi and of the Kimhis
was perpetuated. It is not simply a group of communities
which is in question, but a whole distinctive Jewish civilization. The culture of the Jews of Provence was a unique
one. They had their own customs, their own patois, their
own folklore, their own tradition of synagogue-construction,
their own *hazzanut,* their own rite of prayers, their own
style of calligraphy, their own method of pronouncing
Hebrew. With an incredible fortitude this exiguous Jewish
group—numbering perhaps between 2,000 and 3,000 at the
most—was able to withstand the persecutions of centuries,
preserving its traditions and its identity unimpaired. If
perpetuity seemed certain for any branch of the Jewish
people, it was assuredly the case with this, which had given
over fifteen hundred years concrete proof of its fitness for
survival. Yet this intense Jewish life, after withstanding
persecution with such incredible fortitude, was swept away
almost in a moment, after the French Revolution, by the
first breath of freedom. Now, almost nothing is left to
commemorate the existence of this pathetic remnant excepting a romantic tradition, a couple of ancient synagogues of
exquisite beauty, and a vast number of liturgical manuscripts. As one views the ruin, it seems impossible to feel
assured of perpetuity of any branch of the House of Israel.

Let us take another instance. In China the Jews were
already established at the period of the Han dynasty, perhaps from the date of the destruction of Jerusalem by Titus.
From that time onwards, the record is more or less continuous. Communities existed in several of the principal
cities. The Chinese treated their Jewish fellow-citizens
with every consideration. The latter showed their grati-

tude by sloughing off their foreign characteristics and entering into the life of the country. They were admitted into
the mandarin class. They wore pig-tails in the approved
fashion of the time. Their synagogues were built in the
Chinese style and went by a Chinese name. They venerated
their ancestors with their fellow-countrymen. On the other
hand, they adhered punctiliously to Judaism, observing
the Sabbath and feasts with all due rigor, cutting out from
all meat the sinew of the thigh (which they burned with
great solemnity), and industriously copying the sacred books.
The history of this extraordinary community is traceable for
nearly a thousand years. Now, according to latest reports,
it is represented by a few individuals grouped about the
ruins of a synagogue, who know that their fathers were
once Jews, and a couple of clerks preserved in a Shanghai
bank as an historical curiosity. Here then is another Jewish
civilization which has altogether disappeared.

The communities which I have instanced, I will be informed, were minute and isolated and cannot therefore
be taken as precedents for our present conditions and problems. This is not perhaps so sure. Nevertheless, in any case,
it is not the most striking phenomenon of the sort. We
have already seen the example of Hellenistic Jewry, numbered by hundreds of thousands, living under conditions incredibly similar to our own, whose disappearance was even
more complete than that of the other bodies which I have
mentioned: and that in spite of the inspiration of a living
Jewish tradition in Palestine, within easy reach. If a Jewish
civilization such as this can vanish, none of our upstart Jewries of today can consider itself safe.

The Jewish people will assuredly live—but not necessarily that particular section with which we are in touch,
however vast and however wealthy it may be. One is reminded forcibly of that striking passage from the Book of

Esther—from the literary point of view the most remarkable of all biblical works, though so much decried nowadays by those who, oblivious of the existence sometimes of a higher veridicity, allege that it lacks historical accuracy. Mordecai, you will remember, is urging Esther to take action in behalf of her people. "Think not within thyself," said he, "that thou shalt escape, being in the King's house, out of all Jews. For if thou holdest thy peace at this time, then will relief and deliverance arise for the Jews from another place, but thou and thy father's house will perish; and who knoweth whether thou art not come to royal estate for such a time as this?" We are in the same position today. Relief and deliverance and perpetuation will assuredly come about for the Jewish people from some place or the other: of that I am convinced.[4] But, because we live in the lap of luxury and enjoy all possible material advantages and have had the benefit of university education, that is no proof that it is we who will escape in any general catastrophe.

In a thousands years' time, the Temples of New York may have followed the Jewish mandarins of China and the Academies of Alexandria into oblivion and decay. Possibly, in that epoch, the Jewish tradition will be preserved by the descendants of the Falashas of Abyssinia, or the Arabized Jews of the Yemen, or the Sephardim of the Levant and northern Africa, whom we now tend to contemn as the degenerate heirs to a noble inheritance. Possibly the glories of Spanish-speaking Jewry will be revived in the republics of South America, in which Jewish populations have by now taken root. But, whoever preserves the tradition, the Jewish people will assuredly live. If therefore we want to secure our own personal perpetuity as Jews, to guarantee our own identity, it is for us to take steps: not on our people's behalf—they can exist without us—but on our own.

---

[4] This was written before the establishment of the State of Israel.

vi

The question is, wherein the salvation lies. If it is possible to generalize in such matters, one may perhaps make one categoric statement. Though some have been uprooted and destroyed (above all, alas, in our own day), it has never happened that any body of Jews imbued with their ancestral culture has withered away.

The Jews of China have left no literary monuments behind them other than a few ancient Scrolls of the Law and other synagogal paraphernalia. The Jews of Avignon expended the whole of their energies in multiplying manuscript copies of their prayer-book. The Jews of Alexandria were more concerned in justifying their religion to the Gentile than in familiarizing it to the Jew. The ancient tradition of the genuine Jewish scholarship has alone succeeded invariably in perpetuating itself and perpetuating those who immersed themselves in it. The living record may be traced from the Palestinian authorities of the time of the Mishnah and the rabbis of the Gemara, through the age of the Geonim and of the Spanish codifiers and of Rashi and his school in France and the German expositors of the Middle Ages and the Polish *yeshivoth* of more recent times, right down to the present. Jewish learning, while it continues to be cultivated seriously, is the one tried preservative. It is, indeed, the solitary means through which the alternative panaceas, religion and nationalism, have themselves been preserved to our own day. It remains the only thing upon which it is possible for us to rely for our own continuity.

For Historical Judaism has been in the past more than a mere religion, more than nationality, more than a philanthropic brotherhood. It has been a civilization, and a culture: and, without that civilization and that culture, it must inevitably have decayed as so many of its local manifestations have done. The intermittent squabbling which goes on between Reform Judaism and its opponents obscures the real problem of today. Any Judaism, of whatever extremity of orthodoxy or liberalism, is a deformed Judaism so long as it lacks that cultural background which was to our fathers the inseparable adjunct of their lives. The only conceivable guarantee of our future is an informed Judaism.

2. THE JEW AS A EUROPEAN[1]

THAT new tide of antisemitism which had its origin in Nazi Germany, and its repercussions in every other land, is very different from the xenophobia which was at the root of former anti-Jewish prejudice. Its purview is wider—here, more than in anything else, we have the "international" enemy at present poisoning the basis of civilized life. It is not concerned with the function of our people in one country or the other. It attacks the whole body of the Jews as a collectivity, alleging that we constitute an alien "Asiatic" stock, who menace the purity and the cohesion of western life as a whole. It is not enough, therefore, for us today to demonstrate our position as Englishmen, as Frenchmen, or as Italians. We must go a step further, and demonstrate our position as citizens of the Western world.

The growth of geographical knowledge in recent times has rendered possible a fairly clear-cut distinction between the various portions of the world—above all clarifying the major division into continents. America, Africa and Australasia are indeed more or less self-contained and sharply defined. This does not, however, apply to the demarcation between Europe and Asia, which is clearly marked by nature only sporadically. To the north the division is an arbitrary one; it is not altogether wrong, indeed, to define Europe as an irregular peninsula jutting out from the Asiatic mainland north and west of the Caspian Sea. Elsewhere the boundary is more clearly indicated by the Mediterranean

---

1 Presidential address delivered before the Jewish Historical Society of England, 1938, and published thereafter in pamphlet form (London, 1938) and later in revised form in the Transactions of the Society, vol. XIV, pp. 22-38.

Sea and its inlets. One must not overlook the fact, though, that even in remote antiquity a well-navigated and charted sea, regularly traversed by shipping, was more in the nature of a bond of union between distant lands than an insurmountable division. The Isles of Greece were thus in far closer relationship with the Eastern seaboard of the Mediterranean than they were with, for example, the later Germany, or France, or even Italy.

In early Classical times, in fact, the name "Asia" was not applied to the entire continent, but simply to that inconsiderable area in Anatolia watered by the River Cayster, where the Ionian colonists first settled. Incidentally, the very name "Europe," far from having an intolerant and exclusive implication, deriving from an obvious geographical distinction, was of Asiatic—nay, of Palestinian—origin; for it was derived from a Semitic damsel of that name, daughter of a Phoenician king of Tyre, who was carried captive into Crete by Zeus. It is a point, I venture to think, worthy of the antisemites' attention.

What we term Civilization, or, more strictly, "Western Civilization," is in fact by no means a product of Europe alone. It is essentially a product of the Eastern Mediterranean and the adjacent lands. Draw a line from the Strait of Otranto to Alexandria. West of that point the world produced almost nothing that matters in the history of mankind until very shortly before the beginning of the Christian era—and not very much, indeed, for some time after. Yet, east of that point the world had already given birth by then to more than one magnificent culture; and not on the European shores alone. From as early as 3000 B.C.E., Egypt was producing in an unbroken sequence masterpieces of architecture and sculpture which are worthy of comparison with, and in some instances are perhaps superior to, the productions of any age. It is purblind to imagine that subsequent Greek achievement in precisely these same arts was completely unaffected by the precedent; for a culture seldom withers away barren, and the parallels are in this case sometimes too striking to be due to mere coincidence. Recent excavations have shown us that Mesopotamian civilization had already attained a very high level at the time when Abraham was born there, some 3800 years ago. The precise extent of its heritage to the Western world is difficult to trace, but it is certain that it includes something of our mathematics, a good part of our astronomy, and even so fundamental a fact as the seven-day week and our method of measuring time. And at this period Greek history had barely begun, and the rest of Europe was a barbaric waste.

Nor is it proper that we should overlook the part that further Asia played in the advancement of mankind. We may leave aside the store of genius it has produced in the sphere of the spirit, with Confucius and the Buddha, and confine ourselves to the material aspects which the Western world esteems so highly. Our mathematics—in particular our arithmetic—derive from India. We owe the magnet, which has facilitated navigation, and the invention of paper, which alone has rendered possible the universal spread of education, to China—that same China which anticipated the invention of the printing-press and which knew of gunpowder, though it did not turn it to lethal purposes, centuries before Europe. It is absurd to consider that Western Culture, even in its widest interpretation, has contributed all our amenities of life.

Egypt and Mesopotamia, however, were the neighbors of our fathers when the Hebrews became a people. The first period of Jewish history was not enacted in a remote territory of the barbaric world. It was at a focal point of the ancient polity, where Europe and Asia and Africa met, where troops and diplomats and merchants were constantly passing backwards and forwards, bringing fruitful ideas in their train as well as more perishable commodities. It was not in ignorance of the highest material civilization of the day, but in full consciousness of it, that our fathers proclaimed that there were higher considerations for man than physical excellence. That they did not insist on material achievement does not necessarily imply that they were uninterested in it. There is, indeed, a growing body of opinion which holds that the Hebrews were very closely associated with the enterprises and achievements of the Phoenicians—including that colonizing activity which first brought seeds of civilized life to many parts of Western Europe.

ii

At this formative period, that civilization subsequently associated more specifically with Europe knew no precise geographical boundaries. Hellenic culture, to which the modern world owes so profound a debt, was not in the narrow sense of the term "European." It was centered around what we now term the Ionian Sea—but as much on the Asiatic as on the European shore. Of the seven cities which contest the honor of having given birth to Homer, Asiatic Smyrna and semi-Asiatic Chios are the most likely. It was in Asia that the Trojan War, the starting-point for continuous Greek history, was enacted. In the great days of Hellenic culture, the cities along the Phrygian coast were little less important, less cultured, and less beautiful than Athens or Thebes. The Greek Islands, closer to the Asiatic than the European coast, gave birth to Sappho, Pythagoras, Timocreon, Hippocrates; Ephesus in Asia Minor to Heraclitus. Nor must it be forgotten that the preservation of

Greek literature—and indeed of the priceless heritage of Greece as a whole—is largely due to the schools and teachers of the partly Jewish city of Alexandria, in Africa, in which the lamp of learning was religiously tended when in Greece proper it had become dimmed.

The fact of interdependence is brought out strikingly from a detail which, if of little importance in itself, is nevertheless of considerable significance. One of the most remarkable, and perhaps the earliest, of the records of continuous European civilization is the list of victors at the Olympic Games, which goes back without a break from the third century of the Christian era to the year 776 B.C.E., approximately a thousand years before. We are indebted for this to the researches and industry of a writer who lived in the reign of the Emperor Elagabalus (218-222 C.E.). But this writer was not a Greek. He bore, indeed, a Roman name, Julius, but from his surname, Africanus, it is obvious that he originated in Africa. But where did he flourish? By a curious coincidence (it is, of course, no more), *in Palestine.* The name "Europe" is Semitic; European chronology is due to a Palestinian of African origin. Here we have two of the more diverting of the very many indications of the unity of Mediterranean civilization in Classical times, and of the integral role played in that civilization by the Holy Land and its inhabitants.

Even later, in the heyday of the Roman Empire, when civilization had at last made its great stride westward and Rome was the capital of the civilized world, there was still no cultural differentiation between Europe and Asia. The Imperial city recruited its inhabitants from every part of the Empire; the emperors were chosen with sublime indifference from every province; and those great thinkers who were in the fullest sense the Fathers of the Christian Church—Tertullian, Augustine and so on—were Carthaginians, Alexandrians, Antiochians—almost everything, in fact, but "Europeans" in the narrow sense.

When, therefore, the Greek or the Latin spoke of Asia, he thought at the most of a convenient geographical distinction, and not a very sharply defined one at that; he did not, nor could he, think in terms of a cultural differentiation, which did not exist for many centuries after. And Europe represented for him as much (or more) the vast expanse which stretched north of the Balkans and the Alps, largely inhabited by Teutonic "barbarians" (as he considered them), as it did the highly cultured cities of Attica or Sicily. There was thus no question of proceeding from a superior cultural environment to an inferior one when a man crossed from the European shore of the Bosporus to the Asiatic. If the thought of such a differentiation had entered men's minds, it was perhaps an ascension, rather than a descent, that would have been in question.

It is, indeed, only in comparatively recent times that the idea of Europe as a cultural as well as a geographical entity has triumphed. Even so, it has never been possible to apply the distinction too strictly. There was a period, in the Middle Ages, when only two parts of the Western world were civilized. One was Spain; but Spain was largely occupied from the eighth century onwards by an Asiatic people, speaking, writing and studying an Asiatic language. The other was the Byzantine Empire, where the traditions of ancient Hellas and Rome had persisted without serious interruption; but the heart of the Byzantine Empire was in the Asiatic rather than the European provinces. Nor could the differentiation be strictly applied after the period when the Moslems were driven out of Spain; for did not this coincide with the occupation of the eastern provinces of Europe by the Turks—who incidentally, showed themselves in many respects the equals or the superiors of the Western

peoples? It is only during the past two decades, following the
Graeco-Turkish War of 1922-3, that the great interchanges
of population have at last made it possible to draw a more
or less clear-cut division in this part of the world, ethnically,
religiously and politically (except for the Moslem enclaves
in Thrace and Bosnia); though simultaneously the occi-
dentalization of a great part of the Levant has obscured
the difference.

iii

What we term "Civilization," then, had its origin not in
Europe but in the Eastern basin of the Mediterranean.
Thence the distinctive culture now associated with the Western world gradually extended. The Greek colonists were not
the only pioneers; they were often preceded by the Phoenicians, who (as has been indicated above) are now held to
have included in their number many of their Jewish neighbors. Afterwards came the great unifying genius of Rome,
which spread Mediterranean culture as far as the Pillars
of Hercules and beyond, though even now ideas flourished
more in the Levant than in the new centers of material
achievement. With the Middle ages, century after century,
the world's intellectual center was Italy, where the city-
republics demonstrated that extent of territory and force
of arms are not the fundamentals of human achievement.
And Italy continued to lead the world until the discovery
of America reduced the Mediterranean to the condition of
a backwater, instead of being (as she had been since the
beginning of history) the main-stream of the world's communications. At once the countries on the Atlantic seaboard came to the fore. London, Amsterdam and Hamburg
took the place of Venice and Genoa as the great *entrepôts* of
trade. The world's commerce, the world's communications,

the world's culture, were from now Oceanic, not Mediterranean; and the countries of northern Europe, with their
offshoots oversea, henceforth led mankind.

In one respect the Jews were unique among the peoples
who were present with them at the formative period of our
civilization in the Eastern Mediterranean so many centuries
ago. The others were entirely dependent upon their political
status and their association with their land. The Jews, by
reason of their unique religious system, were independent
of this. They were hence able to be mobile and were carried with the tide of culture, thereby being enabled to contribute to it at every stage. As we have seen, they contributed to the intellectual ferment in Alexandria at the
beginning of the Christian era, when that city had almost
supplanted Athens as the center of Greek life. They were
present in Rome, not ineffectively, even before the Augustan
Age. In the Dark Ages they were almost alone among lay-
men in preserving in Western Europe some notion of the
amenities of life and letters. When Europe had forgotten
the existence of Greek literature and science and thought, it
was they who assisted the Arabs in preserving it. When the
culture of the Western world was concentrated in Moslem
Spain, they were there, playing a role of supreme (according to some authorities, decisive) importance: and they
were working with Alfonso the Wise at Toledo when he
desired to raise the low level of cultural life in his dominions and thus initiated the Golden Age of Spain. They
collaborated so far as they were permitted in the Italian
Revival of Learning in the fifteenth century, and more than
in proportion to their numbers in the Revival of Science in
the nineteenth. Thus, of all the groups at present associated
with European culture, their association is not only the
oldest but also the only one that has been continuous.

Let us for the moment neglect the remote period, when the Greek culture was one only of the many that flourished in the Middle East, and come to that later age when Hellenism definitely took the lead. It was in the fourth century B.C.E., with the conquests of Alexander the Great, that Palestine definitely entered the orbit of the Greek world. Even the reaction under the Hasmonaeans was effective only in the spiritual sphere—the first great triumph scored for the principle of religious freedom. Culturally, for better or for worse, the eyes of Palestine henceforth looked towards the West. I have pointed out elsewhere how the country is divided off by a vast sea of desert from the Asiatic territory that surrounds it, united by a familiar and navigable sea to the countries which lie beyond it in the direction of the setting sun. One can hardly imagine any slight geographical change which would have affected mankind more—in the realm of religion and of ethics, of science and of inquiry— than a slight shifting of the sands of the desert, with the result that Palestine would have looked towards the East instead of the West. It is from Europe rather than from further Asia that the country has received its most potent influences, Europe rather than Asia that has been fertilized by its seminal religious and intellectual conceptions, to Europe rather than to Asia that it has sent its children as colonists.

iv

Precisely how ancient the Jewish settlement in Europe is it is difficult to say, but there is documentary evidence to prove that it goes back for over two thousand years. It is probable that the later Prophets envisaged the presence of enslaved compatriots in Greece when they spoke of the extension of the exile as far as the "isles of the sea." In various places inscriptions have been found which date well before the beginning of the Christian era, and in I Maccabees, xv, there is a remarkable list of presumed Jewish settlements all over the Eastern Mediterranean to which in the Hasmonaean period the consul Lucius sent letters of recommendation and safeguard.

It had been a little before this, in 161 B.C.E., that Judas Maccabaeus had first entered into formal relations with Rome. The historicity of this episode has been questioned, but (as it seems from the most recent researches) on insufficient grounds, and in any event the critics are able only to postpone, not to deny, the opening of relations with Rome by the Hasmonaean brothers. The names of these earliest ambassadors, as they are given us in the Apocrypha, were Eupolemus ben Johanan ben Accos and Jason ben Eleazar. Do not think lightly of this apparently dry and unimportant fact. These two are the earliest European Jews known to us by name, and the earliest Jews who are recorded to have traveled beyond the Eastern Mediterranean. They are hence the spiritual ancestors, as it were, of all of us here. And from the date of these pioneers, twenty-one hundred years ago, the record of the Jewish association with Western Europe is absolutely unbroken.

And where were the other denizens of Western Europe at this time? The amalgam that we term the English was not yet dreamed of—it was not to emerge till a thousand years later. Much the same was true of Spain, where the presence of Jews is attested in some numbers as early as the first century (else why should St. Paul have meditated his missionary journey thither?). The ancestors of the Visigothic nobility were skin-clad savages in the frozen steppes of Central Russia. The Franks had not yet entered France, nor the inhabitants of Burgundaholm (Bornholm) wandered south from the Baltic Sea into Burgundy. As for the Germans, they were still the savages—not always noble—whom Tacitus described. It was in Gallic, not Teutonic, territory that the Romans established many years later that colony which was the origin of the present Cologne. Jews were probably present in it almost from the beginning. By the fourth century they had a well-organized community, with its synagogue and its lay-leaders and its rabbis. This is clear from that well known edict of 321 of the Emperor Constantine, regulating certain privileges enjoyed by the Jews of that city in such terms as to make it plain that the congregation was by no means a newly-established one. Nor is this the only, though it is the most striking, evidence which proves the existence of Jews in this region in Roman times. It was only 150 years after this edict of Constantine that the Germans first permanently crossed the Rhine and established themselves in the Roman province. It is a curious consideration that a stranger ignorant of Latin who visited Cologne in the fourth century would probably have had difficulty in finding any person to whom he could have spoken German, but would certainly have been able to make himself understood in Hebrew. Whoever were the strangers on the Rhineland when the Nazis came into power, it was certainly not the Jews—the only representatives in it, perhaps, of its inhabitants of sixteen centuries ago.

Far be it from me, or from any Jew, to speak of the Asiatic ethnic strain or of Asiatic culture with contempt. It may, however, be observed that, if one desires to isolate any Asiatic strain in European life, one should look rather to the Hungarians or to the Finns of today, whose ancestors a bare thousand years ago were wandering about the steppes of Central Asia—at a period when the Jews had already been represented in Europe for a thousand years, and for a thous-

and years more had been in the orbit of the European world. To quote a distinguished authority: *

The Jewish carriers represent perhaps the most continuously civilized element in Europe. European Jewish thinkers in numbers were consciously developing Hellenic philosophy and discussing Plato and Aristotle, the Stoics and Plotinus, while the rest of Europe was, as yet, in its barbaric incoherent childhood. In a cultural sense the Jews were the first Europeans. In a racial sense—if, indeed, there be a Jewish race—the reader may be reminded that the Jews had settled in Western Europe before many of its most typical inhabitants had emerged from Asia and before others had crossed the Central European Plain or had traversed the North Sea to invade the West.

v

The Jews are not merely European; they are in many respects quintessentially European. It was not only that they assimilated themselves to their environment and adopted its language; it was not only that they contributed powerfully to the various literatures; it was that they sometimes occupied, as it were, a strategic point, and thereby determined the battle. Let us bear in mind the fact that as long ago as the first century B.C.E., when Latin literature was despised in the best Roman circles, it was Caecilius of Calacte—one of the first European Jews known to us by name—who defended it, and that this same early pioneer stood out as a champion of the pure Attic style of oratory as against the verbose Asiatic forms then beginning to gain ground. Many centuries later, the Jewish translators at the court of Castile (to whom passing reference has been made above) helped to create modern Spanish as a literary medium.

It is highly significant that the Jew has retained something of his allegiance in this respect even when intolerance

---

* Dr. and Mrs. Charles Singer in *The Legacy of Israel.*

has driven him into exile. Until a generation or so ago, the whole of Jewry (with only a few exceptions), notwithstanding their changed environment, spoke one or the other of two Western European tongues. In the Moslem world, among neighbors familiar only with Arabic and Turkish, the *Sephardim* still clung to the medieval Spanish of their fathers. In Poland or in Russia the *Ashkenazim* constituted a German-speaking island surrounded by a vast Slavonic sea. Nor is this Europeanization in matter of language a new thing. We may deplore, but we must none the less recognize, the fact that the use of Greek had begun to make enormous inroads in Jewish Palestine, even before the fall of Jerusalem. It is almost startling, to those of us who regard the revival of Hebrew as one of the most important achievements of the present rebirth, to see how fifteen centuries ago Palestinian Jews used the tongue of Hellas even for their tombstones and synagogal inscriptions. It has more than once been pointed out that, if a modern student requires specimens of the oldest French, he must have recourse to the biblical glosses of the great medieval Jewish biblical commentator, Rashi,[1] and that the earliest specimen of the Apulian dialect was preserved among a certain section of the Jews of Corfu. But one may go even further. There are many features of Low Latin, as it was spoken in the later phase of the Roman Empire, which are now to be traced only in the Ladino of the Mediterranean basin and the Judeo-Italian which still lingers on in Rome.

The Jews, then, are a European people—more truly than are more than one of the peoples of the Western world. As a European people, moreover, they have been active for untold generations in every manifestation of Western cultural life. In my book, *The Jewish Contribution to Civilization,* I have dealt with this matter in detail. Here I can only call

---

[1] There are some even older specimens in the commentaries of Rabbenu Gershom of Mayence, who died about 1040, but their authenticity is disputed.

attention to the bare fact. The Jewish scriptures were one of
the great formative influences in almost every European
tongue. Jews contributed in an outstanding manner to the
intellectual ferment which reintroduced the classical dis-
ciplines to medieval Europe and brought about the Renaissance. Jews in the Middle Ages were prominent more than
in proportion to their numbers as astronomers, physicians,
scientists. They were instrumental in bringing Indian mathematics to the Arabic-speaking world in the first instance,
and thence in the second instance to Latin Christendom,
thereby sowing the seed of modern Europe's technical and
scientific pre-eminence. Jewish mapmakers and instrument-
makers facilitated the labors of the great explorers whose
activity marked the close of the Middle Ages. Jews were
collaborating in literary life in France, Spain, Germany and
Italy as far back as the thirteenth century. Jews were prominent in Italy when that happy land was the center of the
Renaissance, playing their part in philosophical discussion,
in the world of music, to a limited extent even in the world
of art, and taking a really important share in the nascent
drama. The last King of Portugal generously admitted how
his country was prepared to receive the influence of the
Renaissance only through the presence of a large and cultured Jewish community, who led in scientific inquiry and
(for example) set up a printing-press in the country—not
for the production of Hebrew books only— seven years before
any non-Jew thought it worth while to follow their example.

It is true that religious intolerance limited, and in the
end suppressed, this fruitful collaboration. With the decay
of the walls of the Ghetto, however, it began again. In
science and in chemistry, in medicine and in astronomy, in
literature and in art, in criticism and in politics, in humani-
tarianism and in education, the share of Jews since then
was noteworthy in every land. They studied sedulously at

the feet of non-Jewish scholars, and passed their learning on after them to non-Jewish disciples. Let us not exaggerate. There is no need to claim that the share of the Jew has been in any single branch preponderant. But it has been a share worthy of study and of respect. It is no more possible, moreover, to isolate or to eradicate the Jewish contribution than the English or the French or the German one.

But the Jews were more than collaborators in Western culture. It is not an exaggeration to include them among the pioneers. When, in the Dark Ages, Jewish traders penetrated through untold dangers to the barbarous lands of Northern Europe, importing thither something of the amenities of life of the Mediterranean shores, they brought with them the spirit of European, or of Western, cultural life. When, in the later Middle Ages, Jewish settlers pushed eastward, into the dreary wastes of Poland and the Ukraine, they carried the germs of Western civilization, and the little settlements which they set up were so many centers of humanization. We were at one time induced to believe that the Polish Jews constituted an alien element, of retrograde cultural and political development, to be denied the natural rights of other Poles and to be thrust away into remote islands at the whim of their fellow-countrymen. (Since then the "problem"—if there was one—has been settled in another fashion, so horrible that the mind refuses to accept it.) On the contrary, they were one of the ethnic elements settled in that country from time immemorial, no more alien than the descendants of the Normans in England today, and retrograde only in that they failed to conform quite so readily as some of their neighbors to the dictates of the Machine Age.

So, too, Jews have been in the forefront of European expansion overseas. It is a thrice-told story how the voyages of exploration at the close of the Middle Ages were dependent in large measure on Jewish maps, Jewish nautical instruments and Jewish astronomical tables; how hardy Jewish travellers paved the way for, and skilled Jewish interpreters accompanied, Albuquerque and Vasco da Gama; how Columbus's expedition was both patronized and financed by Jews; how it was a crypto-Jewish sailor who first sighted the New World, and the ex-Jewish interpreter who first set foot on it. Jews were among those who were consulted by Amerigo Vespucci, and among the *Conquistadores* who followed Cortes. The first great Asiatic physician of modern times was Garcia d'Orta, and the greatest Asiatic explorer of the sixteenth century was Pedro Texeira. It is significant that the first books printed by the European method, both in Africa and in Asia, were produced by Jews. Here are one or two illustrations only of what might be expanded to fill a whole volume.

But, we are told, however long we Jews have been in Europe, it does not affect the fact of our ultimate Asiatic origin, and present (it seems a *non-sequitur*) Asiatic character. In considering this point, it must be borne in mind that the ethnic differentiation between the Jew and his neighbor is grossly exaggerated. The number of Jews in the Roman Empire has been estimated as high as 10,000,000, scattered from the Atlantic seaboard to the fringes of Parthia: conservative estimates place the total at 4,000,000 or 5,000,000. In the Middle Ages the number dwindled to as few as 1,500,000. What was the reason for this diminution? Massacre, famine, destitution, cannot entirely account for it. There was also slow assimilation by the environment, accentuated by conversion to Christianity on what must have been, whatever the reason, an enormous scale. And throughout the Middle Ages, while the number of the Jews in the world remained stationary century after century, the process repeated itself. It was considered part of Christian duty to bring the Jews into the arms of the Church. There was continual attrition on the fringes—conversion from necessity, conversion from conviction, conversion from compulsion. Forced baptisms by the score or hundred accompanied every pogrom, and sometimes attained impressionable proportions.[1] In the Iberian Peninsula alone there were three attempts— once under the Visigoths, once under the Catholic sovereigns, once under Manoel of Portugal—to dragoon the whole of the Jewish community into Christianity. Though the experiments were not successful, they nevertheless resulted in the merging of a vast number of Jews into the general body of the Spanish and Portuguese peoples. These are the most notorious of such cases, but the same took place in almost every other country. Even in England the Jewish converts to Christianity were alleged in the thirteenth century to constitute a "problem." No country, however, encouraged conversion from Judaism quite so sedulously as Germany— in the Middle Ages by force, later by the bait of social emancipation and admission to office. The Jewish strain in the German people must necessarily be stronger than even the most fanatical Nazi was willing to admit.

vi

What has been said thus far is universally recognized, though not universally appreciated. It is less generally realized, on the other hand, that the same process was repeated in the reverse direction—that is to say, the infiltration of non-Jewish blood among the Jews. For that too has been continuous, though necessarily on a far smaller scale. Even in the darkest hour of Jewish history there were not wanting those who saw fresh spiritual potentialities in Judaism and threw in their lot with our faith.

---

[1] This aspect is dealt with in greater detail in the next paper, *The Unassimilable Jew*, pp. 37 ff.; on conversions to Judaism, see *Proselytes of Righteousness*, pp. 143 ff.

It is not suggested that this process ever attained really considerable dimensions, in recent times at least (though in Imperial Rome, and in the Kingdom of the Chazars, the reverse was the case). But an infiltration of this sort, continuous over many centuries, must necessarily have qualified any purity of blood that may originally have existed. In the year 1000, it has been reckoned by a mathematician, we each had one billion ancestors—in other words, each of us is today descended probably from every Jew who was in the world, or, at least, in the Western world, at that period and whose progeny still survive. Can there be any doubt that among these multifarious ancestors we all have one or more of these Proselytes of Righteousness of many centuries ago? Hence, just as the blood of almost all Western Europeans must necessarily have been modified by the constant procession of Jewish converts to Christianity, so we Jews must needs have in our veins some tincture at least of the blood of these Christian converts to Judaism.

We Jews are sometimes informed that we have no right to complain of Racialism, as our whole history is an exposition of the racial principle. Israel Zangwill, twenty years ago, exposed the absurdity of the comparison in his brilliant lecture, *Chosen Peoples*. Indeed, the Prophet anticipated him many centuries before: "You only have I known of all the families of the earth; *therefore* I will visit upon you all your iniquities"—in other words, our Choice implies not privilege, but Responsibility. The point I desire to make here, however, is the qualification of the racial principle which our ancestors admitted in their acceptance of proselytes as "children of Abraham our Father." It is in that sense, as the spiritual progeny of the Patriarchs—not merely their physical descendants—that we Jews have our ethnic unity, as one of the peoples of the Western world.

3. THE UNASSIMILABLE JEW[1]

IN THE course of the new antisemitic campaign which was launched some years ago in Germany and has since spread to other countries, a number of new charges against the Jews, of sins imaginable and unimaginable, have been given prominence. The variability of these would be amusing, if they had not become tragic. They vary from country to country and from age to age. The very things that the Jews were advised to do a few years ago in order to give the lie to the accusations then made against them, have now themselves given rise to new charges.[2] Not seldom they are simultaneously accused of two diametrically opposite and contradictory enormities. Nevertheless, though the charges may alter, they must be met and refuted as they arise, lest the case go by default. And this is so in particular as regards everything connected with this new conception of race, which, however untenable scientifically and however childish in its developments, has had, whether we like to admit it or not, a profound influence on the popular mind.

One of the pillars of this absurd conception is the allegation that the Jew in Europe constitutes an unassimilable

---

[1] Originally published, under the title "Are the Jews Unassimilable," in *Jewish Social Studies*, III (1944), pp. 3-14.

[2] Thus the poet Crabbe (1754-1832), reflecting the opinions of Hanoverian England, wrote,

> "No War nor Wisdom yields our Jews delight,
> They will not study, and they dare not fight."

It was to oppose this attitude of mind that English Jewry made a conscious effort to divert their children from commerce to the professions, not imagining that their grandchildren would be blamed for this very propensity. As far as the second part of the sneer goes, though it persisted in spite of Jewish participation with his fellow-countrymen in recent wars, it cannot very well survive the events of 1948 in Palestine.

element. Race ideology starts from the Hegelian conception
that identifies country, people and state, and proceeds from
that to the corollary that those whose origin is perceptibly
different from that of the majority of the inhabitants of the
country can have and can play no part in the state. There
is an easy retort to this, and the Jews and their defenders
were quick to make it. There is no country of Western
Europe the population of which is homogeneous, the Jews
being only one of the many ethnic elements that have collaborated in building up Germany and France and Italy and
England as we know them. To this truism, a specious answer
was made in Italy. It is perfectly true, said the racialists, that
immigrants from other countries may have assisted in the
past in building up our own. But, unlike the Jews, they
entered completely into our national life and lost their
identity; only the Jews have remained unassimilable.

ii

The best way to approach this question (a fantasy can
hardly be dignified with the name of "problem") is statistical.
Most persons are quite ignorant of how the Jewish population of the world has fluctuated during the past two millen-
nia. Above all, it is not realized that in the heyday of the
Roman Empire the Jewish population of the world was, in
relative terms, roughly comparable to that of our own day—
or to be more exact let us say of our grandfathers' day.
Moreover, *it is the only period of history when the figures
have been comparable*. The latest investigations suggest that
in the period of the First Temple—say 700 B.C.E.— the population of Palestine was roughly 2,000,000, having risen during
the period of the Israelitish occupation from half that number. In the reign of Herod, tranquility, a strong rule and

intensive cultivation again increased the country's economic potentialities after an interlude of comparative distress. By the time of Jesus the figure had risen to 2,500,000, of whom some 300,000 were Samaritans and Greeks.

To compensate for the latter, however, there was even at that time a very considerable body of Jews living outside Palestine. Some of these were the descendants of the exiles of long ago who had remained in Egypt, in Rome and in all the coastlands of the eastern Mediterranean. An ancient report indicates that at the time of the Emperor Claudius (first century C.E.) there were ascertained to be 6,944,000 Jews in the Roman Empire; and this, though it sounds unreasonable, is by no means inconsistent with other facts and figures as we know them. Add to these at least a million more for Mesopotamia, Persia and other regions not under Roman rule, and it will be seen that a total of 8,000,000 for the entire world in antiquity is within the bounds of possibility.

The figures given here (as elsewhere in this article) are those arrived at by Professor Baron, of Columbia University, a scholar whose opinion is to be regarded with the utmost respect. Other estimates do not differ very widely from this. Edwyn Bevan accepted a figure of between four and seven millions for the Jewish population of the Roman Empire. Juster, author of the classical work on the Jews under the Romans, placed the figure between six and seven millions. The total population of the Empire has been estimated at between 55,000,000 and 100,000,000. Jews thus constituted, according to a consensus of opinion, not less than seven per cent, and possibly as much as ten per cent, of the total population of the Empire.

The number of those who retained their allegiance to Judaism rapidly fell with the rise of Christianity. In the Dark and Middle Ages it does not seem that the Jewish population of the world ever much exceeded one million, or a million and a half at the outside. This figure seems to have remained almost constant between, say, the tenth century and the seventeenth. Thus, between the heyday of the Roman Empire in the third century and that of the Papacy in the thirteenth, the number of Jews in the world dwindled by 66 per cent on a conservative estimate, and 85 per cent on a less cautious one.

What happened to the residue? There was, of course, a general diminution in population during the period under discussion, but it was by no means so marked as was the case with the Jews. That people was subject to massacre and violence; but this was more characteristic of the Middle Ages than of the preceding period, and cannot have been the decisive factor. (It must be recalled that generally speaking only the population of Palestine was affected by the bloody campaigns of Vespasian and Titus.) One is driven to the conclusion, therefore, that what was principally responsible for this striking diminution was *assimilation into the general body of the population.* Even in the classical period it was not an unknown phenomenon for Jews to throw off their ancestral faith and adopt the religion of the majority.[3] When Christianity began its career it was among Jews that it had its first field of activity and it was against Jews that it subsequently directed its strongest attack; and when it finally triumphed and obtained control it exerted every ounce of its strength to make the Jews abandon their opposition—first by persuasion and ultimately by compulsion. Hence there was a constant stream of converts. The chroniclers record instance after instance, throughout the Dark Ages, when Jews relinquished their "superstition" and went over to Christianity *en masse,* as a result of the preaching of an eloquent

---

[3] It is enough to think of that nephew of Philo of Alexandria, the most earnest Diaspora Jew of his generation, who became chief of staff to Titus.

missionary or the stern measures adopted by a zealous ruler, who would give his Jewish subjects the alternatives of expulsion and baptism, or death and baptism.

Much the same happened with the spread of Islam, when all over the Middle East and northern Africa individual Jews or entire communities were persuaded or compelled to embrace the triumphant faith. Here then we have the explanation, why between the birth of Jesus and the year 1000, while the general population of the western world diminished perhaps by 25 to 50 per cent, the number of Jews diminished, notwithstanding their purely legendary prolificness, by 66 to 85 per cent.

And the process was not ended. From the year 1000, or not very long after, the population of the western world slowly increased. That of the Jewish world, on the other hand, remained stationary or dwindled further. There were in England in the twelfth century, for example, some 1,500,-000 souls. In the seventeenth, notwithstanding the great pestilences which had meanwhile intervened, there were rather more than 5,000,000. The Jews, on the other hand, who may have numbered between a million and a million and a half (as we have seen) in the year 1000, diminished rather than increased. In the middle of the seventeenth century, after the devastation caused by the Cossack massacres in Poland, it has been estimated that there were no more than 900,000 all told (650,000 in Europe and 250,000 elsewhere). The total population of Europe at this time has been reckoned at 100,000,000. Hence, whereas the Jews were some 7 to 10 per cent of the population of the western world in the days of the Roman Empire, they had diminished at this period to less than one per cent.

What was the reason for this curious contrast, between the Christian increase and the Jewish decrease? The answer is as before. There were, of course, everywhere frequent and bloody massacres. But the massacres were accompanied or succeeded in many instances by conversions *en masse*. At other times, mass-conversion took place without the massacres, as was the case, for example, in Portugal at the close of the fifteenth century, when this was responsible for the disappearance of an entire community. And in the intervals, there was the constant pressure of environment, of temptation, of bribery, of argument, of kidnapping, of social advantage, of conviction, of petty annoyances, of Ghetto pressure, of conversionist sermons and the rest of an elaborate system organized mainly with a view to breaking down the resistance of the Jew. It was not only a question of the spectacular apostasy of entire communities, such as was sometimes recorded; there was also the gradual seepage of individuals, not many at a time, but in the long run very numerous. Sometimes, doubtless, the original converts retained their former beliefs in their hearts, but it was not so easy to transmit them to their children, and in the long or the short run the offspring in most instances lost all knowledge and realization of their Jewish affiliation. Jewish antiquarians pride themselves, and not unjustly, on the heroism of those who, like the Marranos of Portugal today, have retained through the ages some inkling of their ancestral loyalties. More numerous by far, however, were those who lost them. It was this more than massacre which kept down the numbers of the Jewish population, generation after generation and century after century.

iii

Let us consider one country that is peculiarly significant, partly because our knowledge of it is so detailed, partly because its Jewish associations have been so continuous, and partly because it was not so long since infected with the racial mania and forced ostensibly (though the inhabitants

regarded the matter with their usual scepticism) to neglect
the obvious implications of its own history. The Jewish
associations of Italy are the oldest in Europe, and Italy is
the only country of Europe (save Germany) in which these
traditions were unbroken down to our own day. Jews first
arrived in Rome under the Maccabees, in the second century
before the Christian era. They suffered occasional maltreatment, but it may be said that from that time to the present
Jews have never been absent from Italy. Under Tiberius,
according to Juster's calculation, there must have been in
Rome between 50,000 and 60,000 Jews, out of a total population of about 1,000,000. Suetonius tells us that the Emperor enrolled 4,000 young Jews to serve against the bandits
in Sardinia, while 8,000 accompanied a Palestinian deputation to the Palatine in the time of Augustus. Moreover,
there were in Italy outside the capital some forty places in
which we know Jewish communities to have existed in
classical or immediately post-classical times.

Now, Italy never figures in Jewish history as a land of
violent persecution, and never in consequence as a land of
mass emigration.[4] One might, therefore, imagine that, even
had there been no immigration at all, the Jewish population
today would have been very high indeed, as the result of
natural increase. But in fact, far from increasing, the Jewish
population has tended to remain stationary. This is all the
more remarkable in view of the continuous immigration into
the country, though, indeed, this has never been so great as
to modify to any appreciable extent the quasi-autochthonous
nature of Italian Jewry (especially in the central provinces)
and their title to represent, with less modification than any
other, an ethnic element present in the country since Roman
times.

---

4 If we omit Sicily and Naples, from which Aragonese intolerance brought
about a wholesale expulsion under King Ferdinand the Catholic.

In the early part of the seventeenth century, Italian Jewry numbered (according to an extremely acute contemporary observer) about 25,000. A reliable conjecture for 1810 is 27,500; for 1820, 29,000; for 1830, 30,000. During the last century the number has been reinforced not only by immigration, but also by the addition of various communities in the provinces annexed from Austria after the war of 1914-1918; even so, the census of 1921 gave a total population of only 47,825. There has thus been an inconsiderable increase during the past three hundred years, and a considerable decrease as compared with eighteen hundred years ago. Proportionately, the figures are even more striking. Whereas in 1638 the Jews of Italy constituted about two in a thousand of the entire population, in 1938 they were barely one in a thousand. Or, to put it in another fashion, whereas during the course of the past three centuries the Italian population has increased fourfold, the Jewish population has barely doubled.

What is the reason for this discrepancy? Once again, we can answer with more precision for Italy than for other parts of the world. It was not that Italian Jews emigrated on a large scale during the period under discussion. They did not. It was not that Italian Jews were massacred. They were not. One can draw up a list of the number of Italian Jews who lost their lives in religious upheavals since the Renaissance, and it does not approach one hundred. (The greatest tragedy in Italian-Jewish history was the mass deportation by the Germans during World War II.) But though there was little actual violence, there was the steady, unremitting temptation of the Italian environment, the pressure of the Church, and the nightmare of the ghetto system. During all those centuries, from the Middle Ages to the *Risorgimento,* there was every temptation for the Italian Jews to abandon their faith and to become absorbed in the majority; and they did so continuously. There was a perpetual procession from the Synagogue to the Church. Between 1634 and 1700 no fewer than 1,195 Jews were baptized in Rome alone. At Ferrara, with a small Jewish community, the annual average of converts at the close of the seventeenth century was 6.8. In the Duchy of Modena, with a bare handful, the total in the relatively tolerant period between 1831 and 1840 rose to 48. And these figures neglect those who, finding Judaism a burden too great to bear, but not liking the idea of baptism, quietly merged in the general population in some part of the country where they were unknown.

These facts sufficiently explain the phenomenon we are discussing. There can be very few among the population of the Italian towns in whose veins there does not run the blood of some of these converts. Indeed, seeing that the neophytes generally assumed the surname of some noble family who stood their sponsor at baptism, there is almost as much possibility today that those humbler citizens who now bear these historic names are descended from the former denizens of the ghetto as that they are the heirs to the swashbuckler condottieri and unscrupulous bankers of the Renaissance.

iv

In the course of the past three centuries the general phenomenon has changed. In the first place, for the first and only time since early in the Christian era the number of Jews began to increase. At last, some time between 1850 and 1900, there were once more in the world as many Jews as there had been at the time of the Roman Empire. While during the course of the next generation, this figure was exceeded; yet—and this, the second point, is perhaps the more important—this increase was largely illusory. It was accompanied by a corresponding loosening of Jewish religious and social ties, so that left to themselves a very large proportion of the world's Jews would have been likely to assimilate with the majority in the course of a generation or so. This process has of course already proceeded a long way in the countries of greatest enlightenment. Jews have been resident in England now for nearly three centuries, since the Resettlement under Cromwell. But very few English Jews trace their ancestry in this country back so long; the majority are descended from the refugees who arrived at the close of the last century and the beginning of this one, fleeing before the outbreaks of violence in Russia. What, then, has happened to the descendants of the Anglo-Jewish community of a century, two centuries, three centuries ago? The answer is, of course, that to a large extent they have assimilated, in an atmosphere of decreasing prejudice, greater toleration and loosening religious bonds. There have been many conversions, there has been much intermarriage, there has been, on an even larger scale, imperceptible merging with the majority. One can trace the descendants of some families who were established here at the formative period of the Anglo-Jewish community, and though some of their descendants are still inside the Synagogue, there can be little doubt that the majority of them are outside. Conversely, of the aristocratic English families who set the tone to the country as a whole and whose genealogical ramifications are most easily ascertained, there are few—from the Duke of Norfolk and the Marquess of Salisbury downwards—who have no Jewish admixture or alliance. Again, certain names which were once characteristically Jewish—Ricardo, Aguilar, Lopes, Schomberg—are now barely ever met with inside the Jewish community, but are common outside it, mainly in the upper strata of society. But the same necessarily applies elsewhere, and among the bourgeoisie and even the proletariat inquiry shows that Jewish connections or half-forgotten Jewish ancestry are incredibly common.

This process has been singularly comprehensive. The descendants of the former pillars of the Synagogue merged completely and without qualification with their neighbors. The British Army families of Jewish extraction—Pereira, Aguilar, Barrow—are today indistinguishable in type as well as in mentality from other families who traditionally follow the same calling. The famous Victorian wit, Bernal Osborne, descended from a Jewish Bernal who played some part in synagogal life in London, could be described in Lady Dorothy Neville's *Memoirs* as a wild Irishman, and Lord Roborough, head of the Lopes family which became converted rather more than a century ago, was called by the *Times* when he died a "leader of Devon men." It does not even seem that Jewish mental characteristics survive in any marked measure in such cases any more than the Jewish physical characteristics—recessive, as scientists inform us— have done. The traditional Jewish acumen is itself in all probability nothing more than a reassertion of natural vigor after generations of ghetto depression; and there does not seem to be any marked persistence of it in the descendants of assimilated families, or, indeed, in Jewish families long soaked in their environment. Nor is there discernible any sociological or economic distinctiveness, other than a tendency to urbanization which, in view of the origins of the families in question, is inevitable.

v

It must be pointed out, in order to avoid misconceptions, that the process was reciprocal. Just as there was a constant procession from Jewry to Christendom and Islam, so there was (on a smaller scale but also into a much smaller population) a continuous trickle from Christendom and Islam to Jewry. Even in the darkest hour of Jewish history, when to embrace Judaism was to court death, there was no period in which there were no converts to Judaism, in greater or in smaller numbers, impelled either by conviction or by passion; and these converts were accepted whole-heartedly and unreservedly by the Jewish communities, into whose midst their descendants became completely and inextricably merged.[5] A process of the sort, continuous over many centuries and into a small community, must necessarily have modified the purity of the Jewish strain. Thus, what with the non-Jewish strain among the Jews, and the Jewish strain among non-Jews, the Jew and his neighbor have had far more common ancestors in these centuries than is generally imagined. The only unimpeachable differentiation is in fact the religious one, whether that be applied to the present generation, as has generally been the case, or (as has become fashionable in the last few years) retrospectively for one or more generations.

Here, then, we have the answer to the allegation that Jews are unassimilable. Clearly, the reverse is the case. Were it not so, their number in the world today would be at least ten times what it is. The mere fact that only in the comparative tranquility of the nineteenth century the total again equalled what it had been in the heyday of the Roman Empire proves definitely that in all the intervening period Jews had assimilated. Having assimilated, they have disappeared from our ken. Only in one or two instances do occidental families of today preserve recollections of their Jewish origin centuries ago. The rest have become absorbed, lost without trace, in the general mass of the population in which they live. Only a minority has remained faithful to

---

[5] See the essay, "Proselytes of Righteousness" elsewhere in this volume, pp. 143 ff.

their religion, and it is they or their immediate descendants who are today termed "Jews."

In Nazi Germany, an arbitrary dividing line was taken. Conversion before 1800 was admitted as valid; after 1800 it was not recognized, and the descendants had to bear the stigma which attached in that country to persons of Jewish extraction. The reason for this (apart from sheer physical difficulty of continuing genealogical research indefinitely) was the assumption that before the age of emancipation the line of demarcation between the Jews and their neighbors was so strong that there was virtually no admixture. That is to say, in order to prove that the Jews are "unassimilable," and that ostensible assimilation during the past 150 years was fraudulent and may therefore be disregarded, it was postulated that before this date the phenomenon was unknown. But this is demonstrably untrue. It is clear that, as one goes back further the circle widens. In 1933 the number of Jews in Germany was about half a million, of "non-Aryans" some two millions. But if one were to fix the line of demarcation at 1700 instead of 1800—an equally logical or illogical date—it is probable that the number of the latter would be doubled, and if one goes back far enough it would presumably embrace the totality of the population of the country. For the process of assimilation of and by Jews in Germany—as in other countries—was continuous ever since the dawn of history. At the risk of repetition, I want to make it quite clear that assimilation was not due only to pressure; during the past hundred years or so, it has been a spontaneous process. Nor is it a question, generally speaking, of the greater attractions of some other religion, such as (in the western world) Christianity. It is the result rather of the loss of positive attitude towards Judaism, itself largely dependent on the rapid decline in Jewish educational standards and the general decline of religious belief.

There is no indication that this process has ended. It is true that the violent pressure which existed in previous generations, and which compelled or tempted innumerable Jews to abandon their faith, has disappeared. But the influence of the environment, on the one hand, and the breaking down of the religious bond, on the other, have been even more potent. Conversions are relatively less frequent today perhaps than they have ever been for the past twenty centuries. But, on the other hand, the abandonment of Jewish tradition and absorption in the environment, inter-marriage accompanied by absorption, the bringing up of children without any notion of the Jewish religion, with its inevitable consequence of absorption, have become more and more widespread. There are some places where, according to statistics, more Jews marry non-Jews than Jews. There are others where it is almost unusual for a Jewish child to be given even the most elementary religious training or induction into his ancestral faith. Everywhere, Jews living among non-Jews are abandoning more or less completely all trace of their Jewish individuality. In Russia, the communist experiment of breaking down Jewish economic distinctiveness and of undermining the traditional Jewish occupations, coupled with the legal prohibition of antisemitism and the quasi-prohibition of religious teaching, has resulted in a very few years in the destruction of much of the individuality and a great deal more of the probability of survival of what was until recently one of the numerically greatest and most religiously devoted of the world's Jewries.[6] Moreover, unlike their ancestors, who set up synagogues and religious organizations in every new center to which they penetrated, the Jewish pioneers of today are isolated human

---

[6] The situation in the USSR has changed in several respects since this essay was written in 1941.

beings, whose offspring are likely to be lost to the community to which their ancestors belonged.

Hence, apart from the horrible losses that the Jewish people suffered at German hands between 1939 and 1945, there is not only the possibility but also the probability that, left to their own devices, there will be a further catastrophic decline in their numbers in the course of the next generation or so. This will be in part due to the fact that the Jews belong in the main to the urban elements and to the petty bourgeoisie, among whom the birth-rate has declined so rapidly and who are committing race-suicide. This tendency, it may be observed, is even more marked among the Jews than among their neighbors, and is accentuated, moreover, by the fact that the former have no rural reservoirs from which to be reinforced. Indeed, were Nazism to have left the German Jews alone, it seems likely that in the course of a generation or so the Jewish "problem" in Germany would have been solved, neatly and completely, by the disappearance of the Jews.

More drastic is the force of assimilation, the inroads of which seem likely to make away with a majority of those whom race-suicide may leave. In small communities the process is already in action and is very rapid indeed. In the larger, where the Jews constitute a fairly compact body, it is not quite so marked. Thus, in a city like New York, where the Jews form one-quarter of the population, it is inevitable that for the moment the tendency should still be for Jewish social life to remain fairly homogeneous, and a considerable Jewish population must continue to exist for some time to come. But in smaller communities, where the Jews constitute ten or five or one per cent of the total number, the forces of assimilation are overwhelmingly strong. With the progress of acclimatization and the weakening of the force of religious tradition, they may score in the end an overwhelming triumph. This indeed is the argument of one school of Zionists, who see only in Palestine the guarantee for continuing to live Jewish lives with good hope of transmitting the Jewish tradition and Jewish ideals to future generations.

The events of the past few years have, of course, modified this state of affairs. The Nazi government in Germany and its imitators elsewhere proclaimed in no uncertain tones— and largely on the ground that the Jew is unassimilable!— that assimilation was to end, while in other countries the spread of the racial idea, on the one hand, and the consequent renewal of Jewish consciousness on the other, did something to slow down the process and even thrust back into the Jewish fold persons who a few years back seemed to be lost to Judaism for good

However that may be, the charge that the Jew is unassimilable is demonstrably untrue. He has assimilated with his environment, continuously and vigorously, during the past two thousand years. The Jews of today are simply the religiously unassimilated residue left by this process who were, until a few years ago, continuing it at almost suicidal speed. Far from being unassimilable, then, the Jews are— from the Jewish point of view—only too assimilable.

That, however, is their own problem.

4. THE MEDIEVAL CONCEPTION
OF THE JEW[1]

i

THE problem which I am endeavoring to solve in this paper is one which must have impressed many other students of the Middle Ages, but which I have never seen formulated, namely, that of the amazing mentality which contemporary literature, records and chronicles appear to ascribe to the Jew. Close examination shows that according to these sources he does not seem either to think or to act like other human beings. His behaviour in matters of the utmost significance is completely irrational. He is proof, apparently, not only against logic and argument, but even against ocular demonstration. Nevertheless, he is prepared to maintain his absurd opinions, and to persist in his preposterous conduct, to the death. He is, of course, depicted as an enemy of Christendom—that goes without saying. But he gives expression to his enmity under circumstances, and in a fashion, conceivable in no ordinary man: and he persists in his attitude even when publicly proved in the wrong.

Let us take, as a point of departure, the curious spectacle presented by the medieval "Disputations" between Jews and Christians. In most cases, these are misnamed. I am not for the moment alluding to the fact that they were so one-sided, that the verity of Christianity was assumed by the sponsors to be beyond all question, and that any fair debating reply on the part of the Jews to the obloquy heaped

1 Originally published in *Essays and Studies in Memory of Linda R. Miller* (New York, 1938), pp. 171-190. The thesis has since been developed systematically by Dr. Joshua Trachtenberg in his fascinating volume, *The Devil and the Jews* (New Haven, 1943).

upon their heads would be characterized, and punished, as blasphemy. Quite apart from this, these discussions did not necessarily center upon the merits and verities of the two faiths. They were in many instances attempts to prove *from the Talmud and kindred writings* (the italicised clause is all-important) that the Messiah promised in the Bible had already appeared in the person of Jesus. This was the case, in particular, in the Disputation of Tortosa in 1413/4— the most spectacular of all those of the Middle Ages—when the apostate Mestre Geronimo de Santa Fé pitted himself against the flower of Spanish Jewish scholarship, in the presence of the anti-Pope Benedict XIII and his *curia*. On this occasion, the efforts of the champion of Christianity were concentrated in an endeavor to convince his opponents not out of the Bible, but out of rabbinical literature, that the Christian religion was the true one, and Jesus the Messiah. This argument postulated, in effect, that the rabbis of the first centuries of the Christian era had admitted the messiahship of Jesus, realized the verity of Christianity, and even given their ideas literary expression, while at the same time organizing Judaism as a separate faith, based upon the denial (not to say the blasphemy) of the Redeemer whom they knew to have appeared! [2]

All this appears to the modern mind utterly absurd. There are, as it seems to me, three possible explanations.

---

[2] The contemporary records are too prolix to permit the quotation in full of passages to prove this point. Cf. however Moses Nahmanides' account of the Disputation of Barcelona of 1263: "Then again said Brother Paul [i.e., Pablo Christiani, the Christian protagonist] that in the Talmud it is written that the Messiah is already come; and he brought evidence from the Midrash on the Lamentations of Jeremiah . . . Then again Brother Paul said that it is stated explicitly in the Talmud that Rabbi Joshua ben Levi [learned from the Prophet Elijah that the Messiah was to be found among the sick in Rome] . . . And he is Jesus." See also Baer's study on the Disputation of Tortosa in a recent issue of the *Spanische Forschungen,* and his documents, p. 331: "Talmudice auctoritates per magistrum Jeronymum contra judeum allegate . . ." For the Disputation of Barcelona, see now my article in *Harvard Theological Review,* xliii (1950), pp. 117-144.

One is to deny the authenticity of the records—which in the case just mentioned, at least, are unimpeachable. The second is to question the sanity of the theologians who put forward this point of view, of the pontiff and prelates who applauded it and of the Christendom which admitted it. Yet the medieval mind was as keen, as logical and as eminently reasonable as is ours. The last alternative is to discover the premise which permitted this line of argument, and (as we shall see) much else traceable to it.

ii

I have found it, I think, in the conception which I now wish to submit for consideration. We are accustomed, at the present time, to the phenomenon of the person who does not conform to the state religion. Even in rigidly Catholic countries, such as Spain or Portugal, non-Catholics are known and tolerated. The Jew is regarded in consequence simply as a dissenter—different perhaps in degree, but not essentially in kind, from the Wesleyan or the Baptist or the Adventist. In the Middle Ages, of course, the picture was entirely different. In Western Europe, where the most important Jewish communities were to be found, the Catholic Church was everywhere supreme. The residue of the old pagan faiths had been rooted out, or else forced to conform. Heresy was fiercely suppressed. The only exception which qualified the universal homogeneity of faith was, therefore, the Jew. The very conception of dissent being strange, he could not be fitted into that category. He was not a heretic— one who professed himself a Christian, but refused to conform to Catholic doctrine. Moreover, he knew the Scripture, he lived among Christian people, he was not ignorant of Christianity. He was in this respect completely dissimilar from the benighted, ignorant paynim. He was neither a heretic, on the one hand, nor a heathen, on the other. He was something more—an unbeliever: nay *a deliberate unbeliever*. Unlike the unfortunate Hindu or Moslem who had never known the truth, he was one who, knowing the truth, refused to recognize it.

Here we have, as I believe, the solution to the problem which I have endeavored to propound. This explains why the verities of Christianity might be proved from the Talmud; for the rabbis of that age realized them and did not scruple to put them on record in their recondite Aramaic compilations, for the information (not, of course, for the guidance!) of posterity.

The Jews (so many Christians argued) had witnessed the life and activities of Jesus. They had seen all the prophecies of their ancient seers fulfilled in and by him. They had personal experience of the miracles by which his claims were so amply substantiated. But, in spite of all this, they refused to give him the recognition which was his due. They had gone further. They had crucified him, because he did not live up to the standard of earthly splendor which they had anticipated. Their medieval descendants, had they been present at the time, would *ex hypothesi* have acted in a precisely similar manner, for the attitude was one inherent in the Jewish nature in all ages.

The perpetuation of the enmity against them, generation after generation, was not therefore entirely unreasoning nor (granted the premises) illogical. The Jews were not blamed (as is generally believed) simply for the crime committed by their ancestors. They were blamed for a crime which was the inevitable outcome of their stubborn national temperament—one which, had circumstances permitted, they themselves would certainly have condoned, and which they were prepared to repeat at any time if they had the oppor-

tunity. The "unbelieving Jew" (not the unbelieving Mus-
sulman, or the unbelieving heathen) thus became a by-
word. After the forced conversions in Spain and Portugal,
in the fourteenth and fifteenth centuries, the same physical
and moral characteristics which had marked the Jews, and
the same qualities of deliberate misbelief, were considered
typical of the New Christians, their descendants: [3] and in the
long succession of anti-semitic literature written to assail the
Marranos of the Peninsula, exactly the same charges figure.
It is not suggested that this was the universal conception
of the Jew—Gregory the Great, or Bernard of Clairvaux, or
Thomas Aquinas, obviously thought differently. But it
must have been a very widespread conception, particularly
among the less educated; and it explains a good deal in the
medieval religious mentality which otherwise remains
incomprehensible.[4]

There were numerous natural signs which clearly indicated to the popular mind that the Jews were a race apart,
cursed for all eternity. The Jews had tails—a superstition
credited in remote parts even now. They were distinguished
from the rest of mankind by a bloody flux and a peculiar
odor which disappeared automatically on the administration
of the waters of baptism! This was enough, surely, to make
rational beings realize the error of Judaism. But the Jews
were not rational beings, and it was preposterous to regard
them as such.

A striking illustration of this attitude is provided by the
story of Ahasuerus, the Wandering Jew. When Jesus was

---

[3] In the case of the "Old Christian" Martyr of the seventeenth century
[see pp. 182 ff.], Don Lope de Vera, who was of unsullied *limpieza*, it was
suggested that the milk imbibed from the breast of his Marrano foster-mother
sufficed to infect him permanently with Jewish disbelief!

[4] More than one Pontiff and scholar of the Middle Ages, indeed, went
out of his way to teach that the Jews were men like any others, and should
be treated as such. Possibly, this was intended to controvert the popular
view of the Jew here outlined.

on his way to crucifixion, according to an almost universal medieval legend, a Jewish shoemaker pushed him and told him tauntingly to go on. In punishment, the Savior in turn condemned him to go on forever, "till I come back." In consequence, the Wandering Jew was believed immortal. He reappeared at intervals thoughout the Old World and the New, but could not die. No person, assuredly, could have had more convincing proof than this eyewitness of the messiahship and divinity of Jesus. But, notwithstanding this fact, the Wandering Jew remains eternally a Jew. He does not profess repentance. He is dressed in characteristic Jewish garb; and he never accepts baptism.

In this, as in so much else, the Wandering Jew is typical of his people: for the Jews of more recent times were as intentional in their disbelief as their ancestors had been at the time of the Crucifixion. The pretensions of Jesus were incontrovertibly proved (it was considered) from the Holy Writ; but the Jews did not scruple to tamper with many such passages in the hope of obscuring the evidence. In the heyday of the Renaissance, an Italian Jewish scholar named Lazzaro de Viterbo felt impelled to write a treatise for the Cardinal Sirleto vindicating the integrity of the Hebrew Scriptures. St. Jerome himself accused them of suppressing the doctrine of the Trinity in a number of verses of the Prophets. St. Justin asserted that they eliminated certain incriminating statements from Ezra and Nehemiah. Even in the year 1932, a Catholic scholar could express implicit belief in this charge. Under the circumstances, it is little wonder that, in the Middle Ages, the Jews were suspected of wholesale suppression and misinterpretation of any biblical prophecies which might prove them in the wrong. They *were* in the wrong. They knew it. But they staunchly refused to admit it, even at the cost of eternal suffering in this world and the next.

iii

It was not only the Scriptures that they were willing to distort for their own ends. As we have seen, they were as unscrupulous in their treatment, and their interpretation, of their own recondite Jewish authorities. The controversies which center upon them were thus no ordinary disputes. They were attempts to tear away the veil of hypocrisy behind which the Jews had taken refuge, and to show the world that their own teachers realized (even if they did not recognize) the essential truth of Christian doctrine. Similarly, the pioneer Christian students of Hebrew, Pico della Mirandola and Johannes Reuchlin, were able to justify their interest in such suspicious lore only by demonstrating that, though the Jews refused to admit it, Jesus was plainly indicated in the cabala.

Nor was it from the Talmud and the allied literature alone that the Jews could be confuted. Their great historian, Josephus, bore eloquent testimony to the life and miracles of Jesus. Naturally, they not only refused to pay any attention to these passages, but in case of need would even suppress them. An anecdote of Giraldus Cambrensis (*Opera* VIII. 65), describing an alleged episode of the twelfth century, is eloquent in this respect:

"But it is thus clear how great is the malice of the Jews, and how obstinate and obdurate is their teaching against their own weal, that even the testimony of their historian, whose books they have in Hebrew, and consider authentic, they will not accept about Christ. But Master Robert, the Prior of St. Frideswide at Oxford, whom we have seen, and who was a man old and trustworthy, whose latter years coincided with our earlier ones, was a man of letters and skilled in the Scriptures, nor was he ignorant of the Hebrew tongue. Now he sent to diverse towns and cities of England in which Jews have dwelling, from whom he collected many Josephuses written in Hebrew, gaining them with difficulty, since they were acquainted with him because of his knowing the Hebrew tongue. And in two of them he found this testimony about Christ written fully and at length, but as if recently scratched out; but in all the rest removed earlier, and as if never there. And when this was shown to the Jews of Oxford summoned for that purpose, they were convicted and confused at this fraudulent malice and bad faith towards Christ." [5]

One of the most common, most tragic and most widely-believed of all charges brought against the Jews in the Middle Ages was that of desecrating the Host. From the thirteenth century down to the eighteenth, this accusation continually made its appearance in various parts of Europe and was the occasion for massacres, expulsions and judicial murders galore. It was alleged that the consecrated elements were stolen and ritually outraged by torture, stabbing, or flagellation. This is, perhaps, the most preposterous of all accusations of the sort. It is perfectly obvious that such action in a Jew would be completely paradoxical. It presupposes a degree of belief in the supernatural qualities of the sacrament which he could not conceivably hold, if he retained his religious convictions. If (as the result of some curious mental aberration) he desired to show his contempt of Christianity in some tangible manner, an unconsecrated wafer (obtainable with far less difficulty and danger) would have served his purpose equally well. So, at least, it would appear to the modern mind.

But the medieval point of view was quite different. Of course, the Jew believed in the supernatural qualities of the Host—no rational being could do otherwise. Of course, he was perfectly aware that after consecration the wafer became

---

[5] Robert Eisler ingeniously, though unconvincingly, suggested that the MSS in question actually contained an elaborated version of the *Testimonium Flavianum*, such as may be found in the Slavonic Josephus.

transformed into the very body of Christ. It was for that very reason that he desired to get it into his possession and to torture it, making it know once again the sufferings of the Passion. The offense was generally said to come to light because of the astounding reactions of the Host to its maltreatment. It would spontaneously rise into the air, or bring about an earthquake, or above all—in a majority of cases—shed blood in discernible quantity (a phenomenon for which a scientific explanation is in fact available, in the *micrococcus prodigiosus* which may appear on stale food kept in a damp place). On one occasion, we are informed, while some Jews were burying pieces of a pierced Host in a meadow, the fragments changed into butterflies which began to heal cripples and restore the sight of the blind. On another, they fluttered out of a swamp, and a herd of grazing oxen did homage before them. On another, when the wafer was being burned in a stove, angels and doves flew out. In an early legend, we are told that the wafer whimpered like an infant on being pierced. Similarly, in another account, the blood is said to have splashed over the foreheads of the Jews who were engaged in the torment, leaving an indelible mark which betrayed their crime.

In consequence of tales such as these, myriads of innocent persons perished in the long centuries which followed the first tragedy at Belitz (near Berlin) in 1243, when a large number of Jews were burned at the stake on the spot subsequently known as the *Judenberg*. Yet in barely a single one of these instances is it reported that any individual was sufficiently impressed by the miracle to request baptism, even though this would certainly have saved his life.[6] Some-

---

[6] Considering the inherent dangers, it was difficult even for medieval naiveté to ascribe an adequate reason for such behavior on the part of the Jews. One was found, sufficiently preposterous to fit the crime, in the assumption that the blood which flowed from the Host could cure the Jews of their unpleasant smell, the *foetor judaicus*, or endow them with the fresh complexion denied them by nature!

times they are reported to have been surprised, but no more than a Christian would be at a similar happening. Why was this? The answer is not difficult to find on the hypothesis which I am attempting to propound. They knew that the Host actually *was* the body of Christ (it was for this reason only that they went to such risks to obtain it). It was therefore natural, even in their eyes, that it should react in a human fashion when cut with knives or tortured. There was no reason why, on that account, they should change their attitude towards Christianity, which was one of deliberate defiance; and they mounted the pyre or the gallows still continuing in their sacrilegious negation of what they knew to be true.

Closely akin to this accusation in its essential paradoxicality and incredibility was another of a like nature. A charge frequently brought up (not so much, it seems against the Jews themselves, as against the New Christians or Marranos, who were left behind in the Iberian Peninsula when the Jews were expelled) was that of scourging and otherwise maltreating crucifixes or images of the Madonna as part of a religious ceremonial. Thus, for example, the principal sufferers in the great auto-de-fé held at Madrid on July 4th, 1632, were the supporters of a secret synagogue which had been discovered in the Calle de las Infantas.[7] Part of the procedure at these illicit assemblies is said to have been the flogging of an effigy of Christ. It manifested its sufferings by shedding blood and thrice chiding the delinquents. It might have been imagined that, under such circumstances, the latter would have repented wholeheartedly of their misdoing. Instead, they consumed the object with fire. Inquisitors and Grandees of Spain vied with one another in their zeal to destroy the building in which so heinous an action

---

[7] Lea, in his *History of the Inquisition in Spain*, III, 130/1 and 310, duplicates this episode, ascribing some lurid details to 1732.

had taken place; and the Capuchin convent subsequently erected on the site was known as La Paciencia, in rememberance of the patience with which Christ had borne the indignities inflicted upon his image.

iv

The case was not dissimilar with regard to the alleged Ritual Murders, committed on the person of an innocent child. With regard to this ghastly libel, which unhappily still haunts the Jews in many parts of the world even at the present day, a great deal of confusion has arisen, through which the real issue has become obscured. The terms "ritual murder" and "blood accusation" are today used interchangeably. They actually denote, however, two completely different conceptions. The Blood Accusation is the charge levied against the Jews of obtaining Christian blood (generally, but not invariably, as the result of homicide) for use in manufacturing their unleavened bread or other ritual requirements at the Passover period. The motive, according to Thomas of Cantimpré in his *Bonum Universale de Apibus,* was rational enough. Ever since the Jews had called out to Pilate "His Blood be upon us and on our children," they had been afflicted with haemorrhoids. A sage had informed them that they could be cured *solo sanguine Christiano*— that is, through the blood of the Messiah whom they had rejected. Through wilful blindness, however (here we find further support for the hypothesis I am endeavoring to establish in this paper), they preferred to interpret this advice literally. Hence some congregation in each province (the choice being made, according to another account, by a conference of rabbis which assembled at Narbonne) undertook to slaughter a Christian each year in order to obtain blood for distribution amongst their co-religionists far and near.

Why, however, was this imagined crime associated with the Passover? And why was the putative victim always, or almost always, a boy, hardly ever being ascribed to the opposite sex? In order to answer these questions, we must direct our attention to the other conception which (as I have shown elsewhere [8]) is the earlier—that of Ritual Murder. In spite of all the efforts of the Council of Nicaea, the Jewish Passover still approximates to, and sometimes even coincides with, the Christian Easter. It is with this that the atrocious charge levelled against the Jews was originally associated, the Passover connection and the consumption of blood (now considered axiomatic) being later developments. Christian Europe was first made acquainted with the idea in 1144, on the occasion of the discovery of the body of little William, a tanner's apprentice, in a wood outside Norwich. The day, on which the murder was said to have been committed, was the Wednesday in Holy Week (March 22nd). This happened in that year to coincide with the *second* day of the Jewish feast, when the major solemnities were already concluded. According to the envenomed oration made before the Synod by the priest Godwin, as reported by Thomas of Monmouth, the outrage was so fixed because of the incidence of the occasion, not in the Jewish but in the Christian calendar (*dominice passionis ebdomada*) on which account the Jews were bound to carry out such practises (*ex dierum quibus tale quid a iudaeis fieri debuerit habitudine*). The murder of the child was thus in imitation of the Passion, and without any connection with the Passover, on the one hand, or with the ritual use of the blood,

---

[8] "The Feast of Purim and the Origins of the Blood Accusation" in *Speculum*, October 1933.

on the other. These two elements began to figure only at a later period, after the close approximation of the Jewish and Christian solemnities began to be noted; and for a long time, though the two ideas were confused, the earlier remained paramount.

It must be admitted that, granted the premises (that is, the Jew's deliberate disbelief and his hatred of the Messiah whom he had wittingly rejected and slain), the earlier idea is the more logical; and it enables us to realize at last the origin of what has hitherto seemed a particularly stupid and pointless libel. It enables us to see why the alleged victim is always a boy, and never a girl. It explains the origin of so many of the grotesque accompanying details which are so frequently found—for example, the perpetration on the victim of tortures reminiscent of the Passion, and the conclusion of the outrage by a reenactment of the Crucifixion. It provides the clue, moreover, to one mysterious sequel which had previously been peculiarly perplexing. The victims were generally revered by the populace as martyrs; and in some instances the Church itself unwillingly acquiesced. The cases of "St." William of Norwich, "St." Andreas of Rinn, "St." Hugh of Lincoln, "St." Simon of Trent, and El Santo Niño de la Guardia (dramatized by Lope de Vera) will readily come to mind: yet they are only a few out of many. In these cases, there is one detail which appears supremely illogical. A child of three or four years, perhaps, as yet unexposed to the trials and temptations of existence, can hardly have had the opportunity to show supernal perfection in his daily life. The mere fact that he was put to death, unwillingly, at the hands of the Jews would not appear to give him *per se* a title to the adoration of the faithful, any more than falling in battle against the Saracen did to the average crusader. If, however, the children were purported to be slain, not merely in a spirit of hatred or in order to obtain their blood, but as a quasi-religious ceremony in imitation of the Crucifixion (exactly similar, therefore, to the alleged crime of desecrating the host) it is obvious that the case was different. Something of the divinity of Jesus himself descended upon the innocent boy, who had ostensibly suffered in a ceremonial reenactment of his Passion. Beatification (in the popular heart, at least) was thus a foregone conclusion.

In these instances, too, it may be noted, the conduct of the Jews after the discovery of the alleged outrage is significant. The crime was generally said to be made manifest by miracles performed by the tortured body. Thus, when "Little St. Hugh" was martyred at Lincoln in 1255, it was found impossible to bury the corpse, which rose spontaneously, time after time, to the surface of the ground. On other occasions, the body gives out a sweet odor, or the child continues to chant the *Ave Maria* (as in Chaucer's "Prioress's Tale"), or the church bells ring without human agency. But such phenomena seldom persuaded the Jews of the exceptional heinousness of their action—a fact of which they were already abundantly aware; and they were considered willing to stage a similar parody without qualms in the following year. How different all this was from the attitude of ordinary non-Christians, who would go in droves to the baptismal font for conversion to Christianity in consequence of the slightest manifestation of supernatural phenomena! Nothing, indeed, was generally required to open the eyes of the latter to the light but the preaching of any earnest missionary—whose main difficulty, according to the chronicles, was to secure a hearing. It was not, therefore, that the Jews did not believe in Christianity, in the same sense as Moslems or heathens did not believe in it. It was that they were constitutional antagonists of Jesus Christ—of a Jesus whom they knew to have existed and to have been justified in his divine claims, but whom they had crucified rather than admit to be their king.

v

The Jews, then, deliberately rejected Christianity, while realizing to the full the implications of their attitude. Small wonder then, that their professions of religion were not always taken seriously. They were hardly considered to be, in fact, worshippers of the Most High. They were followers rather, in a literal sense, of Beelzebub, on whose support and favor they counted to save them from the divine anger which was the natural consequence of their sins.

Conscious misbelievers such as these were plainly less than human. Individuals whose whole life was a perpetual conflict against Jesus and his followers were capable of any crime, imaginable or unimaginable. They were prepared to assassinate without compunction any of their co-religionists, or even their own children, who desired to pass over to Christianity. They did not scruple to butcher non-Jews for the purposes of their infernal rites. At time of pestilence, it was they who had poisoned the wells. At time of war, they were prepared to betray Christendom to the Moslems or to the Tartars. They exported large quantities of weapons from Germany to arm the latter, concealed in barrels. Their physicians were suspected of the intention of murdering all patients who came under their charge. (There was a New Christian physician in Lisbon who was said to have boasted that he had brought about the death of no less than 2,000 true sons of the Church in the course of his professional career.) They were the declared enemies of God, of the Christian faith and of the human kind.

The popular medieval conception of the Jew, as a deliberate miscreant rather than as a mere unbeliever, thus explains to some extent the bitterness, as well as the psychology, of the persecutions of that age. When persons of this nature were concerned, it was impossible to feel consideration or fellow-feeling. They could hardly be considered human beings, and human sentiments were out of place where they were concerned. Atrocity could be repaid with atrocity. They might be expelled and despoiled, without compunction, by any Christian monarch, who in persecuting them performed a duty rather than committed a crime. They could be attacked and exterminated by the mob, with no more hesitation than a pack of wolves. On the assumption advanced in the foregoing pages, it is possible to acquit the ordinary man of the Middle Ages of unreasoning cruelty in his relations with a people whom he was encouraged to consider in so distorted a light; but not our own contemporaries, who revived an equally preposterous conception in this ostensibly enlightened age.

5. THE ETERNAL PROTESTANT[1]

i

AMONG the perennial problems of modern life is that of Jewish survival. Time was (and not so very long ago) when assimilationists were asking, scornfully, why on earth the Jew should survive; time is, thanks to Hitler, when some of the same persons are asking, querulously, why the Jews must survive. After all, the question is not one which can be easily dismissed. There are millions who cling tenaciously to their Jewish heritage because it is theirs, regarding it as treacherous to surrender, in the hundred-and-first generation, what has successfully resisted the erosion of the past hundred. Yet it is not so easy to justify that persistence logically. Liberal Judaism, indeed, endeavors to do so by the "Mission of Israel" theory. But, even from the religious angle (and still more from the irreligious!) this is open to question. It can be maintained that the Jew has served his purpose, from the spiritual point of view, by destroying the revolting polytheism of former days, and implanting ideas of morality in the world. Some forms of Judaism and advanced Christianity are in effect hardly distinguishable: and the lessons of the Hebrew prophets are now the common property of the entire human race. It is not as though we live up adequately to the standards which we profess to have set humanity. Many Jews make themselves prominent in objectionable ways which need not be specified—so different from the superb idealism of Isaiah. We speak speciously about our contribution to modern civilization: but is our quota of great men really so considerable

---

[1] Originally published in *Opinion*, September 1934.

as to justify our existence? At the best, we have produced a great *French* philosopher, a great *British* statesman, a great *German* scientist, a great *Austrian* physician, a great *American* judge. Would not their roles have been equally important had they lacked the Jewish background? Even the Zionist achievement in Palestine (the most significant among recent developments) bids fair to produce nothing more memorable than another "lesser nationality," to join Bulgaria and Greece in diversifying the cockpit of the Near East.

I do not want it to be imagined that the above represents my view: but it represents a view which is widely held, and which cannot be dismissed with scorn. It is not contested that the Jewish people has made an imperishable contribution to humanity in the past. But we cannot always live in the past. What of the future? How would humanity suffer if the Jews were now to disappear?

ii

The answer to this question lies, I think, in an examination of what has been one of the most obvious and important functions of the Jew in history, since Biblical times. With my taste for the romantic, I always seem to find my parallels in the Book of Esther: and there, in the figure of Mordecai, I see the prototype of the historic Jew: *"And all the king's servants that were in the king's gate bowed and reverenced Haman. . . . But Mordecai bowed not, nor did he do reverence."* Israel, more intimately than China, has watched the legions thunder past, the juggernauts of civilization roll unwieldily along, fetish succeeding fetish and -ism succeeding -ism. All have commanded universal obedience in their days: each in turn has momentarily appeared to represent the acme of human progress. But, even at the height of their authority, Israel (and Israel alone) has not bowed down nor done reverence. It has provided the still, small voice of scepticism which in the end has undermined the foundations of the idol of the moment, thus saving the world from the curse, first of uniformity, and then of stagnation. It is this, the role of the Eternal Protestant, which has justified the Jewish existence for the past two thousand years.

In the second century before the Christian era, a little band of devotees on the hills of Judea took it into their heads to resist the advance of culture and civilization in their backward country. Creasey does not count the Battle of Emmaus in 165 B.C.E. among the Fifteen Decisive Battles of the World. Nevertheless, it certainly deserves to rank in their number, more than Hastings or even Waterloo: for it was this which saved humanity from the unquestioned victory, inexorably followed by the tyranny, of Hellenism. Contemporaries no doubt regarded Antiochus's reverse much in the same light as our fathers did a French or English setback in one of our "colonial" wars against "uncivilized" fanatics. Judea, at the time of the birth of Jesus, would very likely have been a more pleasant country to live in, had the Hasmonaean brothers never risen in revolt, or had they been crushed at the outset. In fact, however, they were successful (though not perhaps quite so successful as was once thought, seeing that political intrigue had as much to do with the outcome as victory in the field). Their action saved Judaism—hence the annual celebration of *Hanukkah*. But it is not too much to add that it saved humanity. But for it, the triumph of Hellenism would have been complete, and its sway undisputed throughout the Mediterranean. The synthesis which goes to make up modern civilization would have lacked one of its most important components—the Legacy of Israel, both in its direct expression and in its

Christian dilution. Above all, the western world would have lain under the incubus of an unchallenged uniformity—which, however specious and attractive at the outset, must have ended by becoming an obsession.

iii

In point of fact, uniformity was never so much a reality as in the medieval world, when the power of the Roman Catholic Church was supreme in Western Europe and all men, from the Arctic to the Straits of Bizerta, believed and thought in an identical fashion. This unquestioned hegemony was broken by the two allied movements, which we term the Renaissance and the Reformation—the former undermining the foundations of the medieval world by scientific criticism, and the latter extending that process to the study of the Bible and to theological dogma.

In both phases Jewish influence may be traced. The inception of the Renaissance came about when Christian Europe rediscovered part of the lore of the schools of Athens, which had been preserved in Arabic versions in the schools of Cairo and Cordova. The part which the Jews played in this process is well known. It was from them that Christian Europe heard of the existence of these treasures: and they were largely responsible for the translations, *via* Arabic and Hebrew into Latin, which made them available to Dante and his contemporaries. The intellectual history of Europe would have been fundamentally different but for the activities of men like Jacob Anatoli and Johannes ibn Daud. Had it not been for them, it is doubtful whether the Italian savants would have realized the opportunities afforded them in the fifteenth century, when the fall of Constantinople flooded their country with scholarly Greeks.

In the Reformation, the part played by the Jews was less direct: but it was not less important. Much has been written regarding the Jewish influence on Christian reform movements. I personally venture to regard as somewhat exaggerated the views put forward by Rabbi, Louis I. Newman, in his weighty monograph on the subject: but there is certainly a good deal to be said to support his thesis. The Roman Catholic Church, indeed, had no hesitation in associating the Jews with those movements which threatened its supremacy. In consequence, its traditionally tolerant policy was qualified, after every reforming outburst, by legislation which aimed at thrusting the Jew back upon himself and preventing him from contaminating Christendom further by the taint of his disbelief. Thus the growth of Albigensianism was followed by the formulation at the third and fourth Lateran Councils (1179 and 1215) of the terrible repressive code associated especially with the name of Pope Innocent III. This, seldom consistently enforced, was reverted to at the beginning of the fifteenth century, at the period of the growth of the Hussite movement, with all its fatal potentialities as far as Roman Catholicism was concerned. It was finally put into effect, to the accompaniment of all the horrors of the Ghetto system, as part of the considered policy with which the Counter-Reformation of the sixteenth century answered Luther.

This timidity of the Church was not entirely unjustified. The historian cannot agree with the view put forward, from entirely opposite angles, by some Catholic apologists and some Jewish pamphleteers, in accordance with which Jews were continually working to implant, to foster, to spread the seeds of disbelief which were undermining the authority of the Church. On the other hand, it is impossible to deny that so often, on these occasions, appeals for support were made to Jewish tradition, and some Jewish teacher was hovering in the background. For these movements were based upon the conception of free enquiry into the true meaning of Holy Writ, for which the example, the counsel and the tacit support of the Jews was invaluable.

It is not easy for us today to realize the degree of regimentation which prevailed in the medieval world. It was not so much that every man believed the same, as that the possibility of believing differently hardly occurred to the ordinary person. From every pulpit in Christendom, the same doctrine was proclaimed as axiomatic. But in every city in Christendom there was to be found a handful of persons who, against all reason, persisted in holding to their own "preposterous" tenets. They were as intelligent as their neighbors, as learned as their neighbors: yet nevertheless they refused to do as their neighbors did, or to believe as the Church bade them believe. The populace, perhaps, could dismiss them as "unbelieving Jews." But their presence forced the more intelligent to think for themselves, in order to find out why these neighbors of theirs, cooped up in the *Judengasse,* persisted in opinions which the world branded as preposterous. The conclusion to which they came was not identical with the Hebraic view: yet, had not the Jew been present, it was doubtful whether they would have realized that there was a problem to solve, or reached any conclusion at all. It was not that the Jews deliberately fostered the Reformation: it was that their presence rendered reformation inevitable.

The classical case in point, in this connection, is of course that of Johann von Reuchlin. He came to the Jews to study their literature, himself remaining scrupulously and unquestionably orthodox to the end. Yet the stand which he made in the world of scholarship, as champion of Hebrew literature, resulted in the great battle of books which began with his disputation with Pfefferkorn, reached its climax in the

Epistolae Obscurorum Virorum, and so led, by an uninterrupted chain, to Luther and his epoch-making revolt. *Pace*
the majority of historians, the new Protestant states showed
themselves, at the beginning at least, no more friendly towards the Jews than their Catholic rivals: yet it is doubtful whether the Reformed faith would have come into being
but for the challenge which the existence of the Jews flung
to the spiritual and religious ideals which had previously
prevailed. It is interesting, in this connection, to compare the
stagnation of seventeenth and eighteenth century Spain with
contemporary conditions in the rest of Europe. No doubt
this was due, in part, to the benumbing influence of the
Inquisition. But may we not ascribe it also to the fact that
the Jew, with his stimulating scepticism, was in exile?

iv

This is not intended as a merely antiquarian study, con-
centrating upon the past. It remains to be seen how far the
Jew is perpetuating this traditional "Protestant" role of his
in the modern world. As a matter of fact, this, under slightly
different nomenclature, constitutes one of the commonplace
accusations levelled against him even today. He is, we are
perpetually told, destructive rather than constructive. He
produces nothing essentially great in literature, in music
or in art. Yet nearly all the most penetrating critics, literary
and musical and artistic, are Jews. By their questioning of
existing political and economic institutions, rather than by
their positive contributions, they contributed materially to
the upbuilding of the new world which came into being
after the Napoleonic wars. The work of Karl Marx and of
Albert Einstein was more potent, if not more important,
on the negative side than on the positive. Without Jewish
criticism—that is, without the spirit of protestantism innate

in him—the world of yesterday would have been a very different thing.

And today?

Once again (to a greater extent than in the Dark Ages—for the spiritual element is now entirely absent) the world is suffering from the danger of Authoritarianism. Its roots are in politics: but its tendrils are penetrating to every corner of our intellectual life, establishing a stranglehold with unbelievable rapidity.

The Jew, however, is still the Mordecai, who refuses to bow down or to do reverence: still the Eternal Protestant. It is not simply a question of the traditional Jewish "passion for righteousness," or of the invincible human potentialities of the Jewish heart, so much as the spirit of free enquiry which is innate in him. "No Jew is really a Fascist," an Italian once said to me. She was wrong, superficially: yet in a profounder sense she was right. However loyal a Jew may be to an authoritarian state as a momentary expedient, he is sentimentally incapable of accepting it as a permanent ideal. The Jewish spirit within him will continue to question—perhaps to mock: and his questions must one day find practical expression.

Jacob Wasserman's superb spiritual autobiography, *My Life as German and Jew,* contains one passage which is extraordinarily significant in this connection:—

The unfortunate fact is that one cannot dispute the truth that the persecutors, prompted agents and volunteers alike, had something to go upon. Every iconoclastic incident, every convulsion, every social challenge has seen, and still sees, Jews in the front line. Wherever a peremptory demand or a clean sweep is made, wherever the idea of governmental metamorphoses is to be translated into action with frenzied zeal, Jews have been and still are the leaders . . .

Personally, I must confess that I abominate much of this activity sentimentally, as much as I regret it politically. Yet at the same time it seems to me that one should welcome the mental attitude of which it is the manifestation. (Jacques Maritain approaches the same conception with his idea of the Jewish "ferment.") It is the modern expression of the spirit of the Eternal Protestant, who always refuses to be satisfied with the present condition of affairs, and will never surrender himself entirely to the prevailing current in ideas, in ideals, in political theory. Today, he happens to be most prominent, perhaps, in the revolutionary cause. Yet the tyranny of the Left is as alien to his conceptions as that of the Right. The undermining of the conceptions of the orthodox Marxianism, tomorrow, is no less likely to be the work of some Jewish spirit than was the undermining of orthodox Capitalism yesterday. One may endeavor to explain away, for reasons of expediency, the existence of these Jewish stormy petrels: yet, in one's heart of hearts, one must be glad that they are making their presence manifest. As the Jew, by the fact of his existence, preserved the world from stagnation in the Dark Ages, so his existence is a perpetual challenge to the benumbing Authoritarianism of today. Jews are still protestants—protestants against the modern deification of the State as they were against the deification of the Church four centuries ago, and against the Juggernaut of Hellenism before the Christian era began. In no narrowly theological sense, it may be said that the survival of Judaism may yet mean the salvation of civilization.

6. FOLKLORE OF THE GHETTO[1]

IT IS not my intention to give here a comprehensive survey of the subject of Jewish folklore. That would be out of the question in the space at my disposal, even if it were within the compass of my ability. For very much has been written upon this fascinating topic from various angles: it is enough for me to refer to the periodical published for so many years in Germany by Dr. M. Grünwald (*Mitteilungen zur jüdischen Volkskunde*, Hamburg, etc., 1898-1929, succeeded by his *Jahrbuch für jüdische Volkskunde*, Berlin-Vienna, 1923, 1924-5), which later had its counterpart in Palestine in the absorbingly interesting quarterly, *Edoth* ("Communities"), published in Hebrew and English under the editorship of Dr. R. Patai. All that I can do is to call attention to certain aspects which have impressed themselves upon my notice in connection with my own studies. And, my studies being centered upon Western Europe, it is with Western Europe that I will naturally deal especially: not with the Central and Eastern European masses, now almost obliterated out of existence through the ghastly tragedy of the past few years, who had absorbed so much of the folkways of the peoples among whom they lived and in some cases added to them much of their own. At the same time, I will not deal with any specifically religious practices, or practices that obtained a religious sanction: for by this very fact they ceased to be dependent on folk-memory and thus lost what is obviously the essential quality of folklore.

But, even if we accept this restriction, there are certain Jewish practices which demonstrate a folk-memory which

1 Lecture delivered before the Folk-Lore Society in London, November 19, 1947; published in *Folk-Lore*, LIX, pp. 75-83.

perpetuated itself, as it were, underground over a period of very many centuries. Recent archaeological investigation has brought to light an extraordinary instance of this. One of the well-known Jewish dietary taboos which has received religious sanction forbids the consumption of meat and milk together, or of the latter immediately after the former. The reason for this is given in the rabbinical literature as an extension of the thrice-repeated biblical prohibition of seething a kid in its mother's milk (Exodus, 23. 19; 34. 26: Deuteronomy, 14. 21), which was fantastically elaborated. But the rabbis were no half-wits, and it is probable that they sought in the Bible a justification for a practice that was already well-established. For the basic prohibition against "seething a kid in its mother's milk" was presumably not based merely on humanitarian and sentimental grounds, but at the same time was a revulsion against an established heathen practice. This, conjectured many centuries ago by Moses Maimonides, who may be considered the father of the study of comparative religion, has now been finally established by the discovery at Ras-Shamra, in Phoenicia, of the prescriptions of a heathen cult going back to 2000 B.C.E., which, among other things, prescribed the seething of a kid in its mother's milk as part of the celebration of the Feast of First-Fruits, corresponding to the Pentecost. But here we have an amazing survival. The hyper-orthodox Ghetto Jew who normally waited for six hours after meat before consuming milk or cheese waived this on the Pentecost and partook of the one quite soon after the other, milk and milk products being, in fact, the dish prescribed by tradition for this festival. The ridiculously tenuous reason given for this is that Pentecost is associated with the giving of the Law, which is compared to milk and honey: but in view of the recent discovery which I have mentioned, we can hardly doubt that it is the survival of a very ancient prescription, wholly unrecorded in the meantime; the result of a folk-memory, which links together Palestinian Baal-worship and the simple piety and dietetic practice of the Ghetto Jew, the twentieth century B.C.E. with our own day.

Here we have, I think, a striking instance of chronological continuity. My next instance will illustrate not association with antiquity, but association with the environment. The domestic service held on Passover Eve, the *Seder,* is rich in folkloristic elements: for example, the egg, which figures among the unused and, as it were, superfluous appurtenances of the ceremonial, is clearly to be identified with the Easter egg, itself a pre-Christian reminiscence. The ritual recited on this occasion is called the *Haggadah,* or "Recounting," and it contains folk-hymns such as the *Had Gadya,* or "One Only Kid," which is a Jewish form of the "House that Jack Built," and a "madrigal of numbers," *Who Knows One?* which is the counterpart of *Green Grow the Rushes, Ho!* etc. (but, un-like it, goes up to thirteen!). Much has been written about this, but I desire to call attention to something which so far as I know is completely novel. The *Haggadah* was one of the few works in the Jewish tradition which was commonly, or even usually, illuminated or illustrated, from the Middle Ages onwards. The illustrations follow a certain definite convention: for example, they show the events leading up to the Exodus, with plentiful legendary elements introduced in some cases, such as Pharaoh's bath in the blood of Jewish children in order to cure his leprosy: or the "negromancers" shown, owing to confused folk-etymology, as negroes. Now, in the German and Central European manuscript *Haggadahs* of the Middle Ages, and in the earliest printed versions of the sixteenth century, one of the conventional illustrations depicts a hare-hunt. This is obviously out of place in a religious work: all the more so since Jews did not normally have either taste or opportunity to indulge in hunting, and anyway would not have wasted their efforts on a hare, which they considered a "forbidden" animal. But a curious reason for the inclusion of this scene was to hand. If Passover started on the conclusion of a Sabbath, a sequence of benedictions at the beginning of the service had to be in the following order: first *Yayin*—Wine; then *Kiddush* or Sanctification; then *Ner* or Blessing over the light; then *Habdalah* or ceremony of the conclusion of the Sabbath; finally *Zeman* or blessing of the festive season. The initials of these five words, *YKNHZ* was vaguely similar to *Jakenhas*, contracted from *Jag'den Has'*—"hunt the hare." Hence (one was informed) the reason for this illumination, which gave the pious householder guidance through an involved portion of the service.

Surely a less complicated expedient might have been found; and in editing the *Haggadah* service I was profoundly dissatisfied with the explanation that I had to give. But, when I recently read Mr. John Layard's absorbing study, *The Lady of the Hare* (London, 1944), I found the true explanation. In connection with a psychoanalytical problem that had presented itself to him, he brought together a great deal of material dealing with the Hunting of the Hare which especially in Central Europe, attained a symbolical significance and for this reason figures even in stone carvings in many churches. In Pomerania it was customary to eat a hare at Eastertide; in England a hare-hunt traditionally took place on Good Friday, and elsewhere on Easter Monday. All this, be it noted, was especially associated with the Easter season. There cannot be the slightest doubt that this usage was as familiar to the Central European Jews as it was to their neighbors, and that it was for this reason that they introduced it into their conventional religious art, precisely in the Passover (i.e., Easter) season. An ingenious mnemonic was discovered by which the illustration could be brought into some sort of preposterously tenuous relation with the text: but it is clear that this was only secondary.

Another very interesting analogy with the folklore of a remote antiquity is to be found in a practice in vogue, until recently, among the almost-extinct Jewish communities of Avignon and the Comtat Venaissin, and still practised by those of Italy, though not apparently elsewhere. It is customary here to prepare some little time before the New Year festival, in September-October, a plate containing a few grains of corn, which are covered with water sufficiently to keep them damp. On the Eve of the New Year, when they have begun to sprout, they are placed on the festive supper-table and left there until after the Day of Atonement, ten days later, or the Feast of Tabernacles which follows soon after: they are then thrown away. Here we obviously have an echo in Jewish custom of the very ancient tradition of the Gardens of Adonis, which still lives in varying forms in many parts of Italy and Provence—the same areas, that is, where the Jewish usage recorded above has survived. It is customary that on or about some religious feast (mid-Lent in Sicily, Good Friday in Tuscany, St. John's Day in Sardinia) the peasant women prepare plates containing grain, which is moistened; when it has sprouted, they are taken to adorn the Holy Sepulchre in the churches. It is an interesting point to speculate whether this is a case of imitation by the Jews of the folk-ways of their neighbors in Europe, or whether they themselves brought the practice with them independently from Babylon and Palestine. In either case, this is obviously a relic, now given an orthodox religious tinge, of the "pleasant plants" or "plantings of Adonis" so resented by the prophet Isaiah (17.10).[1] In the original form the Gardens of Adonis

---

[1] "For thou hast forgotten the God of thy salvation, and thou hast not been mindful of the Rock of thy stronghold; therefore thou didst plant plants of pleasantness, and didst set it with slips of a stranger" (that is, of a strange god).

were prepared by sowing grain or any other rapidly-growing seed in earthenware or other receptacles (sometimes in costly silver vases). In due course, when they had sprouted, they were displayed in the funeral ceremonies that were held each year for the god who was dead and would now arise; subsequently they were thrown into the sea, or else in running water. It would take us too long to demonstrate how this practice (mentioned, too, in the eleventh century *Arukh* of Nathan of Rome in a slightly different form) links up with the rite of *Tashlikh,* or the throwing of crumbs (formerly grains of corn) into running water on the New Year, ostensibly as a symbol of God's casting the faithful's sins into the depths of the sea. It is a far cry between the long-bearded Eastern European Jew, piously emptying his pockets at the water's edge on the afternoon of the New Year, and the lamentations for Adonis in ancient Syria: but the continuity of tradition is hardly to be doubted.

But this is not all. In another curious survival, very much disapproved by some of the greatest rabbinical authorities, it was customary to perform a quasi-sacrificial ceremony on the eve of the Day of Atonement, waving a fowl (as a rule a cock for a male and a hen for a female) round the penitent's head to the accompaniment of soul-stirring verses from the Bible; the animal was then slaughtered and it or its value given to the poor. Clearly, this whirling of the religious object round the head, at the same season of the year, is another relic of the ceremony associated with the Gardens of Adonis; at one period of antiquity, indeed, it was performed not with fowls but with plants.

Another demonstration of the close interconnection of the folklore of the Jews and that of their neighbors may be seen in the prevalence of amulets and charms, which received a powerful impetus after the cabala established so intimate a hold from the sixteenth century onward. These, however, would vary from country to country, the rude inelegance of the written formulas that were usual in Eastern Europe contrasting vividly with the Hand of Fatima, etc., known in the Moslem countries and the extremely artistic silver objects which are sometimes found in Italy. The Jews were indeed considered among their neighbors to be specialists in this sort of thing, but the influence of the environment on them was extremely marked. I have, for example, seen the word square

S	A	T	O	R
A	R	E	P	O
T	E	N	E	T
O	P	E	R	A
R	O	T	A	S

transliterated into Hebrew as a charm for specific use, but with an uneven number of letters, and thereby losing all of its former mystical symmetry.

To a certain extent, the folk-practices of the Ghetto were dictated by obedience to or reaction from religious prescriptions. To sit on a stool or on the ground was considered unlucky: for one sat thus when one was in mourning for a parent, and it was as it were an evil omen to do so at other times. To kneel was considered objectionable: for Christians knelt in church, and Jews should not do so, therefore, in any circumstances. It was an orphan who recited the Memorial Prayer known as the *Kaddish:* therefore, one whose parents were still living should not do so. Similarly, there was a taboo, not indeed universal, against calling a child by the name of a living parent or grandparent, originating in the idea that in such cases the name of the latter would be bandied about in the house in a derogatory manner.

The elaborateness and universal observance of Jewish religious prescriptions, not monopolized by a priest or confined to a place of worship, were a fruitful source of Jewish folklore. It is natural, I imagine, for popular superstitions to cluster round any object used for ritual purposes once its function has ended, folklore abhorring a vacuum as much as nature does. For example, on the Feast of Tabernacles a citron was taken to synagogue, with a palm-branch, in obedience to biblical prescription (Leviticus, 23, 40). But what can be done with it when Tabernacles is over? It now enters into the realm of folklore: it would be used as the handle of a circumcisional knife, or given to bite to a pregnant woman, who would then assuredly bear a male child. Similarly, the ritual meal on Passover Eve ended with a fragment of unleavened bread, which still goes by the Greek name of *Aphikomen* (*'επίκωμσί* dessert) : for this whole celebration is in its way a fossilized festal meal preserved from classical times. Eaten at the very end, when people were supposed to be sated, it was natural that fragments were left over, which were slipped into the service-books and kept from year to year. Around this, now, a whole body of unofficial lore clustered. To eat it was said to prolong life. Carried about the person, it was a precaution against the evil eye. In Italy it was regarded as a safeguard against the terrors of a thunderstorm, and the Jews would throw it from the house-tops to conjure away hail. I have been informed that Sir Moses Montefiore once used it similarly, to his complete satisfaction, during a tempest in the Mediterranean.

There is one very curious and long-lived piece of Jewish folklore which may also have its origin in a trivial religious prescription. On *Hoshanna Rabba,* the last day of the Feast of Tabernacles proper, before the two nominally separate days of final celebration, it is customary to take willow-branches into the synagogue, this being a reflection of an ancient temple practice. But that which is used for a religious purpose should not be tainted by any suspicion, however remote, of dishonesty. Hence these branches had to be acquired by purchase and, since Jews were not rooted on the land, by purchase from a Gentile. Whether it was because of this or no, or whether it was a revulsion from the great and perhaps promiscuous festive gathering that had formerly taken place on this night in the temple at Jerusalem, or whether, conversely, the specification that the acquisition must be made from a Gentile was the result of this, it ultimately came to be regarded as unlucky for a man to venture outside the door of his house on this night, which in Jewish tradition was the night of the final divine judgment on mankind year by year. For, if a man looked at his shadow in the moonlight (the moon was at this season just beyond the full) he could see what fate had been decreed for him in the coming twelve months. If the shadow lacked a limb, it betokened that he would be mutilated; if it lacked a head (God forbid!) it betokened that he would die. This popular superstition, which I have traced in Spain in the Middle Ages (and has its parallel among German Christians), seems to have become very firmly established in due course: and in the Customaries (*Minhagim*), published in northern Europe as late as the eighteenth century, the stereotyped engraving to illustrate *Hoshanna Rabba* shows a group of men, willow-branches in hand, standing in the moonlight, one of them with a weirdly-drawn headless shadow, like a partial Peter Schlemihl.

It is not my intention here to go into the extraordinarily fascinating subject of the folk-stories of the Ghetto, but it should at least be mentioned that they are to be found in colorful profusion in every land: stories such as the appearance of the Patriarch Abraham in Synagogue at Hebron

to make up the quorum of ten for prayer, or of the kidnapped Jewish child who became Pope, or of the sage who
saved the Ghetto from sack, or the synagogue from the
flames, by inscribing mystical divine names on the doorposts, or of the venerable and venerated Scroll of the Law
that floated ashore of its own volition when a ship was
sunk off the North African coast, or the whole cycle of tales
associated with the *Golem* of Prague, or (but this is, of
course, Gentile lore, though associated with the Ghetto)
of how the Madonna appeared in synagogue in order to
save the sacred scrolls from desecration during a pogrom.[1]
It is a subject that demands, not a paper, but rather a volume.

The folklore of the Ghetto penetrated to England, too.
There is a remarkable account of the folk-customs of English Jewry in the eighteenth century, which loses nothing
in the telling, in *The Book of Religion, Ceremonies and
Prayers of the Jews,* by Gamaliel ben Pedahzur, Gent.
(London, 1738) —in fact, the production of a spiteful apostate named Abraham Mears. His account, written with the
obvious object of bringing his erstwhile co-religionists into
disrepute, does not differentiate in the slightest between
religious prescriptions and mere superstitions: this, perhaps, giving it an additional value, though we must, of
course, make allowance for both ignorance and exaggeration. The value of this from the point of view of folklore
may be gauged from the fact that a second edition of the
descriptive material, republished in 1753 under the title
The Jewish Ritual, has recently been studied exhaustively
with a view to its analogies with the folklore of the Penn-
sylvania-Germans in the U.S.A.[2]

---

[1] See *The Madonna of the Scroll* in this volume, pp. 305 ff.
[2] A. M. Aurand, *Little Known Facts about the Ritual of the Jews . . .
an impartial examination of the folklore of the Pennsylvania Germans, dili-
gently compared with an English interpretation of the Jewish Ritual, or the
Religious Customs and Ceremonies of the Jews . . . published in London
in 1753* (Harrisburg, 1939).

I will quote one or two samples of Gamaliel ben Pedahzur's material: If any person desires to ask pardon of the
dead for any differences that were between them in his
lifetime, he stands at the foot of the coffin and takes hold
of the great-toe of the corpse, praying his forgiveness; violent bleeding at the nose shows that this is witheld [3] (p. 9,
ed. 1753). The deceased is thought to hear and know
everything that is said or done about him, until the last
spade of earth is flung over him: his spirit is supposed to
visit the apartment where he died during the following
week (p. 12). If a man loses a tooth, etc., it is saved and
buried with him (*ibid.*: in fact, in the ancient Jewish cemetery at Chatham there is an elaborate tombstone recording
that the stone that had been cut from a man was buried
at his head). As is well-known, it is customary to break a
glass at Jewish weddings—symbolically a symbol of mor-
tality, folkloristically an expiatory sacrifice to bad luck:
but Gamaliel tells us that "the Batchelors generally strive
to carry off a Bit of the broken Pipkin, believing it likely
to promote their being married soon after." He gives in
some detail what he terms "The Opinions of the Jews concerning Apparitions," which they considered to have power
to appear visibly and injure any one single person who was
by himself and in the dark: where there were two persons,
the apparition could show itself, but do no harm; where
there were three, or a lighted flambeau, neither the one
or the other was possible.[4] Evil spirits were to be found in
whirls of dust or rubbish heaps, which are therefore avoided
(obviously a sound hygienic principle). The London Jews
believed that witches could harm them if they found, tied

---

[3] This must have been a very wide-spread practice: I have now seen it
depicted in an engraving of Venetian Jewish life by Giovanni la Pian
(eighteenth century). Once again, there is no need to stress the analogies:
it is enough to think of the story of Richard I at his father's bier.

[4] This belief, like some of the other mentioned, is talmudic in origin,
but Gamaliel records it as though it were very much alive in his day.

together in a bunch, the tops of any greens, such as turnips, carrots, parsnips etc., which had been flung away: or in eggshells or pieces of earthenware discarded without being broken into minute pieces. But, of course, there were remedies against such untoward contingencies, as we read in Gamaliel's most delightful passage: "There are some women among them that pretend to cure all Distempers, which they believe to proceed from an evil Eye, by the Sympathy of Fumigation: Some Part of the Garment worn by the Patient is sent to the said Doctoress, which she holds over some certain smoking Stuff of her own Composure, muttering some few words over the Garment, under the Operation, and that Garment being return'd in a few minutes to the Patient, to wear immediately, never fails of giving Relief, unless their Ailment has been of too long Standing before the old Woman smoak'd them. The usual Price for smoking of a Child's Cap, is a Shilling. A Woman's Petticoat, two Shillings. A Man's Pair of Breeches, half a Crown. *N. B.* The *Spanish Jews* pay more, because the *Smoakers* are *Germans*" (pp. 51-2).

There must, of course, have been much more of this sort that at one time became established in the London Ghetto. A century ago, the beadle of the Great Synagogue in London used to knock thrice with his key at the door of the place of worship before he opened it for service every morning, so as to give notice to the spirits of the departed who had gone there during the night that it was time to depart. The tale is told by an old Anglo-Jewish historian, Moses Margoliouth, that the cemetery of the now long-defunct community of Ipswich received the last remains of a brace of pigeons whose post-mortem conduct (for they ran about moaning after their throats had been cut) caused them to be regarded as the recipients of transmigrated souls: this may, however, be a misinterpretation of a practice at one time common, and itself interesting from the point of view of folklore, of inaugurating a new cemetery by the burial of birds before any human interment took place.

But such lore or practice was, in every case, imported to this country from abroad, and could not stand up for long to the cold light of English rationalism. Today it is difficult to find among the English-born Jews any relics of such beliefs or practices, their place having been taken in many cases by those of the environment—for example, the common prejudice against sitting down thirteen at table. I have known this to be adhered to almost with frenzy even in the religious gathering of Passover Eve—a vagary which, in view of the Paschal associations of the superstition (in connection with the Last Supper) is hardly credible. Obviously, in the long run, Environment is more powerful than Tradition.

7. THE MEDIEVAL UNIVERSITY AND THE JEW[1]

i

ON THE whole, the connection of the Jew with the medieval university[2] was, to say the least, non-academic. For the most part it consisted of the professional relations inevitable between the ubiquitous moneylender of medieval times and that most impecunious of all classes—the university student. We read frequent injunctions limiting the amount of usury which the Jew might be permitted to charge students; until finally, in Spain, he was prohibited from making them any loans at all. Add to these professional considerations the general odium in which the Jew was held, and it is not surprising that he should have furnished that unruly fellow, the medieval student, with an object for attack, even more to his liking than the ordinary townsman, on any occasion of academic ebullition, and that the Jews were the principal victims in countless student riots.

---

1 Originally published in the *Memorah Journal*, vol. XVII (1930), pp. 127-141. The subject has also been dealt with by Dr. H. Friedenwald in an essay, "The Jews and the Old Universities," in his valuable collection, *The Jews and Medicine*, vol. I, pp. 221-240. See also "Jews and the University of Montpellier," *ibid.*, pp. 241-242; and Guido Kisch, *Die Prager Universitaet und die Juden*, Maerisch-Ostrau, 1935. I have since dealt with the relations between the Jews and the University of Oxford in the Middle Ages, in very great detail in my volume *The Jews of Medieval Oxford*, Oxford, 1950; and with the general problem of the qualification of Jewish physicians in the Middle Ages in a lengthy article in *Speculum*, 1953.

2 The term "medieval university" is advisedly used in this essay in place of "the university of the Middle Ages"; for the medieval regime, in university life, lasted generally till well on in the eighteenth century. It was, indeed, coeval with the medieval conception of the Jew, which became general only at the dawn of the Renaissance and was widely broken down only at the period of the French Revolution.

Indeed, there were some places where this traditional student activity developed into a university custom which received semi-official authorization. Thus, in Italy, it was a universal student prerogative to bombard the Jews with snowballs on the occasion of the first snowfall of the year— a right which was compounded at Turin by an annual payment of twenty-five ducats, and at Mantua by a heavy ransom of confectionery and writing paper. At Padua, besides paying a tribute of confetti on this occasion, the Jews had to give a number of fat capons, or the equivalent, on St. Martin's Day. At Pisa, down to the beginning of the nineteenth century, it was customary for the students to weigh the fattest Jew they could find each year on the day of St. Catherine (November 25th—the official beginning of winter), and to exact his weight in sweetmeats from the rest of the community as a ransom. In Bologna, as early as 1401, the Jews were compelled to give twenty-four lire every year to the undergraduates for a special banquet.

There was one particular student grievance against the Jews in the university community. Jewish respect for the bodies of the dead made them unwilling to contribute to the medical school their quota of corpses for dissection, and in some places they paid heavily to be excused from doing so. Despite this, the students resented the invidious discrimination; and repeated riots occurred in consequence, culminating sometimes in the interruption of funerals and the desecration of burial grounds—just as in Eastern Europe in more recent times.

In one or two other points, there was some incidental contact between the medieval university and the Jews. The constant danger of attack drove the Jews to build houses of especial strength, often of stone: an art of which they were, as a matter of fact, among the first exponents in western Europe. These were much sought after in Gentile circles:

so much so that when Walter de Merton founded his model college at Oxford, he used as its kernel a house which he purchased from Jacob, son of Rabbi Moses de Londres. (It is the original bilingual deed of sale, still preserved, which inspired D'Blossiers Tovey to his famous remark that "The *Graven Image* upon this seal can't be thought a Breach of the *Second Commandment;* for in it is the Likeness of nothing that is in *Heaven, Earth or Water,*") Other of the Jews' residences seem to have been used as lodging-houses for the students: witness the names of Moysey's, Lombard's and Jacob's Hall (all near the "Great Jewry" of the Middle Ages), which remained at Oxford until comparatively recent times.[1] Jews were well known, in fact, as property-owners; hence, they were familiar as University landlords, this perhaps being responsible in the first place for the "Halls" which bear their names. The forfeited pledges which fell into their hands included many codices and, as a result, they seem to have been active as bookdealers. Similarly, the University of Heidelberg in its early days was considerably enriched by a grant of the property taken from the Jews on their expulsion in 1390. Their manuscripts went to the University Library, while the synagogue became converted into the University Chapel.

ii

Scholastically, however, the relations between the Jew and the medieval university had degenerated from the standard of a previous era.

In the classical antiquity, it is not likely that there had been any restriction upon the Jew in the academies of

---

[1] I have now dealt with this subject in very great detail in my book, *The Jews of Medieval Oxford*, Oxford, 1950.

learning of the time, excepting such as his own sensitiveness might impose. There is little doubt, though positive evidence is lacking, that he could attend lectures freely and that, if he developed into a really able scholar, he might in turn become a recognized lecturer. Philo of Alexandria, for example, must have been able to study in the ordinary schools, and it is highly probable that his subsequent lectures were attended by Gentiles as well as by Jews. The Arabic universities were in theory less liberal. In 853, the Caliph, inspired by the Byzantine and Persian prohibition of the practice of physic by the Jews, forbade the Jews to teach or study medicine in any language other than Hebrew and Syriac. Nevertheless, the actuality was, as usual, more tolerant; and the names of many Jewish scholars are included in the list of those who taught in the schools of Bagdad and elsewhere, starting with the semi-mythical figure of a second Joshua, son of Nun.

In the Christian world, however, conditions were radically different. The position of the Jewish student in the scholastic life of medieval Europe is sufficiently indicated by the very name "University." The Latin term was "Universitas"—the inclusive whole, the *corporation,* of students and teachers. From any such corporative body, throughout Christendom, the Jew was inevitably excluded. "Excluded" is perhaps the wrong word, for it implies too conscious and too deliberate a process. The possibility of admittance did not in most cases so much as cross his mind—much less that of his Gentile neighbor. It must be remembered in connection with this that the rise of the great universities of Western Europe coincides with that period, after the First Crusade, when the systematic degradation of the Jew had begun. The Jew was not considered a burgher of the town in which he lived; nor could he become a member of any of the guilds which existed for the purposes of trade or of industry—and conditions were clearly even more absolute with regard to those yet closer fellowships which were coming into existence for the purpose of study. He would have been regarded as an intruder, and he would have felt uncomfortably out of place. A Jew attending a university in the thirteenth century would have been considered almost as much a phenomenon as an anthropoid ape, escaped from the zoological gardens, enrolling in Harvard today.

The general unfavorable attitude of the times to the Jew hardly required reinforcement, but there was one additional fact which by itself would have been effective to exclude the Jew from the medieval universities. Education and theology were in the Middle Ages very closely intertwined. (A sufficient reminder of the fact lies in the "benefit of the clergy" through which, down to the dawn of the nineteenth century, many a secular scoundrel escaped the gallows in England merely by proving that he could read.) Indeed, the universities of medieval Europe were almost without exception essentially ecclesiastical foundations. The oldest were for the most part developments of the primitive educational foundations attached to the cathedral churches, and papal license was necessary before such "schools" could be elevated to university status. The Chancellor was invariably a Churchman. The degree ceremony was essentially feudal, and *ipso facto* semi-religious. To enter the life of a university was not very different in kind from entering the life of a monastery. The obstacles to the participation of the Jew in university education were thus insuperable, notwithstanding Martin V's tolerant injunction of 1429 that no obstacle should be put in the way of Jewish would-be students. Indeed, in 1434, the Council of Basle crystallized existing practice by specifically prohibiting Jews to be admitted to a degree at any university (a provision which was afterwards adopted at some places in the Peninsula also with regard to persons of Jewish descent). Henceforth, it would seem there was no loophole for escape.

As a matter of fact, the whole of the discussion hitherto has been very largely pointless. Why discuss the conditions of the Jew's admission when that privilege, if granted, would have been almost entirely useless to him? In his own schools the Jew could obtain an education more catholic by far—in the truest sense of the word—than anything outside. Supposing, however, that some Jewish youth had thought that study in some university could broaden his mind, and that he had been admitted as a student without demur, he would have had the utmost difficulty in finding a subject to study. Not only were the universities essentially Christian in composition and idea, but their interests were extraordinarily limited. The principal subjects studied were essentially and narrowly sectarian. For the Jew, theology, which was the predilection of all of the greatest minds of the time, was obviously ruled out. Philosophy was equally excluded, since the current conception of philosophy was hardly distinguishable from theology, centering as it did upon the writings of Thomas Aquinas and his school, or else upon that of opponents who started from the same premises. Canon law was obviously useless to the Jew—it would, indeed, have been reckoned little short of blasphemous for him to attend lectures on the subject. Civil law was, to be sure, another matter. But among themselves the Jews preferred to be guided by the prescriptions of the Talmud and their own codes; and in interdenominational cases it was clearly unwise to handicap oneself with a Jewish lawyer, who would necessarily prejudice the court unfavorably. Of course, no Christian would see fit to consult a Jewish lawyer—there was an exception to this rule only in the island of Corfu, where the Jews enjoyed the unique prerogative of acting as advocates on behalf both of their own coreligionists and of Gentiles. As for the faculties of Arts, of Logic and of Rhetoric, they were studied at only a few universities, and were everywhere looked down upon as inferior; anyhow, they were of no practical importance to the Jew, whose humanistic interests centered about his own ancestral literature. Thus the only faculty that remained in which the Jew could have any practical interest was that of medicine; and it is around medicine that the discussion of the participation of the Jew in the life of the medieval university must, in effect, be centered.

iii

From the Byzantine era the Jews had been forbidden to practice medicine upon the persons of true believers: a prohibition which was re-enacted time after time by the medieval Church. The reasons for this were plain. The physician had an authority over his patients which no infidel should be allowed to exercise. He had influence which he might use to bring about apostasy. Above all, on the deathbed he might even prevent the administration of the last sacraments of the Church. Hence, in theory, the exercise of the medical profession was to be confined to persons of unimpeachable orthodoxy.

The practice, nevertheless, was very different. For the Jews were famous as medical practitioners in medieval Europe. Indeed, medicine was fully as universal and as characteristic a Jewish occupation as the exercise of usury. No amount of legislation could possibly have excluded the Jew from a sphere for which he was so pre-eminently qualified; and in the case of illness most persons preferred to risk the possibility of excommunication at the hands of the Church than the probability of death through unskilful treatment by a Christian. Prelates and princes vied with one another to secure the services of Jewish doctors; and, the canons of the Church notwithstanding, a whole succession of them practised even in the Vatican itself.

Under such circumstances, it was inevitable that the Jews should have played a prominent part in the study of medicine in medieval Europe. In this, and in this alone, their share in university life was really important. And not as students only. This was especially true in the early part of the era. For, in the Dark Ages and the centuries immediately succeeding them, when Arabic medicine was supreme in the whole of Europe, it was perforce necessary to go to the Jews, those great intermediaries of medieval intellectual life, for the exposition as well as for the practice of the art. To learn only from persons of orthodox principles would have been, at this period, no less than ridiculous.

Accordingly, we find a tradition concerning the Jewish participation in the foundation and in the earlier activities of more than one of the great European universities, not as pupils but as teachers. In Salerno, particularly, the first European home of medical studies, the influence of Jews in the earliest days is said to have been decisive. Such reports are undoubtedly exaggerated, but certainly there was some collaboration, because it was inevitable. With regard to one or two places, documentary evidence exists. Thus, at Montpellier, it is persistently reported that Jews played an important role in teaching in the school of medicine, of which, it is said, Jacob ben Machir (otherwise known as Profiat Judaeus) was in 1300 appointed dean. In the fifteenth century, Master Elias Sabot (the same who was summoned to attend on King Henry IV of England) taught at Pavia; in the sixteenth century, the philosopher

Leone Abrabanel was at Naples; his contemporary Jacob
Mantino, the unromantic opponent of the Messianic claims
of Solomon Molcho and of the divorce of Henry VIII of
England, lectured officially in medicine in the University
of Bologna in 1529, and subsequently at the *Sapienza* in
Rome. (Probably 1539-1541). There are similar tales of a
Jewish professor of medicine named Gaudino (Isaac) at
Perugia in the fourteenth century; of one Hercules He-
braeus, who taught at Pisa in the middle of the sixteenth;
and of a certain Emmanuel de Lattes, who was engaged
by the municipality of Avignon to teach in the medical
school there (not, to be sure, of university status) in 1529.
In view of these reports, there is no need to doubt entirely
the persistent tradition that the Jews played an important
role in their earliest days in other universities where no
such definite report exists. It is significant that of the great
medieval universities it is precisely with regard to Paris,
where medicine played a relatively minor role, that no
similar report is preserved. It must be noted, however, that
the instruction given by Jews must generally have been
informal, so that their presence on the official roll of university teachers is exceptional in the extreme; and, on the
other hand, that, whatever element of truth there may be
in some of these reports, the implications have been grossly
exaggerated by some historians.

There were one or two other university subjects in which
the assistance of Jewish scholars must have been especially
welcomed in the early days. Foremost, of course, was the
study of Hebrew, in which their teaching was indispensable. Thus a certain Abraham Gallo taught Hebrew at
Ferrara in the sixteenth century; and over a long period of
time it was usual for some tame Jew to be found in the
Universities of Oxford or of Cambridge as the *praeceptor
linguae sacrae*. (Notable among these at the close of the

seventeenth century was Isaac Abendana, brother of the *Haham* in London.) At the earlier period, their assistance must have been also necessary in very many cases for teaching Arabic or procuring translations from that language, in which the intellectual treasures of ancient Greece were preserved for the medieval world. Nor was Jewish coöperation confined to these subjects. At the close of the fifteenth century, Elijah del Medigo, the tutor of Pico della Mirandola and a great exponent of Aristotelian philosophy, is said to have lectured at the University of Padua, though there is no evidence of his having occupied an official position. A similar tale is told a short time afterwards of Abraham de Balmes; while Judah Minz, one of the most eminent rabbinical authorities of his age, who died in 1508, is reported, apocryphally, to have followed this example so effectively that a statue was erected to him in the Great Hall of the University. In none of these cases is there any trace of an official appointment. Nevertheless, all of these anecdotes are illustrations of what was a matter of fact, to some extent, inevitable. To neglect entirely Jewish brains and Jewish attainments was impossible, even at the height of medieval intolerance. Innumerable scholars must have gone regularly for information, for discussion and for advice to their Jewish neighbors, whose presence contributed in many instances to that atmosphere of intellectual keenness and curiosity which gave birth to the medieval university.

iv

As the Middle Ages drew to their close, however, the participation of Jews in intellectual life, whether as teachers or as pupils, whether formally or informally, was placed in most countries completely outside the bounds of physical possibility. At various dates from the thirteenth to the fifteenth century the Jews were expelled from almost the whole of western Europe. Thus the University of Oxford attained its greatest glory at a period when, in all probability, no professing Jew ever set foot within the city walls. Much the same could be said of Paris. In Spain, where university development was backward, the general expulsion came about in the year of the discovery of America. In Germany, to be sure, there was always a miserable and degraded remnant, but it was outside the bounds of ordinary life; and the universities remained specifically closed to the Jews down to modern times. The same applied to Poland, from the sixteenth century the greatest center of Jewish life in Europe, which excluded Jews by statute from its solitary university at Cracow from the moment of its foundation. There was only one country of Western Europe in which Jewish life continued to flourish and to maintain its contact with the general world; thus the inquiry as to the position of the Jews in university life must in effect be very largely confined geographically to Italy, as it is, in point of subject, chiefly to medicine.

As the Middle Ages advanced, the interest of the Jews in the study of medicine had changed from that of teachers to that of students. The hegemony of Arabian therapeutics, of which they had been among the outstanding exponents, was passing; and it became increasingly necessary for them to go to the ordinary schools to study the latest developments of the art. Moreover, with the spread of standards of organization, a degree from some recognized school became considered an essential requirement of any respectable practitioner. Despite the passing of the age in which their native tradition and their international connections had given them so great an advantage, the Jews, in those countries where they were allowed to remain at all, continued to occupy a position of disproportionate prominence

PHILLIPS MEMORIAL
LIBRARY
PROVIDENCE COLLEGE

in medical practice. Their inherent skill and ability remained; and, repeated papal Bulls and governmental injunctions notwithstanding, their services were eagerly sought
after by princes and rulers, both secular and ecclesiastical.
Moreover, a regular supply of Jewish physicians was necessary to attend upon their own coreligionists in times of sick-
ness; and the opportunity of study could hardly be withheld
from them. For this, recourse had necessarily to be made
to the ordinary universities. Not even the most conservative
rabbis of the time voiced any objection to this, though it was
discussed whether Jewish students ought to wear the academic robes and, if so, whether these should be provided
at the corners with the fringes prescribed by Mosaic law.

For admission as student there was, as a matter of fact,
not much difficulty once the initial social prejudice was
overcome, for the attendant formalities were slight. It was
even generally possible to sit for examinations and thus to
qualify to act as a physician. Formal graduation, however,
was a matter of extreme difficulty. This was vastly increased
after 1564 when, under the stress of the Counter-Reformation, a papal Bull, *In Sacrosancto Beati Petri,* made it necessary for any graduate or candidate for graduation to take an
oath upon the Gospels and to make a public profession of
the Holy Catholic Faith. Exemption was procurable only
in one way. Since the admission of Jewish graduates was
contrary to the canons of the Holy Church, dispensation
could be obtained from the Pope, who was in addition the
natural overlord of any such semi-theological body as a
university and in whose dominions more than one of the
Italian seats of learning was to be found.

Thus, from the close of the fifteenth century, we find a
whole succession of Jewish students petitioning the Pope
or his representative for permission to be admitted to their
degree. By this formality, they became, as *doctores,* nomin-

ally qualified also to teach, though it is improbable in the extreme that they were normally able to exercise the privilege. A typical instance was that of Abraham de Balmes, later famous as grammarian and philosopher, who graduated at Naples in 1492 after receiving a special license from Alexander VI. At Pisa, there is a similar instance in 1554. Marco da Modena, who qualified at Bologna in 1528, and, like all the graduates of his year, was created a Knight of the Golden Spur by the Emperor Charles V who was then in the city, was no doubt licensed in the same way. In Perugia towards the middle of the sixteenth century the papal legate admitted a few Jews to degrees on the presentation of a special petition; after this period, owing no doubt to the Bull *In Sacrosancto Beati Petri,* there are no more instances. Siena was rather more liberal. The first instance of a Jewish graduation there was that of Isaac of Viterbo, in 1543. From 1628 to 1695, ten Jewish doctors were admitted to degrees; but from that date down to the extinction of the institution in 1804, not a single one—a striking illustration of the rise of intolerance in more recent times. In the free port of Leghorn, freedom of study and of graduation was guaranteed by the nineteenth clause of the famous Jewish Charter of 1593, affectionately known to later generations as *La Livornina.* In practice, however, Jews found it impossible to comply with all of the accompanying formalities, and it was not until late in the eighteenth century, when they were permitted to take degrees in "Medicine and Philosophy" (as the faculty was termed) without ecclesiastical intervention, and to take the famous Oath of Hippocrates upon a copy of the Pentateuch instead of a crucifix, that they were able to qualify. Even then, the ordinary fees payable upon graduation were doubled in their case.

But the great Italian center for the study of medicine was the Studio of Padua, an ancient community in whose intellectual life the Jews played a prominent part. An instance of the graduation of a Jew there is reported as early as 1409. This, however, was exceptional, as the statutes of the University expressly excluded any Jew. At this period, moreover, the degree ceremony was little less than a religious function, the accompanying formalities before the *Collegio Sancto* being conducted with great pomp by the bishop, who was *ex officio* the head of the examining body. A special papal license was accordingly necessary, here as elsewhere, before any Jew could graduate. With the Reformation, however, conditions changed. The Venetian government was never over-amenable to interference from Rome. Padua, by virtue of its geographical position, had become the Mecca of medical students from the Teutonic countries beyond the Alps, most of them Protestant. It was necessary to make some provision for the graduation of these heretics. At the beginning, while Catholics continued to appear before the Sacred College as formerly, all non-Catholics including Jews were—like William Harvey in 1602—admitted by the Count Palatine, with a much simpler ceremony, thereafter being designated as *doctores bullati,* instead of *doctores academie promoti.* In 1615 this right was abrogated and the *Collegio Veneto* was instituted for the same purpose.

From the middle of the sixteenth century, Padua was thus the great center for Jewish students of medicine. Many came from the neighboring Italian communities. But the schools of Padua were famous in the *Judengassen* in Germany and in Poland also, and from them came many Jewish students, some of whom achieved remarkable success. A typical instance was Tobias Cohen, author of a famous scientific compendium, who, born in Germany of Polish parentage, lived in France, studied in Italy, became physician to the Grand Vizier in Constantinople, and died in Palestine:

assuredly a typical member of the "tribe of the wandering foot and weary breast"! Frequently promising young men were sent at the expense of the communities of Cracow, Lublin or Grodno to study medicine in Italy so that on their return they might act as congregational physicians. Though in 1654 the Polish section of the student body resolved that henceforth no unbelieving Jew might claim admittance to their "nation," they continued to force them to acquire, at high cost, a certificate of protection. When some of the Jews tried to enroll in the German "nation," the Poles indignantly demanded compensation for this loss of perquisites. It has been conjectured that the influence of the doctors who studied at Padua is responsible for the presence in Yiddish of one or two phrases that seem to be of Italian origin. Besides these medical students, four youths belonging to the community of the city were empowered to be sent to the university to study conveyancing and law, though they were permitted to practice only for their coreligionists.

The Jewish students at the University of Padua possessed one especial privilege: they were exempted from the obligation of wearing the red hat which was supposed to mark off every Jew for contumely from the rest of mankind, and permitted to wear a black headdress like the other students. To compensate for this, they had certain special burdens. Originally, upon the day of graduation, they had to keep an open house with ample food and drink for all who cared to come: and one may readily imagine that some of the more impecunious Gentiles took care to arrange their diet on the previous days in such a way as to do justice to this enforced hospitality. Ultimately, this right was compounded by a fixed tribute. Every Jew, on graduation, had to give the beadle of the university one hundred and seventy pounds of sweetmeats. These were done up in thirty-five packets: one for each of the thirty-one "nations" into which the student-body was divided, with extra rations for the Anglo-Scottish and German sections, as being the most numerous, and for the servants of the university. Thus, it was reckoned that while it cost a Gentile 886 lire to graduate, the corresponding expense for a Jew amounted to no less than 1,650 lire.

All this, however, was an insufficient deterrent. Jewish youths continued to come to Padua for study from all over Europe. From 1517 to 1619, eighty Jews graduated there; from 1619 to 1721, no fewer than one hundred and forty-nine. If the length of the ordinary course was seven years, there must have been an average of about ten Jews always present in the university, besides the few natives studying law. When a Jew graduated, it was considered an occasion for general jubilation among his coreligionists; and numerous odes are still extant, some printed and some in manuscript, by Ghetto poetasters, congratulating some fortunate youth "upon the day that the Crown of Medicine and Philosophy was placed upon his head."

Padua, however, was unique. Elsewhere in Europe, even such slender tolerance as the Jews enjoyed there was impossible, or highly exceptional, down to late in the eighteenth century. At Leghorn, for example, as we have seen, it was not till 1738 that the provisions of the charter of liberties were observed and Jews allowed to take their degree in medicine. In jurisprudence this remained impossible until 1841, when Canon and Civil Law were at last separated. Outside Italy, conditions were most favorable in Holland: but even in this home of liberty the occasional Jewish graduate was permitted to call himself not "Doctor" (implying a license to teach), but *Medicinae Practicus*. A few Jewish students frequented the University of Leyden —mostly members of the local Portuguese community, with a sprinkling from the neighboring German cities, especially Frankfort-on-the-Main.

Their comparatively enlightened treatment was the occasion of pained surprise to contemporary foreign observers further down the Rhine, like Ulrich, the historian of the Jews in Switzerland. For in Germany, the universities remained specifically closed to the Jews; and it required the special intervention of the Great Elector to obtain the admission of a couple of his favorites, upon whom he bestowed a bursary, to the University of Frankfort-on-the-Oder in 1678. These gave expression to their gratitude by presenting their patron with a Hebrew grammar of their own composition. Nevertheless, even his powerful backing was insufficient to enable them to be admitted to a degree, and ultimately they had to go to Padua to graduate. As late as 1730, Simon Adolphus, the pioneer member of a prominent Anglo-American family of physicians, was permitted to graduate in the University of Halle by Frederick William of Prussia only on condition that he would not practice in the country. From the period of enlightenment which began with the Mendelssohnian era, Jewish graduations in Germany became more frequent, though they were for a long time confined to Medicine. In Austria, exclusion remained absolute until the *Toleranzedikt* of Joseph II, in 1782, declared the universities open to Jews.

In England, professing Jews, in common with all other persons who did not conform to the doctrines of the Established Church, were excluded from degrees in the older Universities until the passage of the University Reform Acts of 1854 and 1856; it is not quite true, as is generally believed, that they had to wait until the repeal of the University Tests in 1871. (The diploma said to have been granted two centuries earlier to the son of Manasseh ben Israel at the time of his father's mission to England is ap-

parently apocryphal.)   This was the case, however, only in
the older universities, the traditional homes of lost causes;
Jews were admitted freely to University College, London,
founded after the Napoleonic Wars as a remedy for non-
conformist students, and a few may be traced in the Scottish
universities as far back as (at the latest) 1779.[1]

V

Thus, up to the period of the French Revolution, the
Jews were absolutely excluded from the universities in most
of Europe, being admitted to a very few of them (especially
in Italy) only under highly disadvantageous conditions.
Even so, there were many Jews who objected to the total
immersion in a non-Jewish intellectual environment which
the course of study entailed.   The situation was, in fact, not
dissimilar from that known to prevail in some places even
today.   On the one hand, the Jewish student was excluded
by something not far removed from the modern *numerus
clausus,* which has a long history, as it now appears, behind
it.   On the other hand, when he was admitted, he was exposed
to the forces of assimilation.   It is worth while to examine
how, so many centuries ago, the Jew reacted to problems
very much like those which confront him now.

It must be remembered above all, in spite of contemporary lamentations, that Jews who studied in the ordinary
universities did not lose their contact with Jewish culture.
Hebraic studies almost invariably accompanied the secular.
Most of the Jewish physicians in the Middle Ages and after
were qualified rabbis—one can cite dozens of examples, from

---

[1] I have now dealt with this subject too in greater detail in a separate
essay, "The Jews in the English Universities," published in the volume of
Miscellanies dedicated by the Jewish Historical Society of England to
E. N. Adler.

Maimonides and before down almost to today. Padua was the seat of a Yeshivah for the study of talmudic lore whose fame extended almost as far as that of its medical school; and the Polish students who came to learn at the one frequented the other as well, receiving perhaps their diploma as rabbi at the same time as they graduated as doctors.

This, however, was not enough for the more pious among contemporary observers. The secular influence working upon these young men might after all gain the day. In empowering a certain Jew to graduate at Pisa in 1554, the Pope had openly expressed the hope that this might ultimately open his eyes to the truth of the Christian religion. Indeed, it was notorious that a number of these medical practitioners succumbed during the course of the sixteenth century either to Gentile influences or else to the hopes of advancement, and apostatized to the Catholic faith. Accordingly, at the beginning of the second half of the sixteenth century, the Rabbi of Mantua, David Provenzali, in conjunction with his son Abraham, put forward a daring plan, remarkably analogous to a present-day proposal, intended to rescue Jewish students from the temptations of their environment. What they suggested was the establishment of a sort of Jewish Academy at which the university training could be supplemented and anticipated. There should be regular courses, not merely in Talmud and Hebraic studies, including philosophy, but also in the secular sciences, especially medicine. Meanwhile, the students should obtain clinical experience by attendance on various physicians, Christians as well as Jews. They would leave this academy with a full intellectual equipment, thoroughly imbued with the Jewish spirit. Subsequently, they might formally enter some recognized university and graduate from it after a minimum period of study. Thus, they would have all of the advantages of a university degree without the necessity of wasting all their days and years in the *Studium* among the Gentiles. This plan was formally launched in 1564, a printed prospectus being circulated among the Italian communities. Whether anything actually came of it is uncertain.

The enterprise must have seemed to contemporaries, as it does to us today, original and audacious in the extreme. It had, however, been anticipated and surpassed a full century earlier in the kingdom of Sicily. Here, on the 17th of January 1466, a certain Benjamin Romano received formal authorization from King John to establish a Hebrew University, with its teachers and its professors, and endowed with all of the rights and privileges inherent in any other such body, up to and including the power of conferring degrees in all subjects!

A plan such as this could have come out of Italy only. In Sicily, indeed, the Jews were almost autochthonous, having been established there since Roman times. Now, in the period of the Spanish domination, they numbered between thirty and forty thousand souls. As practitioners, they were famous, a succession of them having served as royal physicians. Indeed, the office of *Dienchelele,* or Chief Rabbi of the Jews of Sicily, was created on behalf of one of them—no doubt in order to secure his emoluments with a minimum of cost to the treasury. From the close of the fourteenth to the close of the fifteenth century well over one hundred and fifty Jewish physicians had been licensed to practice, after an examination before a mixed board, a formality which obtained in a similar form in contemporary Spain. The functions of this body were henceforth, apparently, to be taken over by the new university. But evidently it was not to be confined to medical studies. The presence of jurists on the teaching staff is an ample indication that Law was also to be taught; and, without doubt, some of the humane studies as well. The whole plan is so extraordinary that it is advisable, if only as a vindication of veracity, to quote the actual wording:

The Royal dignity is wont to concede most freely that which appears to educate, sustain, and influence the human mind to fulfil the will of God and to seize upon the knowledge of truth and the way of good living. Therefore, in answer to the petition presented on behalf of the Jewish communities and leaders of Our kingdom of Sicily, through Benjamin Romano, Jew of Our most faithful city of Syracuse, we do hereby, of our certain knowledge and will, concede the license and give full permission to you—the leaders, communities, and individuals thereof—that, without incurring any penalty, at your own cost and expense, according as shall be disposed and ordained by Us or by Our respected Viceroy in the aforesaid realm of Sicily, in that city, town, or place of the said Realm which the Viceroy with your agreement shall choose, *you shall be permitted, enabled, and empowered to found a Studium Generale, to engage and discharge Doctors, Jurists, and others: and in the said Studium to have instruction in all approved sciences for those who seem proper to them and others*: and to do all of those things which appear to apply to the said *Studium Generale,* while you shall do the same as aforementioned, as shall be disposed and ordained by Us or by the said Viceroy. We moreover do hereby of our certain knowledge place and take under Our especial protection all the Doctors, Jurists, Masters, Students and others who shall dwell in the said *Studium Generale* and frequent it for the sake thereof, as well as the said *Studium* itself. . . .

What came of this endeavor it is impossible to say. That such a conception should ever have crossed the medieval mind is, however, in itself a remarkable fact. It is an extraordinary anticipation of recent successful attempts to establish universities intended primarily for the instruction of Jews alone. *Plus ça change. . . .*

8. A COMMUNITY OF SLAVES[1]

O N THE Island of Malta, in the seventeenth and eighteenth centuries, there existed a Jewish community composed exclusively of slaves captured by the Order of St. John, a community protected by the Inquisition and presided over by a Gentile. This is the essence of a fascinating story disclosed by documents in the hands of the present writer.

i

Malta had harbored a Jewish community for almost fifteen centuries after the visit paid to the island by Paul of Tarsus. Catacombs commemorate its existence in Roman times, and government records mark its medieval history. But the island fell, together with Sicily, under the rule of the royal house of Aragon, and the community of Malta shared, in 1492, the fate of the Jews in Spain. There was a brief interval during which there were no Jews on the island. Then followed the amazing interlude of the slaves.

In 1530, Charles V made over Malta to the Knights Hospitaller of the Order of St. John, who had been driven from Rhodes nine years earlier by the Moslems. The whole *raison d'être* of the body and of its tenure of Malta lay in the supposition of a continual state of hostility between the Moslem world and Christendom, of which the members of the Order were, in a sense, the knights-errant. Accordingly, they waged continual maritime warfare, hardly distinguishable from piracy, against the Moslem powers. Seaports were raided and their inhabitants carried off.

1 Originally published in the *Menorah Journal*, vol. XVIII (1931), pp. 219-233, excerpted from my monograph, "The Jews of Malta," in *Transactions of the Jewish Historical Society of England*, vol. XII (1931), pp. 187-251, where full references and documentation will be found.

Shipping was preyed on indiscriminately, captured vessels being brought to Malta, and crews and passengers sold into captivity. Throughout the rule of the Knights, which lasted until they capitulated to the French in 1798, the island was thus a last European refuge of slave traffic and slave labor.

The victims were any persons, of whatever standing, race, age or sex, who happened to be sailing in the captured ships. Jews made up a large proportion of the Levantine merchant class and were hence peculiarly subject to capture. Because of their nomadic way of life, disproportionately large numbers were to be found in any vessel sailing between Eastern ports. Also, they formed a considerable element in the population of the Moslem ports subject to raids. So, soon after the establishment of the Knights there, the name of Malta begins to be found with increasing frequency in Jewish literature, and always with an evil association.

The island became in Jewish eyes a symbol for all that was cruel and hateful in the Christian world. Whatever the truth of the contemporary rumor that the Jews financed the great Turkish siege of Malta in 1565, certainly they watched it with anxious eyes and their disappointment at its failure must have been extreme. "The monks of Malta are still today a snare and trap for the Jews,' sadly records a Jewish chronicler at the end of his account of the siege. A messianic prophecy current early in the seventeenth century further expressed the bitterness of Jewish feeling, recounting how the Redemption would begin with the fall of the four kingdoms of ungodliness, first among which was Malta.

A typical capture, and one of the earliest mentioned in Jewish literature, is related in the *Vale of Tears* by Joseph ha-Cohen:

In the year 5312 (1552), the vessels of the monks of Rhodes, of the order of Malta, cruising to find booty, encountered a ship coming from Salonica, whereon were seventy Jews. They captured it and returned to their island. These unhappy persons had to send to all quarters to collect money for the ransom exacted by these miserable monks. Only after payment were they able to continue their voyage.

In 1567, large numbers of Jews, escaping to the Levant from the persecutions of Pius V, fell victims to the Knights. "Many of the victims sank like lead to the depths of the sea before the fury of the attack. Many others were imprisoned in the Maltese dungeons at this time of desolation," writes the chronicler. It was not only those who went down to the sea in ships over whom the shadow hung. Of the Marranos of Ancona who fell victims to the fanaticism and treachery of Paul IV, thirty-eight who eluded the stake were sent in chains to the galleys of Malta, though they managed to escape on the way.

Arrived in Malta, the captives were only at the beginning of their troubles. A very graphic account of conditions is given by an English traveler, Philip Skippon, who visited the spot in about 1663:

The slaves' prison is a fair square building, cloister'd round, where most of the slaves in Malta are oblig'd to lodge every night, and to be there about Ave Mary time. They have here several sorts of trades, as barbers, taylors, &c. There are about 2,000 that belong to the order, most of which were now abroad in the galleys; and there are about 300 who are servants to private persons. This place being an island, and difficult to escape out of, they wear only an iron ring or foot-lock. Those that are servants, lodge in their masters' houses, when the galleys are at home; but now, lie a-nights in this prison. Jews, Moors and Turks are made slaves here, and are publickly sold in the market.

A stout fellow may be bought (if he is an inferior person) for 120 or 160 scudi of Malta. The Jews are distinguish'd from the rest by a little piece of yellow cloth on their hats or caps, &c. We saw a rich Jew who was taken about a year before, who was sold in the market that morning we visited the prison for 400 scudi; and supposing himself free, by reason of a passport he had from Venice, he struck the merchant that bought him; whereupon he was presently sent hither, his beard and hair shaven off, a great chain clapp'd on his legs, and bastinado'd with 50 blows.

ii

The Holy One, blessed be He, says a well known rabbinic proverb, always prepares a remedy before the affliction. So it was in the present case. Among Jews, the idea that a coreligionist should be enslaved by a Gentile and forced to disregard the practices of his religion, with life and honor in constant danger, was altogether abhorrent. Thus from earliest days the Redemption of Captives had ranked high among the acts of charity which a Jew was called on to execute, and it was considered proper that, should a dying man leave money "for the performance of a good deed," without further directions, it should be devoted to this *Pidyon Shevuyim*, as best deserving the title.

Throughout the Middle Ages this activity continued, leaving ample traces in *Halachic* and historical literature. Generally the organization of relief had been purely sporadic. Whenever need arose, an emergency collection would be made and assistance proferred to the needy. With the establishment of the Knights of Malta, the depredations on Mediterranean shipping were systematized and came to have one main center. It therefore became useful and necessary to set up a permanent organization to cope with the new permanent situation.

Now, the great entrepôt of Mediterranean commerce was still Venice, whose trade with the Levant was carried on largely by Jews. It happened, too, that there was at Venice an important settlement of Jews hailing direct from the Iberian Peninsula, whose genius for organization was famed. Thus it came about that there was set up in Venice in the course of the seventeenth century the first of Confraternities for the Redemption of Captives—*Hebrath Pidyon Shevuyim*—which, in the course of the next hundred years were to spread throughout the great Sephardic communities of the West.

Apparently the terrible Chmielnicki persecutions in Poland and the Ukraine in 1648 served as the immediate occasion. Thousands of Jews were sold into slavery at this time, and at Venice the charitable brothers Aboab started a fund which became permanent. By 1683 it was so successful as to be described as the most wealthy and most highly regarded among Jewish associations in Venice. The organization was under the auspices only of the Levantine and Portuguese congregations; the German and the Italian congregations, though they contributed liberally to the fund, took no official share in the labors of the Confraternity. This was not due to any lack of solidarity: it was that the two Sephardic communities had commercial and social intercourse with the Levant, and were most immediately concerned.

For its funds the association depended only partially on benevolence. Voluntary donations came in, of course, from Venice and from foreign cities as the fame of the association spread. The wealthy Zacharias Porto of Florence, among his immense charitable bequests, left it 1500 piastres. Abraham Texeira, Swedish resident at Hamburg, made an annual subscription during his lifetime, which was continued by his son after his death. Moses

Pinto, another wealthy Hamburg Jew, gave a yearly sub-vention of twenty patacas. The Hamburg community even established an auxiliary society under the name of the *Camara de Cautivos de Veneza,* with its special treasurer or *Gabbai.* On occasions of great urgency, the Confra-ternity would appeal for help to communities as far afield as London and Amsterdam, which were generally glad to assist. On one occasion, in 1705, every community in Italy, except that of Rome, which was racked with oppressive taxation, contributed to the fund. Sometimes, the native city of a captive would be asked to help raise his ransom.

But all this was regarded as extraordinary income. The ordinary came as a matter of business rather than of charity. In the first place, the members of the Confraternity paid into its funds a certain proportion of their annual profits. But, above all, a special tax of 25 per cent was levied on all goods dispatched from Venice (presumably by sea) to Jewish correspondents, and 125 per cent on all goods taken away in person. This high tax is not so surprising as might appear at first sight. For those who paid it were precisely the Levantine merchants who might have occasion for the services of the Confraternity. It was, as a matter of fact, a form of insurance. That this was the case is shown by the fact that, whenever the fund was curtailed, trade with the Levant was seriously hampered.

The funds were kept in two separate chests or *caixete,* for the "Levantines" and the "Ponentines" (Portuguese) respectively. The amounts varied from time to time. About 1742, the total was 3,500 ducats, of which nearly two-thirds was in the possession of the Portuguese. The combined funds were administered by five officials, the *Deputados dos Cautivos,* of whom three were "Ponentine." These were empowered to dispose of sums up to fifty ducats on their own authority. For the disbursement of larger amounts general approbation was required. The separation of the funds having led to constant dispute, in 1742 recourse was had to the Venetian magistracy of the Cattaveri to make a settlement. It was decided that the two *caixete* should be combined; that the joint organization should continue to be governed by three "Ponentines" and two "Levantines"; and that any sum could be disposed of by four voices out of five.

This parade of internal differences had revealed the wealth of the Confraternity and aroused Gentile cupidity. The consequences were not long in showing themselves. In the same year, the *Inquisitori sopra gli Ebrei,* seeking to bolster the failing loan-banks which the Jews were forced to maintain as a condition of their toleration in Venice, confiscated the whole of the fund. A touching appeal was lodged against the raid. The sums, it was urged, were too small to benefit the banks substantially, while the Levantine merchants, deprived of their insurance, would refuse to trade with Venice. Perhaps, also, reprisals would be made in Turkey. The representations were not without effect. Henceforth, however, the organization came under the control of the *Inquisitori,* whose permission became necessary before any disbursement could be made.

iii

The range of the society's activities was immense. In addition to captives in the Mediterranean trade, prisoners in the constant wars on the mainland of Italy or as far afield as Hungary and Poland, slaves rowing in the galleys in the Adriatic and Tyrrhenian seas from Marseilles and Elba to Corfu and Zante, victims of the Cossacks to the north and of the Tartars to the east, unfortunate Jews groaning in servitude in distant Persia or on the Barbary Coast, all turned for succor to the *Parnassim dos Cautivos* in Venice, certain to receive sympathy, and, if humanly possible, deliverance. But though many galley slaves were redeemed at other ports, three-quarters of the Confraternity's work was done at Malta. The story of this work, as disclosed by the original documents, is not only a monument of Jewish charity at its finest but also a pathetic record of the persistence of Jewish life under conditions which could not have been more adverse.

Communication was precarious; sometimes a letter took two or three months in transmission from Venice to Malta. It was therefore necessary to have on the spot someone to represent the Confraternity. Under the Knights the exclusion of Jewish residents from Malta was not absolute (the plot of Marlowe's *Jew of Malta* was not so entirely impossible as has generally been assumed). They were, however, admitted only temporarily and under great restrictions. But the Venetian merchants had at Malta correspondents willing enough to do them a service, and a succession of these acted on their behalf as "consuls." They received no salary but must necessarily have benefited as a result of their good offices, acquiring through them business correspondents of absolute reliability whose support was valuable in dealing with Jews in other parts of the world. They had, moreover, the right to charge a commission of five piastres for every slave liberated through their offices.

The first of these agents of whom there is any record is a certain Baccio Bandinelli, a namesake of the puny rival of Michelangelo, who acted perhaps from the establishment of the Confraternity down to about 1670, when he was forced to give up by reason of his years. He was succeeded by a French merchant, François Garsin, a Judge of the Tribunal of the *Consolato del Mare*. That the agency was considered desirable is shown by the fact that Thomas Luis da Souza, who had assisted Bandinelli, preferred his services in addition. He was accordingly associated with Garsin for a while (1673-74), until the latter indicated that he would prefer to dispense with assistance. Garsin's zeal was not a selfish one. He refused the commission which he had the right to charge for slaves released through his efforts. "All the greater will be your merit before God," wrote the grateful Deputados, "and by Him will you be rewarded all the more, these being of a nation diverse from your own." Nevertheless, Garsin profited from his connection. The Deputados acted as his agents for the dispatch of merchandise from Venice, and in 1671 did their utmost to procure the intervention of the rabbinate of Alexandria with some of Garsin's recalcitrant debtors in that city. Moreover, he received occasional gifts in token of their gratitude.

Garsin died in the autumn of 1706 after more than thirty-five years of devoted service. His son, Jean-Baptiste, writing to tell the Deputados of his loss, offered to carry on the work. This he did until his death thirteen years later. His successor was a certain Filippo Antonio Crespi, who served for a decade. For some years during this period, a Jewish merchant from Leghorn, Samuel Farfara, resided at Malta and aided the "consul."

When the Maltese galleys returned from a marauding expedition, the "consul" would visit the prison to see whether Jews were among the captives. Frequently there were—usually merchants or travelers sailing peacefully between Levantine ports. Sometimes when Jewish booty was in prospect, not even the flags of Christian powers were respected. The case is on record, for example, of the seizure in 1672 by a Tuscan privateer of ten Jews—seven men and

three women—from a Venetian vessel sailing from Alexandria, under the pretext that they were Ottoman subjects.
They were brought to Malta and shamelessly offered for
sale. A petition presented by the Deputados to the Doge
brought about diplomatic representations at the Court of
the Grand Duke of Tuscany which were sufficient to procure
their release.

This, however, was an exceptional case. Generally
there was no short cut out of the difficulty. Thus, on July
23, 1725, there arrived at the island eighteen prisoners
captured while sailing from Salonica to Smyrna. All were
poor excepting one—Jacob Fonseca, brother of Daniel
Fonseca, Voltaire's friend, who had first been a Marrano
priest and later, as a practising Jew, physician to the Grand
Vizier at Constantinople. Fonseca refused to pay ransom,
and was subsequently released at the instance of the French
court with which his brother had great influence. The rest
were left to the charity of their fellow-Jews. Some time previously, in the autumn of 1675, ten poor Jews on their way
to Palestine were captured by the treasurer of Malta and
brought into the island. Five died of the plague in captivity, and the rest were ultimately liberated for 480 pieces-
of-eight. Another great influx came in 1685, when the city
of Coron on the coast of Greece was sacked; twenty-one
Jewish prisoners were brought in. But these are only a
few of the most striking instances. Throughout the period,
and especially in time of war (as, for example, during the
heroic struggle between Venice and Turkey at the close
of the seventeenth century), there was an almost constant
influx of prisoners, mostly poor, to keep alive the Jewish
connection with Malta and to give the Venetian community
an opportunity of exercising its benevolence.

Whenever Jewish captives were found among a batch
of new arrivals, the agent would give them a small sum

on account of the Confraternity to satisfy immediate needs. Besides, each received an allowance of one ducat weekly until the limitation of funds forced a reduction. Even then, every Jewish slave received the equivalent of four pieces-of-eight in cash annually, distributed on the great festivals, particularly the Passover. In case of illness, they were given an additional allowance. They were housed in a special room taken for them by the agent in the *bagnio,* or prison, in which they were confined.

Meanwhile, word would have been sent to Venice at the earliest opportunity to inform the Deputados of the number and quality of the new arrivals and of the sums demanded for their release. When a single individual was in question, there might be enough in hand to ransom him straightway. When a whole shipload came in, it was necessary to have recourse to all sides to collect the amount required. It occasionally happened, too, that one slave would be set free to collect money for the release of the others, or that a wealthy merchant might be able to give satisfactory security for his ransom. But more frequently the victims were indigent, and it was left to the Venetian society to look after their welfare and deliverance.

iv

The mechanism of release was not always simple. The Jew was rarely as rich as he was reputed to be, but his reputation for wealth was greatest precisely where he was least known. The usual price standard of a slave tended, therefore, to disappear whenever a Jew was concerned. He was worth, not his value, but whatever could be extorted from his brethren. Ransom degenerated into blackmail. Fifteen centuries earlier, the rabbis of the Talmud had realized that this was a case in which it was necessary to turn for once a deaf ear to suffering, lest a premium be put on the enslavement of Jews. They ordained, accordingly, that no captive be ransomed for more than his economic value. This was a rule to obey which was hard for Jews, "compassionate sons of compassionate sires," and generally the price paid for a Jew was higher by far than that of a Moslem.

On occasion, the Jews were mercilessly exploited. The owner of one Judah Surnago, a man of seventy-five whose value in the open market would have been negligible, was unable to obtain the sum which he demanded in ransom. Thereupon, he shut him up naked in a cellar for two months, giving him nothing to eat but black bread and water. The old man came out blind and unable to stand. His master* then threatened to load him with chains and to pluck out his beard and eyelashes if the sum asked were not forthcoming. Ultimately, the Deputados redeemed him for 200 ducats. For a certain Aaron Afia of Rhodes, bought in 1703 by a speculating owner, 600 ducats were demanded. To stimulate the zeal of his coreligionists, Afia's owner kept him in chains and threatened him with the galleys. The proprietors would not believe, wrote Garsin in despair, that his kinfolk were poverty-stricken. The Deputados were horrified. "We are not in a condition," they wrote, "to make such exorbitant expenditure. If they do not moderate their price there will be disaster for the poor wretches, who will die in slavery, and the owners will lose their capital." For a certain Rabbi Isaac Moreno of Belgrade with his wife and three children, the Deputados were willing in 1673 to pass their usual limit and pay 300 piastres for which (so low were funds) they would have to dip into their own pockets. The owners demanded 575 piastres. "If the said masters expect to obtain more for a useless old man and a sick woman and three children, one of whom is blind, who have had nothing out of him (saving your reverence!) but lice, they are much mistaken," they wrote the "consul." The owners retaliated by attempting to raise the price. In another, case, when one Abraham Perez and five companions were taken, one, Joseph Levy, was killed under the lash to stimulate the others to greater liberality. The rest were ultimately released, partly through their own efforts.

In 1702, a speculator had purchased three men and a woman of sixty for 350, 304, 299 and 72 ducats respectively. "It astounds us that they could be sold at such extravagant prices," wrote the Deputados. "They can be sure that they will remain on their hands as long as they live, for our resources do not allow us to order their redemption even for as little as sixty. . . . It would be as well to publish abroad what we have told you in this matter, so that no one will desire in future to purchase at such rates."

Encouraged by a governmental order that Jewish slaves should not be sent to the galleys, an attempt was even made (with the help of a few judicious gifts) to obtain an edict fixing a fair price for Jewish slaves and forbidding their sale at public auction. Apparently, little or nothing came of it, for complaints continued without intermission. "Though it displeases us to see the miseries which those unhappy wretches suffer," wrote the Deputados in 1703, "we do not see how to contribute to their release with more than we have offered in the past, by reason of the calamitous times which are on us and the restriction of business. Their masters should moderate the rigorous pretensions which they have for their ransom: for if they do not they will assuredly lose all, by reason of their inevitable death in consequence of their miseries."

Such was liable to be the fate of any wretched Jew who fell into the hands of an extortionate master. Every effort was made, therefore, to purchase prisoners before they had been put up for sale. In the public auctions, the "consul" was empowered (when there was money in hand) to pay up to sixty or seventy ducats without preliminary authorization, or, at moments of especial affluence, even more. Some of the original deeds of sale are extant—or were until recently—for example, that of Abraham de Mordecai Alvo, "white," of Smyrna, aged twenty-two, disposed of by his captors for a sack of bones "according to the use of the corsairs" and bought by the "consul" for the sum of 110 ducats. In 1677, six slaves belonging to the Treasurer were released together for 480 pieces-of-eight. For every sale a notarial agreement and the licence of the Grand Master were essential. Sometimes, the unhappy prisoners were sent to the galleys, in spite of the governmental order to the contrary, and so it occasionally happened that the Deputados had the opportunity of ransoming slaves from Malta in Venice itself. Thus, in 1704, they appealed to the community of Leghorn for assistance in raising 2,000 reals for the release of three victims, on a vessel then in port, from pains "worse than those of death."

V

Despite all efforts, a long period frequently elapsed before slaves could be liberated. Thus a certain Isaac Esicrit who was ransomed for one hundred ducats in 1716 had been captive for five years; and worse cases are recorded.

Consequently, there was frequently in Malta a veritable community of slaves, as distinct from an agglomeration of isolated individuals. In 1672, for example, there were no fewer than sixteen left unredeemed at one time, while the total number of persons bought in that year was twenty-nine.

Perhaps the most remarkable feature in the whole pathetic story is the way in which these miserable captives found it possible to carry on their religious life under such atrocious circumstances.

The authorities on the island were tolerant, as the ecclesiastical arm generally was, regarding Jews. There was an old authorization permitting the Jewish slaves to have their cemetery and synagogue, with Scrolls of the Law. Slave-owners, however, were often less sympathetic, compelling their chattels to work on Sabbaths and holidays. The Deputados professed themselves unable to comprehend how they could do this, since they had acquired only corporal dominion over their slaves. On March 3, 1673, they wrote to the community of Rome suggesting that some action be taken there, at the center of the Catholic faith and of ultimate authority over the Knights, to remedy this state of affairs. It would seem that something was effected, though none too speedily. In 1675 the Inquisitor of Malta issued an order prohibiting that Jewish slaves be compelled to work on their religious holidays. Thus facilities for a minimum of observance were ensured.

In consequence of this tolerant attitude on the one side and of remarkable tenacity on the other, there came into existence what is surely the most remarkable Jewish community that has ever existed—one composed exclusively of slaves, with its numbers continually recruited by prisoners brought in by sheer force, or depleted by releases effected through death or ransom. The Deputados addressed them in Hebrew in full form: *"To all the congregation of the groaning and captive which are in the city of Malta—may the Lord bring them out from anguish to enlargement; Amen, this be His will!"*

The community, however small, required services which could be rendered only by one who was free. Who else was available but the agent of the Venetian society? It is strange to see how this Catholic man of affairs looked after the religious welfare of these unfortunate creatures of a different faith. He worked with a conscientiousness and a fervor which would have been praiseworthy even in a Jew. On the occasion of the Holy Days, he distributed among the slaves some small gratifications, sometimes without the express consent of his principals, who, he knew, would honor whatever he did. It was the agent, too, who made provision for a modest place of worship. He took a room in the *bagnio*, which was fitted up as a synagogue. At first it was used as such only on festivals; later, on the Sabbath as well. Originally, the Jewish slaves slept here, but subsequently a couple of additional rooms were taken for their accommodation. The gaoler acted as caretaker, receiving regular payment. In the autumn of 1673, the Deputados authorized Garsin to have necessary repairs done to the doors of the synagogue, and, two years later, to the reading desk. In the *bagnio*, too, the slaves had their oven—which in 1685 Garsin had been ordered to provide—for baking unleavened bread for the Passover. In 1707, when the number of slaves was small and regular religious worship momentarily ceased, one of the two rooms was given up.

There was a copy of the Scroll of the Law for the use of the slaves, doubtless originally sent from Venice, though it was not unknown for one to find its way to the island with other booty. If the number of slaves fell below the quorum of ten necessary for the full formalities of public worship, the Scroll was looked after by the agent. Thus, in 1696, when the last Jewish slave then in Malta died, the agent was instructed as to the preservation of the Scroll of the Law and other appurtenances of public ritual. When the younger Garsin entered upon his voluntary duties in 1707, he was recommended to take care of the Scroll and other Hebrew books until they were needed.

But, whatever might have been hoped, the days of the Congregation of Slaves were not yet over, for there was a recrudescence of piracy. "Yesterday," wrote the Consul, on May 6, 1713, "they came to take the Law, wishing from now onwards, being eleven in number, to say their Mass. I gave them also stuff to make the mantle: and they stand in need of a table, with the pulpit." Besides these bare necessities, they went to the extravagance of having a Perpetual Lamp to burn in their synagogue and bells wherewith to adorn the Scroll. They had a curtain, too, to hang before the Ark.

Another necessary adjunct of settled religious life was the cemetery, for the conditions of life under which the slaves lived in so insalubrious a climate (Malta was notorious for its fever) made this requisite out of all proportion to their numbers. In 1-674, without applying to headquarters for authorization, Garsin paid for the burial of two poor Jews who had died in an English ship going to Constantinople. This was done, however, in unconsecrated ground. For a short time afterwards the slaves complained to the Deputados that they had no place in which to bury any of their number who might die. On October 26, 1675, Garsin was authorized to purchase a plot of ground for this purpose at a price not exceeding fifty ducats. A couple of years later plague broke out on the island, and, since it was impossible to bury the dead in the ordinary cemetery, a special piece of ground had to be acquired as a plague pit. It was on March 17, 1677, that Garsin, for seventy-five ducats, purchased a plot outside Vittoriosa in the name of the Spanish community at Venice. Five slaves had been buried there previously. Arrangements were made for surrounding the cemetery with a wall. Despite this, in 1727 it was found that it was being treated as a private garden, and Filippo Antonio

Crespi, the new Consul, urged the Deputados to find the
title-deeds. A permanent cemetery was established in 1784
at the expense of the community of Leghorn for the benefit
of the freedmen, as an inscription over the bricked-up gateway still testifies.

vi

Even in the depths of their misery, the slaves found an
opportunity to indulge in the Jewish luxury of charity.
A touching appeal was made by two of the slaves, both
fathers of families, on behalf of one of their companions,
Solomon ben Isaac Azich (Aziz?), of Leghorn, a youth of
seventeen who had been captured while on the way home
from Smyrna. He was in the service of the Grand Master,
being forced to carry intolerably heavy burdens and to work
beyond the limits of his strength. The two elder men urged
that intervention should be made on his behalf, not mentioning their own plight. Despite their miserable material condition, the slaves somehow found the opportunity to translate their charitable sentiments into works, though they
were not always well-directed. The case is on record of
one unmitigated scoundrel, Isaiah Orefice, probably a galley-
slave, who was in the island in 1716 pretending to be a
captive like the rest, and without doubt obtaining relief
from the agent on that score. The tale he told was so piteous
that the compassion of the other slaves was aroused. They
assisted him to get away, not only by entreaties to the Agent,
but also with gifts from their own slender store of money.
He rewarded their benevolence by taking with him the quilt
and cloak of another slave, Abraham Ajet, and the prayer-
books of the synagogue.

Even more touching was the pawning by the slaves in
1672 of the lamps and petty articles of silver which their

Synagogue boasted in order to assist in the ransoming of Moses Messini and Mordecai Maio, two of their brethren in distress. The Deputados rated them roundly for this action, which might have deplorable consequences in the future, and ordered the Christian agent to redeem the articles from pawn. Nevertheless, there seemed to be an undercurrent of admiration in their rebuke.

The religious life of the captured was enriched frequently by the presence on the island of scholarly prisoners. The most eminent scholar of whom we have any record, as well as one of the earliest, was Jacob le-Beth Levi (Jacob ben Israel the Levite), a native of the Morea and translator of the Koran into Hebrew. He was later Rabbi of Zante, where he died in 1634, leaving a considerable body of Responsa. Earlier in his career he was carried off with his household and all his property to the "den of lions and house of imprisonment" at Malta. His deliverance he regarded as a special manifestation of Providence. More than one victim redeemed by the Confraternity is referred to as Rabbi or Haham; for example, that Joseph Cohen Ashkenazi of Constantinople who was redeemed at the close of the seventeenth century for 150 ducats. Another was one Samuel aben Mayor, purchased in Malta by a speculating Armenian and ransomed later through the congregation of Ferrara. "Emissaries of Mercy," on their way to collect alms in the Diaspora for the four Holy Cities of Palestine, were especially liable to interception at sea. Thus, an emissary of Safed was captured irregularly with nine other persons in a Venetian vessel in 1672. In 1666, a party of rabbis from Jerusalem was captured while on their way to convey the glad tidings of the Messianic pretensions of Sabbatai Zevi.

An interesting and tragic figure appears among the slaves in the last decades of the seventeenth century. Moses Azulai was doubtless of the famous Moroccan family of scholars and mystics, some of whom had emigrated to Palestine. How he was brought to Malta it has been impossible to trace, but his presence there is attested at least as early as 1671. He must have fallen into the hands of a mild master, for there is some indication that he engaged in trade on his behalf, nor did he make appeal for ransom. His preoccupations were not for himself but for others, and for a long time he was coadjutor to the worthy Garsin. He would report what captives had been brought in, what steps were being taken to release them and who had been ransomed. The Deputados had perfect trust in him, advising their agent to rely on him implicitly for the regulation of the internal affairs of the slaves. He seems to have been a man of some learning, who corresponded occasionally in Hebrew and could not support captivity without the solace of Jewish literature. He is, indeed, first mentioned in connection with the dispatch to Malta of a copy of the *Midrash Tanhuma*. He was probably ringleader of the slaves who requested a perpetual calendar (*Sefer Iburim*), and some time after we find him obtaining another calendrical work, the *Tikkun Issachar*. A work of practical utility in another direction which was sent him was the *Pitron Halomot,* or Interpretation of Dreams, as well as the liturgical subsidiary, *Maamadot,* with a commentary. His rabbinical knowledge was at times of practical use. In 1673 and again in 1685 he was called on by fellow-slaves to draw up bills of divorcement. It was owing to his insistence that the oven for unleavened bread was provided. When any of the slaves were refractory (as, considering their misery, quite apart from their race, was no matter for surprise), it was he who was enjoined to restore discipline. From all this it would appear that he acted as religious leader of the community during the period he was on the island.

Azulai seems for all these years to have made no effort to obtain his freedom. Apparently he was content to remain in his position as guide to the captive Jews who came and departed, to maintain his post—the one constant in the shifting population.

At the beginning of the last decade of the seventeenth century, however, there came about a change in the condition of the Jewish slaves in Malta that altered also his apparent determination to make the island his home. The maritime war in the Levant was not being carried on with much vigor. Victims were fewer. The slaves remaining on the island were released one by one. The calls on the Deputados at Venice became more and more rare, the total of their outgoing letters being reduced from a maximum of forty in 1673 to as few as two twenty years later. By the end of 1691, Azulai had only one companion left—a certain Moses Joseph of Safed. He began to feel lonely, and after twenty years of captivity, during which he had been in constant communication with Venice, he asked for the first time for his own release. He was advanced in years and had for a long time served unstintingly, without recompense. He had seen scores of fellow-slaves liberated while he remained in uncomplaining captivity. His demand now could not be refused. The Deputados of Leghorn added forty reals to the fifty contributed by those of Venice, and Garsin was instructed to go as high as 120 if necessary. So that Azulai's companion should not be left in utter solitude, Garsin was to negotiate his release as well. In the latter case there was rapid success and the Palestinian prisoner sailed for freedom on a French ship for Tripoli after 180 ducats had ransomed him. But over the unhappy Azulai, thus left in complete loneliness, there was some difficulty, for the anxiety of the Deputados increased the expectations of his owner. An additional contribution was elicited with-

out much difficulty from Leghorn, and Garsin was authorized to go up to 150 reals. Success seemed at last assured.
Instructions were given for the care of the communal
property. Garsin was to retain the keys of the synagogue
and the custodianship of the oven and burial grounds. The
Scroll of the Law and books and other ritual objects were
to be placed by Azulai in a sealed chest and entrusted to
the agent's keeping until opportunity should offer for dis-
patching it to Venice. For the expenses of his voyage,
Azulai was to be given five reals. At last, in July 1694, it
seemed that his long sufferings were at an end. But when
the Deputados at Venice were expecting to hear of his final
release, they received instead the information of his death
(April 1696).

Out of the horrors of slavery there was always one easy
escape—baptism. But this simple expedient was an alternative rarely chosen by the slaves. An exception was one
Jacob Cardiel of Tunis. When the ship on which he was
sailing was captured he fought to defend it. Fearing ill-
treatment in consequence, if his religion should be discovered, he passed as a Moslem for the first year or more
of his captivity. Realizing, perhaps, that he had better
chance of release as a Jew, he declared himself as one, after
fourteen months. The Deputados, informed of this, instructed their agent to make inquiries. Ultimately his
claims were accepted; but when matters moved more slowly
than he had hoped, Cardiel decided to take the shortest
road out of his trouble. After three years' captivity, he was
baptized—more, wrote the "consul," from desperation than
from zeal. Another convert, Guiseppe Antonio Cohen
(though there is no definite proof he was a slave) attained
some fame, as well as a commemorative tablet and a small
annuity, by betraying the Turkish Plot of 1749—a curiously
contradictory historical parallel to the *Jew of Malta*.

Once a person had apostatized, the Deputados naturally lost interest in his fate. "As for the young woman from Coron, whom you were to ransom," they wrote the "consul" in 1688, "since she has passed to another religion, you are to remove her utterly from your mind."

It was not only human captives that the association felt moved to redeem. At the raid in Coron in 1685, during the Turco-Venetian War, besides the twenty-one individuals captured (mostly women and children), large numbers of books, with Scrolls of the Law and their trappings, were carried away among the spoil. The Deputados were careful to instruct their representative on the island to attempt to redeem these. In 1699, Garsin gave a woman ten ducats for five Hebrew books of the nature of which he had no idea, sure of the approval of his principals. Rabbi Jacob le-Beth Levi, a century before, was able to bring away from the island an ancient Scroll of the Law, no doubt a redeemed captive like himself.

vii

Precisely how long the Community of Slaves continued its intermittent existence it is impossible to say. In 1749 the slaves in the island were still so numerous as to make possible the Turkish Plot which nearly brought Malta under the Crescent at last. With the growth of international peace and humanitarian ideas, the traffic necessarily diminished, but conditions were not fundamentally changed. The case is recorded of the release by the Deputados of Venice of Daniel de Benjamin Silva and his wife Judith as late as 1752 for the sum of 200 ducats, probably from Malta. Even in 1768, the community of London forwarded to Leghorn the sum of £80 to assist in ransoming a batch of no fewer than fourteen prisoners, then in captivity at Malta.

Similar conditions must have prevailed in some degree as late as the period of the French Revolutionary wars.

Slavery ceased in Malta only at the dawn of the nineteenth century, the slaves being freed on the overthrow of the Knights, and their release being confirmed officially on May 15, 1800.

In their last days, the Knights began to show greater tolerance, and a few Jewish merchants settled in this commercially attractive center. Even some redeemed slaves remained and settled as freemen. So, when the British came into possession in 1802, there was the nucleus of a Jewish community already on hand. Under British rule it prospered and increased. Though today on the downward grade, it appears still firmly established, with a rabbi and a synagogue. Among its members, however, I have not found descendants of the slaves, who introduced a new and heartrending element into the tragic story of Israel, and founded a community the like of which no other place or age has known.

9. WAS HEBREW EVER A DEAD LANGUAGE?[1]

i

I
T would not be easy to exaggerate the significance of that
marvelous revival which, within living memory, has restored Hebrew to its position as the language of the Jewish
nucleus in Palestine and the medium of communication between thousands of Jews all the world over. Yet it is only fair
to view the question in its proper perspective and to ask:
Was Hebrew ever a dead language?

There is no need to embark here upon an account of the
phenomenally advanced educational system which obtained
among the Jews in former generations, based of course upon
the study of Hebrew language and Hebrew literature. But it
must be emphasized that every Jew was introduced to the
study of Hebrew at an extremely early and impressionable
age. "At the age of three," a fond sixteenth-century father
jotted down on one of the fly-leaves of his prayer-book, in the
collection of the present writer, "My son Joseph recognized
his Creator, for he began to study."

That wayward prodigy, Leone da Modena, was even
more precocious, for at the age of two and a half he chanted
the *Haftarah* in synagogue. Now, to persons introduced to
their studies so early, it is obvious that Hebrew must have
become second nature—more intimate, in its way, than the
language in every-day use. Indeed, the Hebrew alphabet
alone was so generally familiar in Jewish circles that in al-

---

1 Originally published in *The Jewish Chronicle* of London, November
23, 1934; republished in *The New Palestine*, New York,

most every country the vernacular was written, and even printed, in Hebrew characters.

The use of the ancestral tongue was not confined to the synagogue and the house of study. Throughout the Middle Ages and after, it was customary for Jews to keep their accounts in Hebrew. When marriage or betrothal took place in some prominent family, in the smallest Italian Ghetto, a flood of Hebrew verses, unimpeachably correct in diction and prosody, was poured out by the local poetasters, who could plainly count upon a wide and appreciative audience. Every community had its notary, who drew up wills, contracts of bethrothal, deeds of sale, articles of apprenticeship, and similar business documents in Hebrew. It goes without saying that synagogal business and rabbinical correspondence were transacted in the same tongue. We have a whole series of English private letters (written to Nottingham, of all places!) dating back to the thirteenth century; while prisoners carved their names and personal notes, on the wall of Winchester Castle or the White Tower of Issoudun, in the same tongue. Indeed, it may be said that in northern Europe at this period, whatever language Jews spoke among themselves, it seemed natural for them to slip into Hebrew as soon as they took pen or chisel in hand. Throughout the seventeenth and eighteenth centuries, the sumptuary laws for communal taxation at Mantua (to cite only one place) were drawn up and circulated in pure Hebrew. Since the most implicit obedience was requisite, and was indeed enforced by every sanction available, the use of the "sacred tongue" for the purpose was plainly no antiquarian diversion. It was assumed that most members of the community could understand every intricate detail.

It is true that by now, Hebrew had been partially displaced as a popular medium by Yiddish in northern Europe, and by Ladino in the Levant. Yet these dialects themselves bore eloquent testimony to the vitality of the primitive inheritance. Not only were they written or printed in Hebrew characters, but they contained very large numbers of Hebrew words. Sometimes, indeed, the proportion of the latter element was enormously high. The first clause in the code of laws drawn up by the Western Synagogue, London, in 1809, though its syntax was Teutonic, contained upwards of 90 per cent of Hebrew words and phrases. This, indeed, was exceptional. But the language used in her memoirs by Glückel of Hameln, the German Jewish Pepys, contained 25 to 33 per cent Hebrew. Persons to whom a hybrid so constituted was intelligible cannot have been divorced from the Hebraic tradition.

The development of the Hebrew language during all this period was not entirely suspended. Much of what was written was slavishly based upon biblical or talmudic models; but not all. The prose used by the best medieval stylists is as fine as anything which previous centuries produced. (Some of our most beautiful prayers date from this period.) Moreover, the language was becoming enriched by a continuous influx of new words. The Ibn Tibbon family, in translating various philosophic classics from Arabic into Hebrew, were compelled to invent a new terminology, which has since become an unquestioned part of the vocabulary of the Hebrew language. Other words in every day use were either adapted or else invented. Thus the term *Memron* (probably from the Latin *Membrana*) came to be used for a note-of-hand, and *Perahim* ("flowery coins," as it were) for Florins, named after the City of Flowers: while *Epiphior*, *Hashman*, and *Hegemon* (terms already found, with a different significance in the Bible or Talmud) were applied to Pope, Cardinal, and Bishop respectively.

ii

We have been dealing thus far with the written language. How far was Hebrew spoken during the period in question? Unfortunately, specific documentary testimony now becomes extremely scarce. Nevertheless, it is possible to adduce significant facts, and to hazard certain conjectures. It is known, for example, that there was a great deal of intercommunication in the Jewish world. Wandering rabbis from one country would frequently be invited to teach or to preach in the synagogues of another. What was the medium of communication? A rabbi from Bagdad would indeed find himself at home in Arabic-speaking Cordova, just as a scholar from Vilna did in Yiddish-speaking circles in New York. But in what language did a sage from the Rhineland (for example, Asher ben Yehiel who with his sons revived talmudic studies at Toledo in the fourteenth century) communicate with his colleagues or his disciples in Spain? When pilgrims went from Germany or France to Palestine, via Italy and Northern Africa, what tongue did they speak to the hosts who entertained them on the way? How did they get on with the miscellaneous handful, from every corner of the Jewish world, who kept the banner of Judaism flying in the Holy City? And, when the Palestinian Jewish settlement had grown, and sent out the "Emissaries of the Merciful" to collect funds on its behalf, in every community from Persia to New York, what language did they use on their journeys? There is only one possible answer— Hebrew, the ancient *lingua franca*. Nor are clearer indications entirely absent. The greatest of the "Emissaries of the Merciful" was Hayim Joseph David Azulai, who has left behind him a detailed diary of his travels (including, by the way, a graphic account of London). In 1754, he paid his first visit to Italy, where he records that he delivered a sermon at Pesaro. In what language? In Ladino? They would not have understood him. In Italian? He had not been in Italy long enough to learn it. The conclusion is clear that he must have spoken in Hebrew, and that his audience understood what he said.

iii

Now and again, information is given which permits conjecture to become certainty. There is, for example, no more intimate picture of Jewish life in Germany in the twelfth century than in the anecdotes contained in the *Book of the Pious*. Here we find Hebrew as the habitual medium of communication between native and foreign Jews. Thus we are told (§799) of the elder who attributed his longevity to the fact that, when a stranger who did not understand his own language stayed in his house, he never spoke to him in Hebrew in the bath-house or in any similar place. Again (§902), there is the story of the pious Jew who was taken as captive into a distant land, and saved by two Jews whom he heard speaking Hebrew together. Then (§1368) we are told of the sage who, speaking Hebrew, advised a physician not to disclose the secrets of his art to a priest.

In the Moslem world, the familiarity of Italian and Ashkenazic Jewry with spoken Hebrew was taken for granted. Solomon ben Abraham ibn Parhon, a Spanish philologist of the twelfth century, is explicit on this point. "When travellers arrive in the Christian lands," he points out in his famous lexicon, "they do not understand the native Jews. That is why the latter are forced to converse in the Holy Tongue, which explains their greater proficiency therein." In the Moslem world, on the other hand, Arabic sufficed to carry the traveller almost from end to end.

From the period of the Renaissance on, familiarity with Hebrew was certainly no less in southern Europe and the Sephardic world. Here indeed we are able to leave the legendary element behind and deal with definite historical facts, found in unimpeachable historical documents. In countries like Italy, above all, Hebrew speaking was recognized as one of the necessary accomplishments of the Jewish scholar and gentleman. "Though we all speak Italian here," wrote Azariah de' Rossi, the great Jewish humanist, in the middle of the sixteenth century, "the numerous members of the intellectual class among us meditate, speak, and write in the Holy Tongue." Hebrew was recognized as the natural language in which to converse with a stranger from distant climes. At the beginning of the seventeenth century, a German rabbi, Isaiah Hurwitz, journeyed to Palestine by way of Syria. At Aleppo, he informs us, "their soul longed for my instruction; and morn and eve they came to my door. Their speech is in the Holy Tongue; and, whenever I lectured there, I did so in the Holy Tongue likewise." Such proficiency could not be expected everywhere. Nevertheless, when that romantic messianic adventurer, David Reubeni, was in Italy in 1524, he spoke, and pretended to understand, no language other than Hebrew and found no difficulty in making himself understood as he traveled about Europe using no other tongue.

Rabbi Isaac Luria, "the Lion of the Kabbala," refused at one stage of his life to speak any language other than Hebrew—on the Sabbath, at least. It may be assumed that his example was followed by many of his disciples, in sixteenth and seventeenth-century Safed. Indeed, even in London, within living recollection, there have been religious enthusiasts of the old school who did the same. In the famous Etz Hayim Academy at Amsterdam, in which Menasseh ben Israel and Spinoza had their early education. Hebrew was actually taught by the "direct" method. According to the account of Sabbetai Bass, the children in the fifth class were allowed to speak no other language than Hebrew, excepting that they interpreted the laws in Spanish. The result of this was that, in the Amsterdam Jewish community, there was a succession of young men who could always speak Hebrew if the necessity arose.

iv

It may of course be objected that all this was not very different from the position of Latin, which continued to be spoken by clerics, written by statesmen, and studied by school-boys throughout the Middle Ages and after. But, in fact, there was an enormous difference between the two. Latin, at best, was partially familiar to only a tiny proportion of the total population. But, among the Jews, education was universal, to a degree not equalled in any country until the present generation. Hence the knowledge of Hebrew was spread all but universally; it was used—unlike Latin—for the most ordinary and most strictly secular activities, as well as for the polished and erudite.

It is not desired for one moment to minimize by what has been said the importance of the modern development of Hebrew as a spoken language. Now, for the first time perhaps since the close of the biblical canon, it is the tongue in which the Jewish child, in a Jewish land, babbles its first halting syllables.

10. PROSELYTES OF RIGHTEOUSNESS[1]

i

M UCH HAS been written on the attitude of the Jews towards proselytization. It is well known that there was a time when Judaism was definitely a missionary religion, so that one of the sneers directed in the New Testament against the Pharisees was that they encompassed land and sea in order to secure one proselyte. Later, of course, this attitude was modified—partly through the timidity engendered in the age of persecution, partly from the wholesome realization that the key to heaven is not the exclusive property of any single sect. This is the period when there grew up the practice of solemnly warning any person who desired to enter Judaism of the implications of his action, and doing all else that was possible to discourage him initially. On the other hand, once a person had embraced Judaism, he was treated in every respect as a born Jew—so different from the status of the "New Christians" of Spain and Portugal, or the unfortunate "Non-Aryans" of Nazi Germany. The rabbis were at pains to point out (as no talmudic student could forget) how the grandson of a proselyte might become high priest: and the great Maimonides himself, in a letter to a recent convert, sternly rebuked those who had sneered at his origin:

A man who left father and mother, forsook his birth-place,

---

1 Originally published in the *B'nai B'rith Magazine* (now *The National Jewish Monthly*), January-March, 1935. For the earlier period reference may now be had to Bernard J. Bamberger's *Proselytism in the Talmudic Period* (Cincinnati, 1939) and to a work produced almost simultaneously by William G. Braude, *Jewish Proselytism in the First Centuries of the Christian Era* (Providence, R. I., 1940). A. Yaari has devoted a separate study to "Proselytes in Hebrew Printing," in *Kirjath Sepher*, XIII, pp. 243-8.

his country and its power, and attached himself to this lowly, despised, and enslaved race; who recognized the truth and right-eousness of this people's Law, and cast the things of this world from his heart—shall such a one be called fool? God forbid! Not witless but wise has God called thy name, thou disciple of Abra-ham our father, who also left his father and his kindred and in-clined Godwards. And He who blessed Abraham will bless thee, and will make thee worthy to behold all the consolations destined for Israel: and in all the good that God shall do unto us He will do good unto thee. . . .

That conversionism was not unknown among the Jews of past ages is amply proved by the testimony of the highest authorities of the Catholic Church. From the beginning of the rise of Christianity down to the close of the Middle Ages, Church Fathers inveighed against the familiarity which might spread Jewish influence among Christians. Church Councils elaborated legislation intended to save true be-lievers from the infection of Jewish "perfidy"; and a long succession of Popes enforced a harsh code, the sternness of which they amply realized, with no other object than this in view. The dangers were without doubt exaggerated, as was also the Jewish desire to secure fresh adhesions; yet this testimony cannot be entirely discarded. Outside the bounda-ries of the Catholic (and, to a lesser degree, of the Moslem) world these considerations did not, of course, apply. This is not the place to enquire into the origin of the "Black" Jews of Cochin in South India, of the Beni Israel of Bombay, of the Falashas of Abyssinia. The mere fact of the existence of these colored Jews, however (as, indeed, that of the negro Jews who maintain a number of congregations in America today) is enough to prove that Judaism is to some extent a missionary religion. Picart's delightful engraving of the *Seder* ceremony in Amsterdam, about the year 1700, shows a negro servant at table with the family: a privilege which he would not have been allowed to enjoy had he not become a professing Jew.

Another interesting indication that proselytization was a recognized institution in Jewish life, however much it may have been concealed, is provided in the old liturgies. About the year 1200, a German scholar called Gerson haGozer composed a work containing the regulations for circumcision, in which he advised strongly, on the grounds of expediency, against making Christian proselytes. Yet, immediately the fear of persecution was removed the attitude changed. An Amsterdam liturgy of 1687 devotes a special section to the regulations "for the circumcision of proselytes." This is certainly a sufficient proof that, whatever the reluctance, the objections and the prejudice, the admission of proselytes to Judaism was at this period a fairly common phenomenon. The same rubrics reappear, it is interesting to note, in the prayer book according to the rite of Cochin published as recently as 1917. Similarly, the standard compendium of Jewish law, the *Shulhan Arukh,* devotes a section to the provisions regarding the admission of proselytes. A code, of course, must be prepared for all emergencies; and thus the fact is not perhaps so significant as the other points mentioned above.

In Hebrew a convert was usually termed *ger tzedek* (Righteous Stranger) or, alternatively, "Child of Abraham our Father," the Patriarch being considered the prototype of all who left their kith and kin in order to cleave to the God of Heaven.

In our own days, as is well known, conversions to Judaism generally take place with a view to marriage with a Jew or Jewess. The proportion of such unions in some places is alarmingly high, in view of the notorious fact that mixed marriages so frequently result in apathy, assimilation and, in many cases, total loss. Yet it would be unwise to draw too sweeping a conclusion from these facts, as is done by those anthropologists who assert that the offspring of such unions is invariably lost to Judaism. One occasionally hears of persons who have become converted for reasons in which religion did not enter in the first instance, but whose allegiance to their new faith leaves nothing to be desired.

The number of the offspring of such mixed marriages is increasing rapidly from year to year. One telling set of figures may be cited in order to bring home the significance of these facts. Before 1914, the Austrian province of Styria contained a Jewish population which can hardly have exceeded two or three thousand souls. During the twelve years 1890 to 1902, while about a hundred and seventy Jews in the province embraced Christianity, twenty-one Christians adopted Judaism. Whatever the motive of such conversions, a certain residuum must necessarily have remained within the Jewish community.

ii

In our survey of Jewish proselytization, it would be pointless to go back to the remotest past—to point out how a "mixed multitude" is recorded to have gone forth with the Hebrews from Egypt, how intermarriage with the survivors of the conquered tribes of Palestine was inevitable, how the Maccabaean warrior-kings assimilated by force the border tribes whom they subdued, how Edomites played a decisive role in Jewish history at the period of the great struggle of 66-70. In all these cases, neighboring peoples, of identical stock and speaking a similar language, were in question. It is on record, however, that in a later period, when the Jewish Diaspora had already reached Europe, the process continued. The Roman Empire was familiar with proselytes attracted by the glories of Hebrew monotheism. At one period, there appeared to be the possibility that Judaism would sweep the civilized world, in just the same fashion as Christianity was ultimately to do; and contemporary Latin writers professed to be alarmed at the prospect. Poppaea, the wife of Nero; Aquila of Pontus, who translated the Bible; the Consul, Flavius Clemens, nephew of the Roman Emperor Vespasian, and his wife, Domitilla (Titus' cousin) ; the royal house of Adiabene, whose members fought gallantly for Israel at the period of the First Revolt (when one of the super-patriotic leaders was Simon Bar-Giora, "Son of the Proselyte") —these are a few out of the many outstanding names handed down to us from antiquity. To these, rabbinic fantasy added the Roman Emperors Nero and Marcus Aurelius themselves, as though to demonstrate that Judaism is not exclusive and that it gained adherents in the least likely quarters. Of the two hundred Tannaim, or rabbis of the century before and after the destruction of Jerusalem, seven are recorded as being of Gentile extraction; of the Amoraim (their successors in the following generations) there were at least three. In the funerary inscriptions of classical times, too, quite a number of proselytes are mentioned. Even in the days when Christianity was on its triumphant march to world domination, Judaism often proved itself to be a powerful counter-attraction. The writings of the Church Fathers, and the edicts of the Church Councils, show plainly how much the rivalry of Judaism was feared. At the beginning of the seventh century, a monk who was making expiation in the monastery of Mount Sinai became assailed by doubts as to the truth of Christianity, crossed the desert to Palestine, and offered himself to the community of Tiberias as a proselyte. Ultimately he adopted the name of Abraham, established a Jewish family, and became a zealous advocate of his new religion. Contemporaneously (or perhaps a little earlier) a certain Bishop was converted to Judaism and composed in Arabic a vigorous polemical work defending his action.

It is not necessary to speak always in terms of individuals. Before the rise of Mohammedanism, more than one tribe of the Arabian Peninsula had embraced Judaism. Special mention is deserved by Abu Karib, king of the Yemen, who embraced Judaism in the third century, and his greatgrandson, Harith ibn Amr, who followed his example about a hundred years later; and by their contemporary, Warakah ibn Naufal. Jewish influence here reached its climax with the conversion to Judaism, about the year 515, of King Dhu Nuwas, the ruler of the Yemen. His zeal for his new religion, indeed, brought about his downfall: for a coalition was formed against him by the Abyssinians and Byzantines, leading to his overthrow and death in 525 and the end of the kingdom over which he had ruled. Two centuries later, we have the famous case of the Khazars—a mixed people, with a strong Mongolian strain, who occupied a territory comprised in what is now the Ukraine, between the Caucasus, the Volga, and the Don. For a period of some two hundred years, this was amongst the most important of the independent states which lay to the north of the Byzantine Empire. Early in the eighth century, the reigning Prince, Bulan, recognized the merits of Judaism and formally adopted it as his religion. His example was followed by many of the aristocracy. One of his descendants, Obadiah, was especially memorable for the zeal with which he propagated his faith, constructing synagogues and inviting foreign scholars to settle in the country. The governing classes seem to have become completely Judaized, their example being followed by many of the ordinary people; though, in accordance with the traditional Jewish principles of tolerance, followers of other religions were left undisturbed. Throughout the golden period of the Khazar state, it was considered essentially Jewish by its neighbors. At the beginning of the eleventh century (or somewhat later, according to the most recent researches), it was overwhelmed by an alliance between the Russians and Byzantines: but it is thought that the semi-Mongolian features which are relatively common amongst the Jews of this region to the present day are a legacy from these bygone Proselytes of Righteousness.

Long after this, a vague tendency towards Judaism continued amongst the inhabitants of Russia. At the close of the fifteenth century and the beginning of the sixteenth, this reached its climax in the outbreak of what was known as the "Judaizing Heresy," sedulously fostered by a Jewish teacher from Kiev named Zachariah. For a time it made notable progress in mercantile circles, at court, even amongst the leaders of the Russian Church. Two priests, Denis and Alexius, became eager proselytizers: Helena, daughter of the Grand Duke, was amongst their disciples. In the end, the leaders of the Russian Church became seriously alarmed, and the heresy was stamped out in blood and fire.

Meanwhile, conditions in Western Europe were not entirely dissimilar. Various Church Councils, in almost uninterrupted sequence, prohibited conversion to Judaism under pain of death: secular rulers followed this lead. This, indeed, was one of the pretexts for the relentless persecution of Judaism which now set in. It can barely be imagined that this alarm was based on nothing but sheer nervousness; and the conclusion forces itself upon us that conversions actually took place in some numbers. We are not without actual instances to prove this. We know, for example, that Jews sometimes circumcized the Gentile slaves whom they purchased. Generally, the identity of the converts is shrouded in obscurity; but every now and again a corner of the curtain is lifted and we obtain some actual glimpse of some heroic figure who dared all, and sometimes lost all, for the sake of Judaism. Thus, for example, in 839 the French court was shocked by one episode of the sort. A learned cleric, the deacon Bodo, had received permission from the Empress to go on pilgrimage to Rome. Instead of doing this he (accompanied by a nephew, whose views were similar to his own) made his way to Saragossa, adopted the name Eleazar, and openly espoused Judaism; ultimately marrying a Jewish woman. Not dissimilar was an episode early in the eleventh century, when a German cleric named Wecelin embraced Judaism and engaged in a bitter controversy with one of his former pupils. This occurrence was responsible for a harsh persecution of the Jews in the Rhineland.

To these fairly familiar historical episodes we may add another, dating back to the same period, which has recently come to light as the result of a fortunate *trouvaille* amongst the fragments from the Cairo *Genizah*. Some time in the eleventh century, a girl belonging to a prominent and wealthy non-Jewish family in France decided to embrace Judaism. Forsaking her home and all she possessed, she made her way to Narbonne, where she formally entered the Jewish fold, and ultimately married. Some six months later, hearing that her kindred were seeking her, she escaped with her husband to another city, where she lived for several years. In the end, an attack was delivered upon the Jewish community of this place. David, her husband, was killed in the synagogue, and two of their children taken captive. The unfortunate widow was left penniless and alone, save for a child of a few months old at her breast. In these straits, she was compelled to throw herself for assistance upon the mercy of her new coreligionists; and we may hope that her appeal did not fall upon deaf ears.

Another notable figure, utterly forgotten until a series of documents relating to him was discovered not long since, was a *ger tzedek* named Obadiah, who belonged to a noble Norman family. It is likely enough that he had come to the East as a crusader. Nonetheless, falling under the spell of the ancient faith, he became converted to Judaism in 1102. He studied deeply, became well-versed in Jewish lore, and, when he left Aleppo a little later, brought with him a letter of recommendation from the rabbis of that place conceived in the warmest terms. Of his own literary productions, in Hebrew, there is still extant, in addition to a copy of the Friday evening service which he wrote for his own use, a *Megillah* in which he gives an account of the vicissitudes of the Jewish people at that troubled period and of the various pretenders who had risen to give expression to the age-old Messianic dream. Obadiah too was the name, nearly a century later, of another proselyte who lived in Palestine and was in correspondence with Maimonides, who addressed to him that noble letter part of which has been quoted above.

iii

Throughout the course of the Middle Ages and after, similar characters and similar events may be traced. Amongst the victims of the terrible massacre at Cologne, on the morrow of the Feast of Pentecost in that dark year, 1096, there were at least two proselytes, who were piously recorded in that tragic register, the *Memorbuch* of Nuremberg. The same volume contains records of several others in the same category—for example, Isaac, "son of our Father Abraham," who was burned for the sanctification of the Most High Name (apparently in Nuremberg itself), leaving money for the education of the young; and "the proselyte who was converted at the time of the Lord's anger," martyred in July 1298. There were in addition several others—two at least of them being women. Among the martyrs of Weissenberg, in Alsace, we read of Rabbi Isaac, son of Abraham our Father, of Würzburg, who was burned for the Unity of the Divine Name; and of Rabbi Abraham of Augsburg, "who rejected the gods of the peoples and broke off the heads of the images and was confident in life eternal, and was tortured greatly and was burned for the Unity of the Name" on 21st November, 1264. (More than one poignant elegy was written in his memory.) Most remarkable of all was a French proselyte, known as Abraham, son of Abraham our Father "who had been head [prior] of all the bare-foot Friars" (i.e., Franciscans?) and was put to death in 1268 in the same cruel manner at Sinzig in the Rhineland, the famous Mordecai ben Hillel, the most eminent talmudist of the day, commemorating this tragedy. All told, the names of no fewer than ten proselytes between the years 1264 and 1341—seven men and three women—are recorded in the *Memorbuch* of Mayence, which provides many of the main details here reproduced. It is significant that no less than half of these met martyrs' deaths. Those responsible for the conversions were of course treated no less ferociously than the proselytes themselves. There is every indication that the episode mentioned above brought about a mass persecution at Weissenberg, where several other contemporary martyrdoms are recorded. Contemporaneously, it is recounted how in France a certain Christian named Perrot, converted to Judaism, was buried by the community of Toulouse in their House of Life: and how, in consequence of the enquiry which resulted, the pious Rabbi Issac Males was burned alive (1278).

It is highly significant that quite a number of these proselytes, notwithstanding the advanced age when they embraced Judaism and began to study Jewish lore, made themselves a name as Jewish scholars. The *Tosafoth* mention a twelfth century French savant, named Rabbi Abraham the Proselyte, who made some pertinent observations regarding the different degrees of observance which might be discerned between born Jews and those who joined the Jewish community late in life. Contemporary with him was one Josiphia, whose late introduction to Hebrew studies did not prevent him from writing liturgical poetry in that language. A certain Isaac the Proselyte was author of several medieval exegetical treatises. One begins to see substance in the statement attributed to Rabbi David Kimhi, the famous Franco-Jewish exegete of the thirteenth century, in which he speaks of various French proselytes, saints and sages, who became Jews because of the contradictory passages in the Gospels.

In England, the number of Jews during the Middle Ages was small: yet there may be traced among them quite a number of converts to Judaism. We read, at the time of the massacres of 1190, of the extermination of a "Community of Proselytes." The present writer ventures to believe that this is based upon a copyist's error, *gerim* (proselytes) having been read for *garim* (sojourners) ; but the fact that later generations could accept the erroneous reading demonstrates itself that the idea did not appear out of the question to them. Some time previous to the year 1200 (we are informed in a contemporary chronicle) two Cistercian monks from the north of England turned Jews. "The two wretches might have become Christians," grumbled the witty Walter Mapes. April 17th, 1222, witnessed the burning at Oxford of a certain deacon who had begun to study Hebrew literature and had been led thereby to become a proselyte to Judaism, ultimately marrying a Jewess. It is unlikely that he is to be identified with the Dominican friar, Robert of Reading, *alias* Haggai, about whom a similar story is told in a later generation and who was executed at London. This last episode was reckoned amongst the pretexts for the Expulsion from

England in 1290. When one considers that in all probability only a minority of the cases became known, it will be
realized how imposing is this record, covering as it does so
brief a period.

iv

Other classical examples may be adduced from central
and southern Europe. It will be noticed how many of the converts were Christian priests, whose studies had led them to
a realization of the logical superiority of Judaism. One after
the other of these died at the stake, in almost every country
of Europe. We have already witnessed more than one example from Germany. Italy provides the case of a learned
Franciscan friar living in Rome, named Cornelio da Mon-
talcino, who suffered for his courage and steadfastness on
the notorious Campo dei Fiori, on September 4, 1554.
Three quarters of a century later, and under Protestantism,
it was the turn of Nicholas Antoine, pastor of a little place
near Geneva, who had attempted without success to be admitted to the Jewish fold in Italy but continued his Jewish
principles and practices in his own little community. The
lord of an adjoining manor denounced him; and on April
20, 1632, he perished on the Place de Pleinpalais near
Geneva, imploring the mercy of the God of Abraham as he
died. A pathetic figure makes her appearance about the
year 1600 in the records of the Society for Dowering the
Brides of the Jewish community of Venice, where we read
how full benefits were accorded to "Esther, daughter of
Abraham our Father, whom they burned."

The classical land of Jewish conversionism was of course
Spain. It is insufficiently realized, however, that of the Marranos, who suffered at the stake for secret adherence to the
faith of their fathers or else escaped to profess it openly

abroad, a large proportion were of mixed blood. In the official records, the martyrs and the fugitives are frequently designated as "half" or "quarter" New Christians, indicating that they possessed only that proportion of Jewish blood. Sometimes they were of unqualified Gentile descent. Thus, for example, in an informer's list of the community of Amsterdam in 1617, which the present writer had the good fortune to discover in the archives of the Lisbon Inquisition, one encounters such entries as "Antonio Dias Toscano, of Metola in Alenjejo, Old Christian, formerly in the service of the Grand Inquisitor." Many of the founders of the communities of London, Amsterdam, Hamburg, and New York had wives or mothers in whose veins no drop of Jewish blood was to be traced, or who had themselves begun to realize the verities of Judaism by reason of the ferocity with which its adherents were persecuted and the steadfastness with which they withstood their martyrdom. Moreover, persecution engendered in the crypto-Jews of the Peninsula a proselytizing, missionary spirit such as is seldom met in the history of their people, the Inquisitional records providing ample testimony of the zeal with which some of them propagated their faith, amongst "New" Christians and "Old." Of the most illustrious and devoted victims of the Holy Office, whose memory was so venerated by their Marrano contemporaries, both Fray Diogo da Assunção (who perished gallantly at Lisbon on August 3, 1603) and Antonio Homem (the learned scholar who headed the crypto-Jewish group in the University of Coimbra and was put to death on May 5, 1624) were only partly Jewish by blood. Better known still was the case of Don Lope de Vera, a Spanish youth of gentle birth, with no trace of Jewish blood in his veins. His attention was turned to Judaism by his studies and he became a devoted adherent of the "Law of Moses." Betrayed to the Inquisition, he had the hardihood to circumcise himself with a bone while in prison, assuming the name of Judah the Believer; and he chanted Hebrew psalms on his way to the stake at Valladolid, on July 25, 1644[1]. A more fortunate contemporary of his was Lorenzo Escudero of Cordova, who adopted Judaism at Amsterdam under the name of Abraham Ger (or Peregrino, the Spanish equivalent of this term). He made himself notorious for a gallant resistance to the attempt made by the Governor of the Netherlands to reconvert him; composed a polemical work in defense of his new religion, entitled *The Fortress of Judaism;* and, under the *alias* Juan Gilles, proved a thorn in the side of the Spanish government in the Peninsula.

For it must not be imagined that all those who had the temerity to embrace Judaism paid for it with their lives; though the cases of those who did so are the more notorious. The pride of the University of Marburg, about the year 1600, was Conrad Victor, Professor of Classical Languages at the famous seat of learning. Finding it impossible to accept the Christian dogma of the Trinity or to believe in the divinity of Jesus, he made his way secretly, in 1607, to Salonica. Here he embraced Judaism, under the name of Moses Prado. It was in vain that he solicited from the Duke of Hesse permission to return home to his family, and there enjoy the freedom of conscience which was the right of every man in the Levant: and he remained an exile till his death, some years later. Not unlike this was the case of Johann Peter Spaeth, who, born at Venice and resident at Augsburg, dedicated himself to the study of theology, in which he made great headway. He was the author of an important work defending Catholicism against the attacks of the Reformed Church. But he suddenly became conscious of Israel's long martyrdom, which constituted the whole Jewish people the "Man of Sorrow" of Isaiah's prophecy:

---

[1] See the separate essay, "Judah the Believer," pp. 182 ff. in this volume.

and he became converted to Judaism, under the name "Moses the German" (Moses Germanus). As a Jew, he continued his literary career, publishing amongst other works a doughty onslaught against Spinoza; and he died as a Jew at Amsterdam, in 1701.

Moses Germanus was by no means the only proselyte who figured in this community at this period. More than one, as we have seen, was to be found in the ranks of the Marranos; and in the earliest registers of the cemetery of the Spanish and Portuguese community there figures a long sequence of "children of Abraham our Father." The illustrations to the most popular *Haggadahs* for the domestic service on Passover eve produced at Amsterdam at this period—the prototypes, indeed, of those in general use today—were actually engraved by a proselyte, eloquent token of the degree to which persons included in this category were able to enter into the life of the community. As a matter of fact, an astonishingly large number of learned proselytes to Judaism were engaged in Hebrew printing even as compositors, especially in Holland, at this period, so much so that an entire monograph has been devoted to the subject.

A recently discovered Spanish document provides another instance of a proselyte who fled to the Levant in order to profess Judaism. This was a French aristocrat named Roueries, who possessed no less than three chateaux in the neighborhood of Lyons. Becoming convinced of the superiority of Judaism over other faiths, he made his way to Venice, with his two sons, and there entered the community. Subsequently, he went on to Constantinople, where Don Joseph Nasi, Duke of Naxos, received him and supported him as he deserved. (It was in the course of the last decades of the sixteenth century, when the latter was all-powerful at the Sublime Porte.) Other unscrupulous Jews, on the other hand, took advantage of his condition. French merchants at the Turkish capital were unable to understand how a man could abandon all that he possessed and throw in his lot with a people who treated him thus. His reply was brief and to the point: "I did not come to seek the Hebrews, but the God of the Hebrews and their Law. Of them, you can assuredly say no ill."

Another memorable French proselyte, hitherto unknown to historians, was a certain Aaron d'Antan, a native of a small place in Provence, who became entirely devoted to his new religion. The letters which he addressed to Mathurin Veyssière de la Croix (1661-1739), Royal Librarian at Berlin, justifying the drastic step which he had taken—as yet unpublished—are included in the collection of the present writer.

v

The eighteenth century witnessed three *causes célèbres*—two in the East of Europe, the other in the West. There was living in Russia at this time a tax-farmer named Baruch Leibov, who was in close relations with the Czar's court. During his stay in Moscow, he came into contact with a retired naval captain named Alexander Voznitzin, whom he is alleged to have "seduced" to Jewish ideas. In consequence, he went to the little town of Dubrovna, near Smolensk, where Leibov's son initiated him into the Jewish faith. When the news became known, there was a universal scandal. The Captain and his instructor were arrested and taken to St. Petersburg, where they were subjected to ghastly tortures by the "Chancellery for Secret Inquisitorial Affairs." On July 15, 1738, both were burned, in the presence of a crowd of spectators, on a public square in the capital.

Among Polish Jewry, the memory of no martyr was venerated more than that of Count Valentine Potocki. A member of one of the noblest families in that country, he became convinced of the truth of the Jewish religion while travelling in Western Europe with a companion, a visit to Rome only serving to confirm him in his view. In the free atmosphere of Amsterdam, he formally embraced the Jewish faith. (It was in the first half of the eighteenth century.) Subsequently, he returned to Poland, living among the Jews as one of them under the name of Abraham, son of Abraham our Father. Legend reports that he was betrayed to the authorities by an irate householder whose son he had rebuked for disturbing his studies in the *Beth haMidrash*. He was arrested and every endeavour was made to induce him to repent of his conduct. Even his mother's tears and supplications were brought to bear, but all to no avail. On the second day of Pentecost, in the summer of 1749, he was burned alive in a public square at Vilna. It was unsafe for a Jew to be seen in the vicinity; but a certain Leiser Zhiskes relied on the fact that he was beardless to intermingle with the mob and to secure some of the ashes from the pyre, which were afterwards buried in the Jewish House of Life. It is said that, almost immediately after the execution, a letter of pardon from the king arrived at Vilna—too late to save the victim. The memory of Count Potocki is still revered among the Jews of Poland as the *Ger Tzedek* par excellence. Potocki's companion, it is related—a noble like himself—continued to cherish his memory and not long after left the country with his wife and child and formally entered the Jewish fold in Holland. Subsequently, the family removed to Palestine, where they were merged in the pious, learned community of one or the other of its Holy Cities.

Contemporary with this episode, though significantly different in its consequences, was the famous case of Lord George Gordon. A younger son of the third Duke of Gordon, he had served successively in the army, navy, and House of Commons, and in 1779 became the President of the United Protestant League, formed to oppose (with more bigotry, it is to be feared, than reason) the advance of Roman Catholicism. The agitation which he headed was responsible for the No Popery Riots in London in 1780. These led to his trial for treason, of which he was acquitted in the following year. In 1784, he again appeared as Protestant champion in the quarrel between the Dutch and the Emperor Joseph. But already, as it appears, his mind had been turning to Judaism. The Jewish authorities in London were too nervous to have anything to do with him. Accordingly, he went to Birmingham, where he was initiated into the Abrahamic covenant. From that moment, his life was that of the hyper-orthodox Jew, down to the smallest detail. He was careful to observe the dietary laws, kept his head covered on all possible occasions, allowed his beard to grow, and even objected to receiving Jews who were clean-shaven. This extreme degree of observance continued even during the long period, from 1788 onwards, when he was lodged in Newgate Prison in consequence of libels upon the British Government and Queen Marie Antoinette, and a *minyan* of Polish Jews assembled regularly in his room there for religious services. He died in 1793, and was buried in St. James' Burial Ground, on the Hampstead Road. But, eccentric or not, his real place was obviously in the Jewish House of Life.

Gordon was not by any means the only Anglo-Jewish proselyte of the "modern" period. Only recently details have come to light regarding the followers of the Puritan extremist, John Traske, who preached a return to Old Testament teachings and practices in so uncompromising a fashion that in 1618-20 the whole group was imprisoned on a charge of Judaizing. The accusation was so far from being exaggerated that certain of them settled later in

Amsterdam and formally joined the Synagogue there, the most prominent being a certain Hamlet Jackson (whose name may have some significance for Shakespearean studies, his parents perhaps having been ardent theatre-goers!) In fact, quite a handful of English proselytes may be traced in this city at the time, half a dozen of them being buried in the burial ground of the Spanish and Portuguese community between 1623 and 1625 alone. In 1634, the traveller Brereton met there an English tobacco merchant and his wife who had been converted to Judaism; about the same time the diarist Evelyn made the acquaintance of a Burgundian Jew, "a merry, drunken fellow," who had married a Kentish woman and made for her benefit the earliest recorded English translation of the liturgy. English proselytes are met with elsewhere too. In 1610, Sandys encountered one in the island of Zante, while a Ger from England was assisted by the Hamburg synagogue in 1653. Most significant was the case of the very eminent English miniaturist, Alexander Cooper (brother of the still more famous Samuel), who made his appearance in Stockholm in due course as a Jew with the name Abraham. There can be no doubt that he too had become converted.

At the period of the Resettlement of the Jews in England, one or two converts were included among the London community. Thus, when John Greenhalgh visited the synagogue in Creechurch Lane in 1662, he records that he saw, in addition to "one hundred right Jews," a proselyte as well. This may have been Samuel Swinock, a cooper of Seething Lane, whom we know from another source to have formally embraced Judaism. In 1669, a proselyte named Deborah Israel passed away in London, apparently leaving her property to the congregation.

In the subsequent period, there was much nervousness at the possibly unfavorable repercussions of receiving converts to Judaism. It was reported that Menasseh ben Israel had given an undertaking to Oliver Cromwell about this, which had been repeated after the Restoration to Charles II; and it was believed in official circles long after that this hypothetical agreement had been closely observed. This, however, was far from the case. That a certain nervousness prevailed is of course indisputable. In 1751, the wardens of the Spanish and Portuguese Synagogue addressed a letter to those of the Ashkenazic sister-bodies, calling their attention to the growing perils of the practice of admitting proselytes to the Jewish fold, as exemplified above all in the fact that two or three Christians had recently arrived from Norway with that express purpose. In consequence of this, proclamation was made in the London synagogues to the effect that any person guilty of the offense in future would be expelled from the congregation and deprived of all the privileges of the Jewish faith. Yet this proved an insufficient deterrent, as is revealed in the following entry in the records of the Hambro Synagogue, London, for November 1783:

At a meeting of our vestry held this day it was made known to us that Philip Nathan of Houndsditch did for a certain sum of money circumcise a Christian foreigner, a Native of Flanders, which we hold contrary to the laws of this country. We therefore have excommunicated him from our Society and also excluded him from all the benefits which he has hitherto received.

Notwithstanding this reluctance, there is no doubt that proselytes continued to enter the Anglo-Jewish community in a steady stream—in most cases for the purposes of intermarriage, but frequently from conviction. It is surprising, as a matter of fact, how many "Children of Abraham our Father" figure in the circumcisional and marriage registers of the various communities in London, in and about the

Regency period. In the provinces, conditions must have been identical: it is sufficient to recall the match between Moses Abrahams, of Poole, and the buxom Martha Haynes (daughter of a Dorset farmer), from whom Viscount Samuel is descended. We learn, too, in the *Journals of Ezra Stiles,* President of Yale University, of an entire family from Coventry who, in the middle of the eighteenth century, went to London to become converted to Judaism.

Testimony even more striking is provided by a semi-official list of female converts to Judaism in the same period, preserved in a register in the library of the Jewish Theological Seminary, New York. Over the seven-year period between 1809 and 1816, no less than sixty proselytes—thirty-nine women and twenty-one children—are recorded. In most cases, the conversions were effected with an eye to marriage, the bridegrooms bearing some of the most stately and polysyllabic names in the Spanish and Portuguese community; the provinces, too—Portsmouth, Exeter, Dover, and others—contributed to the number, while one neoproselyte entered the fold on the eve of her departure for America. When one considers that no men are included in this particular record, it will be realized what really high proportions the conversions attained. From 1699 to the beginning of the reign of Queen Victoria, forty-one converts to Judaism (thirty-seven of them being women) were married under the auspices of the Spanish and Portuguese synagogue in London.

vi

This brings us to the verge of modern times. By now, no positive danger was attached to conversion to Judaism. Intermarriage, as we have seen, was increasing apace, and in almost every country of Western Europe and America relatively large numbers of non-Jews, desirous of marrying persons of Jewish birth, embraced their religion as a preliminary. It may be said in these cases that the converts were as a rule no less fervid in their observance (and no more) than the Jewish partner in the marriage; and there are now included in most large Jewish communities persons, sometimes of deep religious feeling and a comparatively high standard of observance, who are only in part Jewish by descent. But, in the period of tolerance, the flow of proselytes who embraced Judaism from conviction did not by any means cease.

The last few generations of comparative toleration, no less than the Middle Ages, have continued to provide a long succession of instances of proselytes who have become spiritual forces in Judaism. The name is recorded, for example, of a certain Isaac Papons, a convert who became rabbi in Eibeschuetz. Some time towards the end of the eighteenth century, an entire family, including three generations—several brothers, their father and grandfather—became converted to Judaism in Amsterdam. The old man died soon thereafter and the rest migrated to Palestine and settled in the city of the mystics, Safed. Here they found a number of other proselytes, and one of the family was authorized later on to travel through Europe collecting funds for the support of this extraordinary group. A member of another family of proselytes lived in the same center of mysticism at the beginning of the nineteenth century. Bearing the name Abraham, son of Abraham our Father, he was also termed "the exalted sage," in an age when such compliments were not easily bestowed. It appears that he had come from some Western country and had, in consequence of his conversion, lost everything he had possessed. So greatly did his pitiful plight impress the rabbis of Safed that, in 1821, they formally authorized him to go among his new coreligionists to make a collection. Another proselyte named Abraham, who became recognized as a rabbinical authority of rank, lived a short while after this at Salonica, where he died in 1870; he is described on his tombstone as "the perfect sage" (*haHakham haShalem*).

An even more remarkable character was Aaron Moses Isaac Graanboom (1736-1807), born at Linköping, in Sweden, at a time when Jews were all but unkown in that country. Of his early history, little is known beyond the fact that he embraced Judaism and must have studied its tenets and its literature with peculiar fervor. So far was this the case that he became one of the *dayyanim,* or ecclesiastical judges, of the community of Amsterdam where he had settled. While acting in this capacity, he published a Hebrew work, *Zera Yitzhak,* of ethical and homiletical content, which achieved some success at the time. When, after the outbreak of the French Revolution, a group sprang up in Amsterdam which favored certain mild reforms in the synagogal service, he threw his weight into the scales in their favor and was appointed rabbi of the synagogue, *Adath Jeshurun,* which they founded. He continued to administer to this until his death in 1807, when he was succeeded in office by his son, Israel Graanboom. A curious parallel to Graanboom's career, a hundred years later, is provided by Aimé Paillière, the well-known French "Proselyte of Righteousness' of our own day. Intended for a clerical career in the Catholic Church, he not only embraced Judaism (though retaining an antinomian viewpoint) but also become one of the ministers of the Liberal Jewish Synagogue in Paris. Here—most remarkable of all— he exerted his influence to strengthen the influence of tradition, and played a noteworthy part in French Jewish life: though in his last years (he died in 1950), he vaguely groped towards a Judaeo-Christian synthesis. He himself magnificently described the spiritual odyssey which led him to Judaism in his autobiographical essay, *The Unknown Sanctuary*.

The United States of America have provided an outstanding representative on this roll in the curious figure of Warder Cresson, of Philadelphia (1798-1860). Of Quaker stock, he made the acquaintance of the Jewish scholar Isaac Leeser, about 1840, and became deeply attached to him. His biblical leanings led him to obtain nomination as first United States consul at Jerusalem. Here, his Jewish interests became more and more pronounced. He assumed the name Michael C. Boaz Israel, contributed to Jewish papers, strongly criticised the methods of the Christian missionaries, and came to be on intimate terms with the principal families in the Sephardi community. At last, in 1848, he took the decisive step, formally entering the Covenant of Abraham. On his return to America to settle his affairs, his wife and son obtained a Commission in Lunacy in order to restrain him: but on appeal, after a memorable law-suit, the decision of the lower court which granted this was reversed. Shortly thereafter he returned to Jerusalem, and devoted the rest of his life to an attempt to secure the agricultural regeneration of a Jewish Palestine, on behalf of which he conducted a vigorous campaign in the columns of *The Occident*. He is hence to be regarded amongst the pioneers of Zionism. He led the life of an observant Oriental Jew, amid the universal respect of the community; and when he died, on November 6, 1860, he was buried on the Mount of Olives with such honors as are paid only to a learned and pious rabbi.

A very similar type, with identical interests, was provided by a burgher of the ancient Baltic city of Danzig, named David Klasen, who was converted to Judaism in 1834. Subsequently he, like Cresson, devoted himself to furthering the cause of Jewish colonization in Palestine.

In the end, he became superintendent of the orange plantations in the Montefiore Gardens near Jaffa, now included in the boundaries of Tel-Aviv. Thus, a Proselyte of Righteousness had a noteworthy share in founding what was to become one of the stable industries of the new Palestine.

Among the residents of Athens, in the middle of the nineteenth century, were two aristocratic French ladies, widow and daughter respectively of the French statesman, the Duc de Plaisance (Piacenza), who had served with distinction under Napoleon. The local atmosphere, at this period, seems to have been conducive to interest in matters Jewish: in any case, there was a Greek proselyte of about 1830, one Abraham Guer, whose biblical expositions are preserved. Whether they came under his influence or no, the two strangers became deeply interested in Jewish matters. They were on very intimate terms with the notorious Don Pacifico, a Gibraltar Jew whose maltreatment by the mob was responsible for the delivery by Lord Palmerston of one of the most famous speeches ever heard in the British Parliament. They became absorbed with the idea of the restoration of the Jewish people to Palestine. In consequence, it was found that when the Duchess of Piacenza died in 1855, she left a considerable fortune, through her Jewish friend, for the furtherance of this object, and a plot of ground in the Valley of Olympia for the erection of a Temple to the God of Israel.

At this period, another famous proselytess was beginning to come before the public eye. This was Adah Isaacs Menken. Actress, dancer, poetess, adventuress; the friend of Charles Dickens, Charles Reade, and Victor Hugo; the lover of Swinburne and Dumas—one of the few constant points in her career was her attachment to Judaism, which she embraced on her marriage, in 1865, to Alexander Isaacs Menken. At one time, she was a contributor to the Cincinnati *Israelite;* she is reported, on a certain memorable occasion, to have delivered a sermon in the old synagogue of New Orleans: and she is said never to have forgotten to kindle the Sabbath candles on Friday evening. A rabbi was in attendance on her when she died; and she was buried, with full Jewish rites, in the Père Lachaise cemetery in Paris.

As far as Great Britain is concerned, an interesting recent case is that of Elizabeth Jane Caulfield, Countess of Charlemont. Born in 1834, she was the only daughter of the first Lord Athlumney, and in 1856 she married James Molyneux, third Earl of Charlemont. Though of course of Christian upbringing, she felt a deep inclination to Judaism. Both in Belfast (near which place she had her country house) and in London, she became a familiar figure in the synagogues; she often resorted to the rabbis for advice; and when she died, in 1882, it was generally understood that she might be considered a professing Jewess.

A woman of our own day fittingly concludes the cycle. "Elisheva" was born in Rjasan, in Russia, in 1889, her name originally being Elisheva Shirkow. She removed to Moscow, came into contact with Jewish life, learned Yiddish and Hebrew, and began to translate into Russian some of the literary treasures of those literatures, from Jehudah haLevi down to Bialik. In 1919, she published a couple of volumes of poetry in her native language. In the following year, she began to feel her way in Hebrew, writing some poems of rare beauty; and, almost as an outcome of her literary feelings, she shortly afterwards embraced Judaism. Henceforth, she lived in Palestine (where she died in 1949), the full, untramelled life of a Palestinian Jewess, and she is numbered amongst the handful of outstanding figures in the contemporary Jewish literary world. What more striking proof of the reality of the Palestinian revival can there be than the case of this female Conrad, who adopted a strange language (to the literature of which she made imperishable contributions) as well as a strange faith?

vii

It has been left to our own day to provide, too, one of the most remarkable, most widely spread, and (curiously enough) least known instances of mass conversion to Judaism. Towards the close of the eighteenth century, in the reign of Catherine II, there began to appear among the Russian peasantry and artisans a sect which held the Old Testament in the utmost reverence, placing it on a footing equal, or even superior, to the New. Little by little, they began to adopt various biblical rites. They observed the dietary laws; they rejected the doctrine of the Trinity; in some cases, they practiced circumcision; but above all, they universally discarded the observance of the Sunday Sabbath in favor of Saturday. It was this which gave them the title by which they became officially known—*Subbotniki,* or Sabbatarians.

Under the old Russian regime, they were persecuted ferociously. Large numbers were deported to the Caucasus or Siberia; many, even as late as the nineteenth century, were put to death. But the new church, like every other, throve on the blood of the martyrs and increased in numbers; so much so, indeed, that the Russian religious leaders professed to regard it as a serious danger. By degrees, many of its followers discarded the few Christian doctrines which they still retained. What was left was no more, and no less, than Judaism. Conversions of individuals, or groups, of whole communities, became more and more common. The government continued to place every obstacle in their way but nevertheless, the movement gathered weight.

There were whole villages in Siberia inhabited by these devoted souls. In appearance and ways of life they were exactly like any other Russian *moujiks*. But, in the middle of the village, a synagogue appeared instead of a church; and some Russian or Polish Jew acted as spiritual factotum of the community, teaching them as much as he could of the traditional Jewish practice. With the Russian Revolution, the floodgates were opened. Exact data are difficult to obtain; but a scholarly enthusiast who devoted a work to the subject some quarter of a century ago suggested that the number of conversions to Judaism of Subbotniki in Russia in recent years had been so vast as to compensate, and more, for all the losses which Judaism had had to suffer during the same period through assimilation and inter-marriage. Since then, however, very little has been heard of them. It is obvious that the spiritual atmosphere behind the Iron Curtain is hardly conducive to such developments.

The importance which these proselytes attach to the Bible explains the intense interest which they have shown always in *Eretz Israel*. The part of the *Ger Tzedek* in building up the new Palestine has been very significant. A really considerable number migrated thither in the 1890's fleeing from the Russian persecutions. Before the World War I, hundreds came from the Southern part of Russia —descendants, no doubt, of the deportees of previous genera-tions—and under the British Mandate frequently applied for the sparse immigration certificates which constituted the key for entry to the land of their hopes. At one time there was talk of their forming a settlement of their own, and, in the colonies of Upper Galilee—Rosh-Pinah, Yesod haMaalah and Mishmar haYarden especially—there are numerous families of proselytes, with nothing Jewish about them save their ideals. There has been a remarkable paral-lel to this movement, though on a far smaller scale, in the amazing recent episode of the devoted group from a South Italian village, San Nicandro, who adopted Judaism during the Fascist regime out of pure conviction (no Jews have lived in that area for five hundred years), made contact with the Jewish Brigade during the Italian campaign and have since removed *en masse* to settle in Israel.

It must once again be emphasized, in conclusion, that the instances brought together in these pages necessarily constitute only an insignificant minority of the whole. Over a long period of years, conversion to Judaism was considered a capital offense over a large portion of the world's surface. Whereas Christendom trumpeted every secession from Judaism as an outstanding triumph for the faith, the Jewish world was compelled to minimize, even to conceal, the accretions which it received from Christianity-victories which, as it knew to its cost, were perpetual incitements to murder, terrorization and bloodshed. Even today, conversion to Judaism is looked upon with intense disapproval by the majority, while the Jew, with eminent sanity, refrains from vaunting it as a triumph for his own creed. Hence those cases which are on record comprise only a few of the most notable, or perhaps of the most militant. The long succession of episodes which have been collected here demonstrate, however, beyond all possibility of doubt, that proselytization on the part of the Jews, and the entry of Gentiles into the Jewish fold, has been practically continuous since Jewish history began. The blood of some proselyte, more remote or less, must course in the veins of every Jew in the world today.

11. THE PEOPLE AND THE BOOK[1]

i

THE KORAN speaks of both Jews and Christians as "Peoples of the Book"—that is, of the Bible. Subsequently, the title was arrogated to the Jews alone. But, based on error though this ascription may be, it is in fact fully justifiable. For the Jews are a People of the Book, very literally and unquestionably, in more senses than one. In the first place, they are no less the creators than the creation of the Book of Books—the Bible (the word itself derives from the Greek *biblia*, "little volumes"). Jewish history and Jewish literature—the most ancient history of any people of the world, and the longest continuous literature that the world can show—are indeed from beginning to end little more than a commentary on the Bible; and the Jew of today is the product of the Bible and of that great religious literature that has received its inspiration from it.

This subject is one pre-eminently for a theologian or a philosopher. My intention here is to deal with another aspect of the question. For the Jews are a People of the Book in another sense as well. They have been, for the past 2,000 years, essentially a literary and an educated people. To an extent unequalled among any other section of humanity, they have been interested in books. In an unlettered world, when kings could not sign their names, they had already developed a system of universal education, so that an illiterate Jew was even in the Dark Ages a contra-

---

1 Originally published, under the title "The Jewish Love of Books," in the London *Jewish Chronicle* in September, 1938, it was republished in the *Jewish Book Annual*, vol. 3 (1944-5), pp. 1-6. A rich collection of material on this subject has been assembled by S. J. Agnon in his charming work, *Sefer, Sofer veSippur*, Jerusalem, 1936, and by S. Asaf in *Reshumoth. I.* 292-316.

diction in terms. Centuries before the modern idea of adult education was evolved, Jews regarded it as a religious duty to band themselves together for study every morning before the labors of the day began and every evening when the ghetto gates closed them off from association with the outside world.

In consequence, the Jew was, from early times, book-conscious. He copied books. He owned books. He patronized literature. He was interested in intellectual life and productions and movements. Thus, even in the most soul-destroying period of oppression, it might be assumed that almost every ghetto Jew, however humble his circumstances and however lowly his calling, was likely to have his modest library. A book was not to him, as to his neighbor, an object of veneration, of mystery, of distrust. It was a sheer necessity of every-day life.

We Jews, above all people, venerate the memory of our martyrs. But even among our martyrs the highest place is held by our literature. If anything excels the brutality with which Jews were treated during past ages, it is the brutality with which their literature was tracked down, condemned, burned and destroyed. From the thirteenth century down to the nineteenth, censors, ecclesiastical and lay, devoted their hateful attention to every work printed with Hebrew characters or dealing with Jews. From 1242 onwards, there was a long series of autos-de-fé, in which Jewish literature was the victim. There were periods when it was a crime for a man to possess any Jewish book whatsoever, excepting the Bible and censored editions of the prayer book, and sometimes even these reservations were overlooked. Down to the close of the eighteenth century, there were frequent searches in ghetto after ghetto, and the few volumes that, in spite of everything, the Jewish householder had been able to bring together were dragged out, submitted

to ruthless examination, and in the end committed to the
pyre. These holocausts were mourned by the Jews no less
bitterly than the loss of their kith and kin; for they realized
that here it was the soul and not the body that was imper-
illed. This long persecution is largely responsible for the fact
that so many Hebrew books once known to exist are now
lost, that Hebrew incunabula (that is, works printed before
1500) are so few, and that the complete text of the Talmud,
for example, is preserved in only one single ancient manuscript. Yet such was the tenacity of our fathers that more
than this was needed to eradicate from their hearts the
passion for their ancestral lore. The persecution served indeed only to strengthen their devotion. In the words of the
ancient martyr-rabbi who suffered death by burning en-
wrapped in a Scroll of the Law: "The parchment is consumed in fire, but the characters form themselves together
anew in the heavens."

In that dark age (not so far past, alas, as one had once
hoped), when the redemption of fellow-Jews enslaved by
land and sea was considered to be among the primary good
actions that a man could perform, there was associated with
that *mitzvah*, the Redemption of Captives, the allied one
of the Redemption of Books—the repurchase of volumes of
Hebrew literature carried off when corsairs raided some
synagogue, or captured a ship in which studious Jews were
sailing peacefully from port to port. Document after document, of the Middle Ages and after, deals with this question. Let us quote one instance only, of special Anglo-
Jewish interest. At the time of the terrible massacre in
York Castle in 1190, we are told by the contemporary
chronicler: "The enemy spoiled gold and silver and beautiful books, of which the Jews of York had written many—
more precious than gold or fine gold, and not to be equalled

in all the world for beauty. These they brought to Cologne and to other places in Germany, and sold to the Jews."

ii

In what light did this persecution of literature appear to contemporaries? I should like to cite a couple of passages which illustrate it as vividly as is possible. The first instance comes from the time of the Expulsion from Spain at the end of the fifteenth century—the greatest tragedy in Jewish history until our own day. The following is from the introduction of an eye-witness, Rabbi Abraham Sebag, to his unpublished exegetical work, *Zeror haKesef*:

Now while I was in Portugal, after having come thither with those expelled from Castille, it came into my mind to compose a commentary on the Five Scrolls, which I did. At that time, the anger of the Lord was kindled against my people in the Second Expulsion, from Portugal. I therefore abandoned all my books, and determined to take with me to Lisbon (the port of embarkation) only the commentary I had composed on the Pentateuch and the commentary on the Five Scrolls, and a commentary on the Ethics of the Fathers, and the work *Hibbur haKesef* that I had composed in my youth. When I arrived in Lisbon, certain Jews came and told me that a proclamation had been issued, that any person in whose possession a Hebrew book was found should be put to death. Forthwith I went and concealed these books of mine beneath a certain olive tree, verdant and fruitful, but in my eyes bitter as wormwood: and I called it the Tree of Weeping, for there I had buried all that I held most dear, my commentaries on the Pentateuch and the Precepts being more precious to me than gold and treasure. Therewith, indeed, I had comforted myself for my two sons, the very walls of my heart, who had been seized by force and baptized: and I saw them no more, for immediately they were thrown into prison.[2] Therefore

---

2 The reading is doubtful, and it seems that there is some scribal confusion. The translation should perhaps run: "and I saw my books no more, for immediately afterwards they threw me into prison."

I said of my books, "Surely these are better for me than sons and daughters." So I remained there for nearly six months, until through the merits of my forefathers God enabled me to reach Fez, where I determined to restore the Chaplet and to attempt to recall a little at least of what was written in my books.

My second instance is slightly later than this. In the autumn of 1553, in consequence of the slanders of a couple of spiteful apostates, a search was made in the houses of all the Jews of Rome and all copies of the Talmud and subsidiary works were seized. The New Year's day, Rosh ha-Shanah, the great solemnity of the Jewish religious year, was chosen by the arch-persecutors to commit these treasures of the Jewish spirit to the flames; and they were burned by the common executioner on the Campo dei Fiori at Rome. The example was followed all over Italy with a ridiculous lack of discrimination, copies of the Bible itself suffering because they happened to be printed in the sacred tongue. Hear, now, the words of an eye-witness taken from the introduction to R. Judah Lerma's *Lehem Jehudah* (Sabionetta, 1554):

This work of mine I published for the first time in Venice. Now on the New Year's Day of the year "for God hath dealt bitterly with me" (i.e. 5314) the Curia of Rome issued an edict in all the countries that owed it obedience, and they burned the Talmud and all works allied thereto. In the month of Marheshvan, the Bitter Month, the edict was published in Venice, and they burned the Talmud and all like works on a Sabbath day, and among them were all the copies of my book which I had just printed, 1,500 volumes in all. Thus I lost everything that I had in Venice, and I did not have even so much as a single leaf from the original or from the printed work as a remembrance. So I was forced to begin all over again and to write it from memory from the very commencement. After I had written three chapters anew, I found one single copy of the printed work in the hands of a non-Jew who had snatched it from the blaze, and I purchased it at a very high price; and I found that by the providence of God I had made the second copy more complete than the first.

A work which represents so vast a sum of human suffering, over which a man labored and wept and yet, undaunted, labored again, surely acquires a sanctity of its own.

iii

The Jewish love of books is demonstrated time after time in the old literature. In the most unexpected sources, one finds quaint illustrations of book-lore, sometimes curiously in advance of their age. It is worth while to assemble a few instances. Let us begin with a charming instance from Hai Gaon. In his *Musar haSekhel,* a rhymed ethical treatise consisting of counsel for guidance in life ("Advice to a Young Man," we would call it today), we find (§ § 32-3) the following characteristic admonition:

> If children thou shouldst bear at length,
>   Reprove them, but with tender thought.
> Purchase them books with all thy strength,
>   And by skilled teachers have them taught.

Or again (ibid, §128):

> To three possessions thou shouldst look:
> Acquire a field, a friend, a book.

A similar attitude of mind is reflected in that typical, but in some ways unenlightened, book of Godly anecdotes, the *Book of the Pious,* composed in the twelfth century by Judah the Saint of Regensburg and his school. We are given much advice about the proper use of books, some of which throws interesting light on contemporary social habits—as, for example, when we are informed (§656) that a man should not kneel on a recalcitrant folio in order to fasten its clasp, or (§649) that pens or note-tablets should not be used as bookmarks, or (§662) that a book should not be used as a missile, a shield, or an instrument of chastisement. "If a man has two sons, one of whom is averse to lending his books while the other does so willingly, he should have no hesitation in leaving all his library to the second son, though he be the younger," runs one recommendation (§875). A gruesome anecdote (§647) recounts how in time of persecution the body of a certain pious man was dug up from his grave and stripped of its shroud and treated with brutal indignity. No one could understand why a person of such exemplary character should have deserved posthumous maltreatment, until he appeared to an acquaintance in a dream and revealed that it was in punishment for the fact that he had neglected to have his books (sacred books, *bien entendu*) properly bound when they became worn. Another pious man, we learn in §676, enjoined his sons on his death-bed that they should not refuse to lend books even to those with whom they had had a serious quarrel, as thereby the cause of learning would suffer. If a man is in reduced circumstances and forced to sell his property, he should (§1,741) dispose first of his gold and jewelry and houses and estates, and only at the very end, when no alternative is left, denude himself of his library.

When a man is travelling on business and finds books that are unknown in his own city, it is his duty to purchase them in preference to anything else and bring them back with him, so that he may be an agent in the diffusion of knowledge (§664). When a man is buying a book, he should not try to reduce the price by saying "This is a bad book"; all he should do is to state the price that he is prepared to

pay without denigrating the quality of the literature (§665).
The whole is succinctly summed up in a pithy general
injunction: "It is a man's duty to have an eye to the honor
of his books."

This conception was carried beyond the present evan-
escent state, for otherwise Paradise would be deprived of
the greatest of possible delights. The Jewish pietists pictured the future world as a vast library, where all the
good books that had ever been written were treasured up
for the posthumous delectation of the righteous. The souls
of the blessed, the *Book of the Pious* informs us (§1,546),
have books lying before them in decent array on tables,
so that they study in death even as they studied in their
lifetime. One Friday evening, we are told, a non-Jew passed
through the Jewish cemetery after dark and there he actually
saw a Jew, who had passed away some time before, sitting
and conning a volume which lay on a desk before him. A
later fantasy informs us how the Heavenly librarian was
the Archangel Metatron, who brought books from the
shelves before the Holy One, Blessed be He, who in turn
handed them for study to the Academy on High. When a certain work was written in the eighteenth century, after the
shelves were already full, the books in the celestial library
pressed themselves together of their own accord to make
room for the newcomer.

As great merit is attached to the lending of books, it
might be imagined that a man acquires vicarious righteousness by borrowing them, purchase being a superfluous
extravagance. But this is by no means the case. A Spanish
rabbi, who lived a century before Christopher Columbus
discovered America, deals with this question trenchantly.
R. Judah Campanton, in his introduction to the Talmud
(c. 1400), wrote:

Of a truth, a man's wisdom goes only as far as his books go. Therefore, one should sell all he possesses and buy books; for, as the sages put it: "He who increases books increases wisdom."

Rashi, of blessed memory, speaks to the same effect in interpreting the injunction of the rabbis: "Acquire thyself a companion." Some read, according to him: "Acquire thyself a book"; for a book is the best of all companions. If a man reads only borrowed books, he is thus in the category of those of whom the Bible speaks: "And thy life shall hang in doubt before thee" (Deuteronomy 28. 66).

iv

The prince of medieval Jewish book-lovers was Judah ibn Tibbon, the great scholar, grammarian and translator, who lived in Provence in the thirteenth century. His will, in the form of last injunctions to his son, deals to a large degree with the treatment of his library. It is worth while to quote one or two passages *in extenso* from the translation by Israel Abrahams:

My son! Make thy books thy companions, let thy bookcases and shelves be thy pleasure grounds and gardens. Bask in their paradise, gather their fruit, pluck their roses, take their spices and their myrrh. If thy soul be satiate and weary, change from garden to garden, from furrow to furrow, from prospect to prospect. . . .

I have honored thee by providing an extensive library for thy use, and have thus relieved thee of the necessity to borrow books. Most students must bustle about to seek books, often without finding them. But thou, thanks be to God, mayest lend and not borrow. Of many books, indeed, thou ownest two or three copies. . . .

Examine thy Hebrew books at every New Moon, the Arabic volumes once in two months, and the bound codices once every quarter. Arrange thy library in fair order, so as to avoid wearying thyself in searching for the book thou needest. Always know the case and the chest where the book should be. A good plan would be to set in each compartment a written list of the books therein contained. If, then, thou art looking for a book, thou canst see from the list the exact shelf it occupies without disarranging all the books in the search for one. And cast thine eye frequently over the catalogue so as to remember what books are in thy library. . . .

Never refuse to lend books to anyone who has not the means to purchase books for himself, but act thus only to those who can be trusted to return the volumes. Thou knowest what our sages said in the Talmud, on the text: "Wealth and riches are in his house; and his merit endureth for ever (Psalm 112.3)." Hence "Withhold not good from him to whom it is due" (Prov. 3.27), and take particular care of thy books. Cover the book-chests with rugs of fine quality; and preserve them from damp and mice, and from all manner of injury, for thy books are thy goodly treasure. If thou lendest a volume, make a memorandum before it leaves thy house, and when it is returned draw thy pen over the entry. Every Passover and Tabernacles call in all books which are on loan.

Similarly, about 1400, the grammarian, chronicler and wit, Profiat Duran, gave advice to the intelligent student in the introduction to his Hebrew grammar, *Maaseh Ephod*. Use works which are brief or systematic, he said—advice which would be fatal to many authors of the present day, especially in view of his further injunction to the reader to keep to one book at a time.

But he goes on with a really memorable piece of advice. Use only books that are beautifully written, on good paper and well and handsomely bound. Read in a pleasant, well-furnished room, and let your eye rest on beautiful objects the whilst, so that you will be brought to love what you read. What an advanced outlook for a provincial student of five centuries ago! It is only in our own day that schools and libraries have begun to catch up with this medieval point of view.

12. JUDAH THE BELIEVER[1]

i

OF ALL the victims of the Inquisition in Spain, none lived more graciously, died more heroically, or was remembered with greater tenacity, than the martyred Don Lope de Vera y Alarcon. The story of his sufferings deserves to be recounted in full detail, upon the basis of the most recent researches, on the tercentenary of his tragic end.

Don Lope was a native of the township of San Clemente, in La Mancha, not far from the city of Cuenca. His father was Don Fernando de Vera y Alarcon—an Old Christian *caballero,* of purest lineage and unsullied *limpieza* on either side, so far as it could be traced. His mother belonged to a family of equal status. While still a mere child, their son Lope (born in 1620) showed utmost intellectual promise. At the age of fourteen, he was sent to the University of Salamanca. Here he not only followed the ordinary course in Arts, but also learned Latin, Greek, Hebrew, and even Chaldaic. Thus, he was led to the study of the Old Testament. He seemed naturally destined for a distinguished career as a theologian, and, indeed, actually matriculated in the Canons. His progress was such that in July 1638, at the age of only nineteen, he competed for a chair in Hebrew. He failed to secure the appointment, but persisted nevertheless in his studies.

Constant reading and rereading of the Old Testament

---

[1] Based *(via* an abbreviated version which appeared in *Liberal Judaism,* April, 1944) on "Le Chant de Cygne de Don Lope de Vera," in *Revue des Etudes Juives,* vol. 97 (1934), pp. 97-113, where the text of the poem is published, accompanied by full references.

text in the original had a gradual influence on him.[2] He began to peruse forbidden works, and to neglect attendance at church. Doubts slowly rose in his mind regarding the interpretation of many scriptural passages, in which, as it seemed to him, Jewish tradition was nearer the truth than the Catholic. Judaism in Spain was a proscribed faith. However, it was notorious that many of the Portuguese were Marranos, descended from the victims of the forced conversion in their native country in 1497, and still faithful to the ancestral tradition, handed on in secret from generation to generation. He began to seek these out, in order to learn their views. For this, the greatest caution was necessary; for the argus-eye of the Inquisition was watching for precisely such lapses as these. Accordingly, he began to communicate with those whom he suspected of being Jews at heart, by way of argument. If this did not help him to attain his object, he would withdraw what he had put forward in the course of disputation. On the other hand, if he obtained a favorable reception, he would become more communicative.

The upshot of all this was, that the handsome young scholar became a convinced adherent of the Law of Moses, for all the world as though he were himself of Jewish descent, instead of being an Old Christian of unquestioned purity of blood. He followed the Pentateuchal laws to the utmost limit of his ability, refrained as far as possible from eating meat, and used to go out into the fields in order to recite without danger the Psalms of David in their Hebrew original.

On one fatal occasion his zeal outstripped his circumspection; but that single slip was fatal. He was in his

---

2 According to the rapid compilation against the Marranos written in the worst anti-Semitic tradition, *Mayor Fiscal contra Judios* (Madrid, 1736), p. 221, Lope de Vera owed his proclivity to the heresy of Judaism to the fact that, when a baby, he had a New Christian as a wet-nurse!

twentieth year when he felt it to be his duty to bring round a fellow student (according to one account, his own brother) to his new way of thinking. The latter, shocked at such heretical disclosures, piously denounced him to the Inquisition of Valladolid. In spite of the fact that there was some corroborative evidence, the *consulta de fé* considered the accusation so improbable that it was not unanimously in favor of opening proceedings; and it was only when the General Council of the Spanish Inquisition (*La Suprema*) intervened that his arrest was ordered. This was carried into effect on June 24, 1639.

ii

Before the Inquisitors, the prisoner freely admitted the truth of the accusations made against him and much more. He denied, however, that he had any evil intention. He asserted that his statements had been simply for the sake of argument; and, in proof of this, he pointed to the fact that he regularly attended confession and communion, and always carried a rosary. The defense was skilful, and might well have been effective. The trial, however, dragged on; and during its wearisome course, the prisoner repented of his duplicity. At audiences on April 16 and May 23, 1641, he repudiated all that he had previously confessed. Then on May 29, he suddenly announced that he wished to be a Jew and to hold all that the Jews believed; for this was the truth revealed to them by God, which he would defend with his life.

His attitude in prison was unflinchingly heroic. It seemed that he was courting death by his defiance of the Inquisitors and their torments. He lost no opportunity, even in jail, of communicating and spreading his ideas. The intervention of his own kinsfolk was useless. When his father was brought in to exercise his powers of persuasion, the intrepid youth actually attempted to convert him. He affirmed publicly, on all possible occasions, that he had hitherto believed the teachings of the Church, but that now he adhered to the one, immutable law, given by God to Israel. The religion of Rome and all other religions were false. No one had taught him this: it was God himself, in His Mercy, who had weaned him from his errors. Formerly, he had never practised any Jewish observances: but he would do so in the future.

Henceforth he refused to eat meat. It continued to be served up to him nevertheless. One day, he abstracted a bone from his ration, and sharpened it upon a stone. On the next morning, the *alcaide* found him lying in a pool of blood: he had circumcised himself overnight. Thus, he boasted, he had won Paradise: and he was now prepared for the worst. From now on he called himself Judah the Believer (Judas el Creyente) and would neither call nor sign himself in any other manner.

A succession of learned men—the most eminent scholars and theologians of the whole Province—were summoned now to persuade him of the error of his ways. He confuted them, however, to his own complete satisfaction, and they retired declaring his pertinacity to be so terrible that, with his knowledge of Hebrew, he was a supreme danger to the faith. He refused to have an advocate or make any defense, saying that he was a Jew and was prepared to die as such, and that his opponents in their ignorance did not understand the plain meaning of the Bible.

The inquisitors requested him to set out the scriptural texts on which he relied, so that they might be refuted. He refused to do this except in writing; and, when a goose-quill was brought to him, rejected it on the ground that, as an animal product, it was forbidden by the Law

of Moses. A bronze pen was accordingly provided; and
with this he set forth his views. His long imprisonment
and sufferings seem to have affected his mental balance.
He intimated that he believed in the transmigration of
souls, he himself being endowed with the immortal essence
of Adam, his father with that of the Prophet Samuel, his
brother Pedro with that of David, and his brother Diego
with that of Aaron.

The Holy Tribunal was genuinely eager to save this
precious soul for Christianity and to deliver it from eternal
torment. Accordingly, it was unremitting in its endeavors
and showed over a long period of time very considerable
patience. Conference followed conference. At last, the
prisoner refused to speak at all. The Tribunal, puzzled,
appealed to the *Suprema* for guidance; and acting on the
latter's advice, ordered fifty lashes to be administered. Even
this failed to loosen his tongue. The trial was thus held
up. It was necessary for the prisoner to ratify his various
confessions; but, when they and the evidence were read
out to him, he put his fingers to his ears and thus effectively
prevented himself from hearing. The suggestion was made
that he should be put to torture; but this was obviously
quite useless, and the *Suprema* advised that the case should
be closed without further formalities.

iii

ON January 27, 1643, the Tribunal unanimously decided to "relax" the prisoner to the secular arm for
"bloodless" punishment—that is, for execution by burning.
The *Suprema* confirmed the sentence. In doing so, however, it ordered that further efforts should be made for conversion. Then, the mental torture recommenced. Every week,

the unhappy youth would be brought up before the inquisitors. He refused, however, to say a word in their presence, excepting "Viva la Ley de Moisen" (Long live the Law of Moses!) : after which he would lapse into a stony silence, which no arguments or persuasions could break.

For a year and a half he lay under sentence. At last, after a total of five years of imprisonment, even the inquisitors became convinced that it was useless to persevere further. On July 25, 1644, a stately *auto-de-fé* was held at Valladolid, in honor of Santiago of Compostella, with twenty-five "penitents." Two of these, accused of bigamy, were sentenced to flogging and a period of forced labor in the galleys. The rest had been found guilty of the heinous charge of Judaizing. All but two had admitted their crime and professed repentance. They were accordingly admitted to "reconciliation," being condemned to wear the garb of shame known as *sambenito* and to serve varying periods of imprisonment. One of the remaining two had saved himself by flight, his effigy being therefore committed to the flames, in token of what should have happened to his body. The remaining victim was Don Lope de Vera y Alarcon: "the greatest Jewish heretic," according to one of the inquisitors, "that has ever been known in the Church."

The ghastly, stately ceremonial followed its usual course. The unhappy delinquent (he was even now only twenty-six years of age) was led before the pulpit to hear his sentence pronounced. To the general amazement, he appeared to glory in his crimes. As the case against him was being set out, he nodded his head in approval, interjecting now and again: "Viva la Ley de Moisen!" It was obvious that he did not feel any shame, and he was looking forward to a martyr's death. In order to forestall any further outburst of "blasphemy" on his part, it was considered advisable to close his mouth with a gag until the ceremonial was over.

The sentence was at last pronounced, and Don Lope was handed over to the civil authorities for punishment. He was sent forthwith to the *quemadero,* or place of burning. As he was led through the streets, mounted on a mule, he continued to chant the Psalms of David, in the original Hebrew, to the astonishment of the onlookers. His extraordinary fortitude continued to the very end. With the usual callous deliberation, he was tied to the stake, and the faggots heaped up around him. He was still obstinate when fire was applied. The flames leaped up in a fiery blaze: and all was still. The long-drawn-out tragedy seemed to be at an end. Suddenly, from the heart of the pyre, a voice was heard reciting the twenty-fifth Psalm: "To Thee, O Lord, I commit my soul." With these words on his lips, the gallant youth expired.

The episode made an indelible impression on the minds of contemporaries. Two days afterwards, the inquisitor, Don Bartholomeo Marques Mirezo, wrote a long letter to the Marchioness of Monterey (herself, as it happened, of remote Jewish ancestry), recounting all that had taken place. Don Lope's obstinacy in his heretical beliefs had horrified him; but a certain degree of grudging admiration is almost discernible through his horror: "Never," he wrote, "was seen such delight in death, nor such confidence in salvation." If this was the impression made upon an inquisitor, it may be imagined how the Crypto-Jews felt about the episode. Many years later a Marrano youth named Juan Pereira, referred to him repeatedly during trial before the Holy Tribunal and declared that he had seen him after death, riding on a mule and glistening with the sweat that was on him when he was taken to the place of burning.

It was not long before the story of this episode penetrated, by some mysterious means, throughout the Marrano Diaspora. In Amsterdam, Antonio Enriquez Gomez, the famous

Spanish dramatist, wrote a long "romance" in celebration of the martyr, Judah *el Creyente* and his heroic end. Another elegy was written by the poet Jacob (Manoel) de Pina. Menasseh ben Israel, in his *Hope of Israel,* gave a dithyrambic account of the tragedy, culminating in "the happy day of glory" when "at last, as a second *Isaac,* (he) offered himself to the flames, contemning life, goods and honors, that he might obtain immortal life and good things that cannot perish." And these were not the only ones.

It is, indeed, a little surprising that such minute details should have been known outside Spain. Some of the particulars recounted in the sources mentioned above can have been familiar to few even in Valladolid. Moreover, the letter of the inquisitor to the Marchioness of Monterey—a personal and confidential document—was actually known to Miguel de Barrios, the poet-in-ordinary to the Amsterdam community, and is moreover to be found *in extenso* in a polemical manuscript written by an Amsterdam Jew of the period. It almost seems as though there was some breach of secrecy in the Palace of the Inquisition itself. That, in any case, is the only ready explanation for the fact that there is to be found in the Library of the Talmud Torah of Leghorn a most pathetic document—the actual memorandum, in verse, which Lope de Vera presented to the inquisitors to justify the attitude which he had assumed: it bears the heading:—

Verses composed by Lope de Vega (*sic*) when he was in the Inquisition in Spain, which he sent to the Grand Inquisitor; wherefore they burned him, to sanctify the name of God in public. May God avenge his death and his blood: Amen!

The contents of these "verses" must be read to be appreciated; they form a shrewd criticism of Catholic doctrine and a magnificent vindication of Jewish monotheism.

The episode of Don Lope de Vera attains a considerable literary interest by reason of its incidental association with the biography of one of the greatest of the scions of the Marrano element in Judaism. Thirty-two years after the event, in a famous letter to his pupil, Albert Burgh, who had urged him to consider the numerous martyrs who had testified to the truth of Catholic doctrine, Benedict Spinoza wrote in reply:—

"They (the Jews) claim that they count far more martyrs than any other nation, and they increase every day the number of those who with singular steadfastness have suffered for the faith which they profess; and with justice. For I myself knew among others a certain Judah, surnamed the Believer, who in the midst of the flames, when he was already thought to be dead, began to sing the psalm, To thee O God I commit my soul; and as he sang, expired." (Epistolae, lxxvi, pp. 321-2.) .

On the basis of this passage, obviously written not without pride, it has often been suggested that Spinoza's forebears came from Valladolid. The present writer is however inclined to doubt the identification. The words used by Spinoza in this letter, *ipse novi,* can only mean: "I was personally acquainted with." Spinoza was never outside Holland, and Don Lope never left Spain; so that the reference can hardly be to him. Moreover, the latter was not, as a matter of fact, of Jewish stock. Hence Spinoza's reasoning as applied to him would have been inadmissible. But, besides him, there were two other famous inquisitional martyrs, to whom the Jewish savants of Amsterdam and elsewhere (Menasseh ben Israel, de Barrios, Cardoso and others) were never tired of alluding. One was Fray Diogo da Assunção, who was burned at Coimbra in 1603, many years before Spinoza's birth. The other was Isaac de Castro Tartas, who was captured in Brazil by the Portuguese and was burned alive in Lisbon on December 15, 1647, at the age of twenty-one. For a long time, the last-named had been resident at Amsterdam, and was familiar with the leading members of the community, as Menasseh ben Israel informs us. When he left, in 1644, Spinoza was already a boy of twelve; and it is not only probable, but almost certain, that the two were personally acquainted. There is every probability then, that the philosopher's memory failed him, and he confused the inquisitional martyr whom he had personally known with the other, Judah *el Creyente,* who went to his death chanting the twenty-fifth psalm.

13. WHO WAS COLUMBUS?[1]

i

ONE OF the few pleasing ironies of contemporary history is furnished by the literature on Christopher Columbus. The Jews were expelled from Spain in 1492 with every circumstance of cruelty. For centuries they were excluded from the Peninsula by the Inquisition and its fires and never referred to by Spaniards without a sneer or a curse. Nevertheless, when in the course of the past generation Spanish writers tried to vindicate as a son of their country the ostensibly Italian explorer who initiated its golden age, some of them found it simplest to postulate that he was of Iberian Jewish stock, and compelled for that reason to conceal or confuse his origin.

Half a dozen authors have elaborated this thesis, with a greater or smaller degree of plausibility. Don Vicente Paredes, for example, tried to show somewhat over-ingeniously that he was a Jew from Estremadura of the tribe of Levi, a member of the famous *converso* (New Christian) family of Santa María whose name he read in the explorer's cryptic signature (of which more anon). Celso García de la Riega agreed that he was of Jewish extraction, but produced evidence that he came from Pontevedra in Galicia (the Spanish province of that name, not the Polish!). José Etrugo,

---

[1] Originally published in *The Menorah Journal*, vol. XXVIII (1940), pp. 279-95. Salvador de Madariaga's thesis, which I examine somewhat light-heartedly in this essay, was summarily rejected by Professor S. E. Morison in his biography of Columbus (*Admiral of the Ocean Sea*, Boston, 1942) and by Rámon Menendez-Pidal in his exacting study on Columbus' language (*La lengua de Cristóbal Colón*, Buenos Aires, 1942). Their criticisms were, however, answered by Madariaga in the second English (and fourth Spanish) edition of his work. My observations, of which he then took full account, deal only with the periphery of the argument.

Otero Sánchez, Nicolás Diaz Perez, and the Marqués de Dosfuentes are other Spanish scholars who have arrived at similar though not identical conclusions. Some years ago a Spanish poet-priest named Rey Soto visited America with documentary evidence which, he claimed, finally proved that Columbus was a Spaniard and a Jew. And there were foreign writers, such as André and Vignaud in France and Duff in England, who were inclined to accept these conclusions. A few Jewish scholars entered the fray also with more or less (though generally less) plausible theories on the same lines. But the evidence advanced was not sufficiently conclusive to permit one to say more than that an interesting case could be made out for the hypothesis.

I must admit that I felt rather skeptical about it when, in the course of a newspaper debate on the subject some while ago, my intervention was invited. The idea always seemed to me a little over-ingenious, and the proofs advanced a little over-elaborate. A year or so back, however, I began to be approached by Spanish scholars of high standing, who were investigating the question from this angle and believed that I might be able to throw some light upon it from my knowledge of the Marrano background. These enquiries convinced me, not that the theory was true, but that it must be taken seriously.

One of these scholars was Don Salvador de Madariaga, whose magnificent work, *Christopher Columbus, Being The Life of The Very Magnificent Lord Don Cristóbal* Colón, first appeared in 1940, and has since been republished more than once. It is witty and wise, vivid and profound, well-planned and superbly well-written, and based upon a masterly and exhaustive study of the sources; and my only criticism of it as a book is that the author seems to have made a deliberate attempt to deprive it of the dignity and amaranthine form which might have made it the standard work on the subject for generations to come. Let this suffice by way of appreciation of the volume; for here I desire only to examine Señor de Madariaga's theory regarding Christopher Columbus's Jewish origin, which, after he propounded it, can never again be lightly dismissed.

ii

Let me say at the outset that Madariaga seems to me to have weakened his thesis by laying too much stress on his personal interpretation of the Jewish psychology, which he sees reflected in that of his hero. "The Jew in Colón," he says, "usually shy and out of the way, comes to the surface, irresistibly attracted as soon as there is a mention of gold or gems in the books he reads." It is rather a sweeping statement, and a tenuous piece of evidence; for, if this is a characteristically Jewish quality, one is driven to the conclusion that the saintly and ascetic Hernando de Talavera, Archbishop of Granada (to take the example of one person only, out of many mentioned in the book), cannot possibly have been of Jewish extraction, unimpeachable documentary evidence notwithstanding. On the other hand, there is this to be said for the author's view. Gem-dealing was a characteristic Jewish occupation in the Middle Ages, as it is today; a member of a Jewish middle-class family is very likely to have had a gem-dealer among his close relatives; and this fact was likely to make him, as it were, "gem-conscious" and quick to notice the lapidary potentialities of any region in which he was interested. Such extenuation cannot, however, be pleaded when the author sees in the fact that Columbus had a keen contractual sense (that is, more or less, that he expected his labors to be rewarded) another ancestral characteristic. I have yet to meet the Christian who doesn't; and

I believe that Judaism is probably the only one of the world's great religions which definitely objects to the service of the Master for the sake of reward, whether here or in the hereafter.

Moreover, having convinced himself that Columbus belonged to a Jewish family, Señor de Madariaga performed some remarkable feats of acrobatics to find confirmation of the fact. For there were always two alternative possibilities open to him, and he seized avidly whichever comes to hand. Either Columbus was acting true to type, in the way one would expect from a Jew; or else, consciously or subconsciously, in the diametrically opposite manner, so as to avert suspicion. For example, at a critical point in his career he seeks out Fray Diego de Deza, of the University of Salamanca, one of the most influential and most learned of Spanish *conversos*. That one may perhaps grant as indicative of common origin and sympathies. But, on his first arrival in Castile, he is found associating with members of the Franciscan order, at the monastery of La Rábida. Why? Because (it is suggested) the Franciscans were the foremost enemies of the *conversos* and the main drive behind the Inquisition, so that it was his obvious course to enter the country under a Franciscan cloak. This is over-ingenious—savoring more of Father Brown than of Sherlock Holmes. Both interpretations cannot very well be true.

Again, we have Columbus's love-affair with Beatriz Enríquez. She may have been a Jewess, we are told (later on, Señor de Madariaga omits the qualification). The evidence? Simply the difference in the conception of sexual morality as it prevailed among Jews and Christians, which resulted in the climax when "young Beatriz does what an Old Christian woman would not have done—she generously gives herself." Here, I must admit, the author seems to me to exceed the boundaries of historical license, which (as all the world should know by now) are wider by far even than those of poetry. I have heard exaggerated claims made regarding the chastity of Jewish women, but this is the first time I have ever heard it suggested—and suggested as a compliment rather than otherwise—that the absence of chastity can be regarded as an indication of Jewish origin.

Enough, however, of these objections, which are all incidental. Let us come to the heart of the matter.

iii

The "official" view regarding Columbus—the view that he belonged to an ordinary bourgeois Genoese family of weavers—is based upon a number of official and semi-official contemporary documents in the local archives, which seem to give a perfectly plausible and consistent story. But, though consistent among themselves, they are not consistent with the explorer's own statements about his origins, which pass the limits even of grandiloquence. For example, though he often referred to himself as "a foreigner," he never once stated in any document that has come down to us that he was Genoese, and he even fought against Genoa at Cape St. Vincent in 1476. If a Genoese, then, he was clearly not an enthusiastic one.

Moreover, though a mass of documents written by him have survived, there is not the slightest evidence that he wrote Italian. The one document that may be brought up as evidence against this is in fact a comic concoction of Italian, Castilian and Portuguese, in which Italian words are not even in the majority. Even when he communicated with the Bank of St. George in Genoa, he used Spanish. What was more, he spoke and wrote Spanish before he came to Spain, for marginal notes from his hand, clearly dated

1481, are in that language. (We must come back to this document again later on, for its significance is particularly great in this connection, though the fact has not been recognized before.) Finally, when this Genoese weaver's son attempted to write in Latin, which he so often did, his errors betray the fact that he was thinking in Spanish, for they are precisely those which a Spaniard might be expected to make.

Spanish, then, was the culture-language of this young Genoese, from his earliest years. There is, it is suggested, only one rational explanation of this curious fact: that the Colombo family were Spanish Jews settled in Genoa who, following the traditions of their race, had remained faithful to the language of their country of origin.

Former writers who attempted to vindicate Columbus's Spanishness tried to show that he was born in Spain—notwithstanding the mass of documents indicating his Genoese origin, which they considered either unreliable or else misinterpreted. Señor de Madariaga, on the other hand, accepts them as substantially authentic, though maintaining that the family came from Spain, having left it probably owing to religious persecution. Now, one knows that this would have been likely enough after the establishment of the Inquisition in Spain in 1480, when an unending stream of New Christians left the Peninsula for more tolerant climes, where their lives would not be endangered. Historians have, however, failed to accentuate the fact that this phenomenon began long before. The Responsa of Rabbi Simon ben Zemah Duran (1361-1444), for example, demonstrate the numbers of the fugitives who settled in Northern Africa at this time. Further afield, traces are less easy to find; but I have records of the arrival of Spanish Jews—forerunners of the expulsion of 1492—long before that date in various parts of Italy: Sicily, Naples, Florence. Thus far, I have not been able to find any trace of them in Genoa; but considering the importance of the commercial relations between that port and Barcelona in particular, it is highly probable that some individuals found their way thither as well. Incidentally, as will be pointed out later on, a considerable amount of evidence may be adduced which seems to point to a Catalan origin for the Colombo family, this again suggesting the neighborhood of Barcelona.

The hypothesis finds its confirmation in a large number of incidental facts and considerations which, curious or even mysterious in themselves, acquire definite consistency on the assumption that Columbus belonged to a family of Jewish stock. Though by no means reluctant to admit his humble extraction, he was always particularly reticent, not to say mendacious, about his origin, and certainly seems to have had something to conceal. As we have seen, though a Genoese, he was curiously un-Genoan in his behavior. He showed himself throughout his career remarkably mobile, going from country to country and allegiance to allegiance in the traditional style of the old Wandering Jew; and his brother Bartolomé resembled him in this. A contemporary biographer, Las Casas, who might be presumed to know some of his secrets, insisted on his orthodoxy as a Christian in such terms as to make the reader imagine that there may have been grounds for suspecting it. He was fond of referring obscurely to the glories of his remote ancestors, in the same way as a Daughter of the American Revolution might do who is descended from an old American Jewish family but prefers not to reveal herself as "non-Aryan." He indubitably had a curious mystical Jewish obsession, and was always referring in his notes to the facts of ancient Jewish history. (To quote only a single instance out of very many: when in mid-Atlantic the sea rose without a wind, thus quietening the discontent of his semi-rebellious crew, he noted: "This high sea was very necessary to me, for this had not happened except at the time of the Jews, when they went out of Egypt.") He similarly had a strange *penchant* for Jewish company—this was realized long ago. Moreover, when all others regarded his ideas as fantastic, it was among the curious freemasonry of New Christians (persons of Jewish descent, whether sympathetically inclined toward Judaism or no) that he found support and encouragement—Sánchez, Santángel, Deza, Cabrero, and so on; and it was through them only that he obtained at last a sympathetic hearing and adequate support from the Catholic monarchs.

It is perfectly true that here and there Columbus hints darkly at the machinations of the *conversos*. But when one knows that in London in 1609, and in Rouen in 1632, the crypto-Jewish community was broken up as a result of internecine quarrels, in the course of which each party denounced the other, one realizes that this is by no means a refutation of the thesis that he was of Jewish origin. Again, in writing to Ferdinand and Isabella about his discovery, he envisaged it as a place of settlement for all "good" Christians. But most other persons in that bigoted age would have spoken of "Old" Christians, so what at first sight seems an objection is in fact just the reverse. Reference should of course be made in addition to that strange clause in the explorer's will, in which he bequeathed "half a silver mark to a Jew who usually stands at the entrance to the Ghetto of Lisbon, or to another who may be named by a priest"— for all the world as though he desired his last earthly function to be associated with an act of Jewish charity.

Most curious of all Columbus's references to Jews is perhaps that well-known passage in the despatch to the King and Queen in which he reported his success: "And thus, having expelled all the Jews from all your kingdoms and dominions, in the same month . . . Your Highnesses commanded me that with a sufficient fleet I should go to the said parts." It is possible to see in this a reflection of a desire to find a place of refuge for his persecuted brethren, though the point should not be labored. On the other hand, a very remarkable fact, which has escaped attention hitherto, is to be noted in this connection. The Jews had to leave Spain on July 31, though some managed to obtain a couple of days' grace, and the ships in which they were conveyed lay hard by Columbus's tiny fleet which was preparing to put to sea. It actually sailed on August 3, just before daybreak—*that is to say, during the night following the Ninth of Ab, the Fast-Day that commemorates the destruction of Jerusalem both by Nebuchadnezzar and by Titus.* Personally, I refuse to attach any exaggerated significance to such details, but I must confess that even as I am writing the significance of some of these coincidences grows upon me. All were embarked, all was prepared for sailing, on August 2, the Ninth of Ab. Why, then, did he wait until the tenth day of the month, half an hour before sunrise? On the former ill-fated day no Jew would begin an enterprise. One who does work on the Ninth of Ab, the rabbis say, will never see a blessing therefrom. Is it possible that Columbus was aware of the anniversary and aware of this ancient tradition? It seems too much to suggest, but it would explain a minor mystery which has never yet been satisfactorily interpreted.

iv

One reason why the previous attempts made to prove Columbus' Jewish origin were so unsatisfactory was because of a complete misunderstanding of the history and psychology of the New Christians of Spain and Portugal. It was assumed that persons in this category were all ardent professing Jews at heart, observing every jot and tittle of Jewish observance in the privacy of their homes. The assumption that Columbus was of Jewish descent therefore implied that he was a Jew by conviction. To demonstrate this, however, in the case of a man who was constantly parading his Christianity, in private and in public, in season and out, who never forewent any opportunity of enthusiastic references to Jesus Christ and the Virgin Mary, who regarded the discovery of America as the preliminary to a Crusade to be led by the Catholic rulers, strained probability to its utmost limits. A greater understanding of the Marrano history and temperament makes this thesis much more plausible. A large proportion of the New Christians, or *conversos,* justified indeed the popular conception, and they were as Jewish at heart after their conversion as they had been before. But there were many others who accepted Christianity, not merely with resignation but with enthusiasm, and attempted by all the means in their power to spread the Gospel they had received among their former coreligionists. One may mention the ex-rabbi Solomon Levi, who as Pablo de Santa Maria, became Bishop of Burgos, and whose son and successor inspired the anti-Jewish legislation of the Council of Constance; Bonafus de la Caballeria, author of *Zelus Christi contra Judaeos,* one of the outstanding anti-Semitic works of the fifteenth century; or Pablo de Heredia and Alfonso de Zamora, both prolific writers against the Jews.

Enough has been said to indicate that there is no need whatsoever to look for any Jewish religious sympathies in a member of a Spanish *converso* family of the fifteenth century, and that any attempt to demonstrate them, in the case of Christopher Columbus, is not only superfluous but confuses the issues. On the other hand, we have seen instances of some of these *conversos* who had a Jewish obsession not unlike that of Columbus, and whose enthusiasm for Christianity did not obscure entirely their pride in the people to whom they owed their origin.

A point worth accentuating, for it increases the likelihood of the general thesis, is that the callings which various members of Columbus' family followed from time to time were without exception associated with Jews and Marranos of this period. As I have shown in my book, *The Jewish Contribution to Civilization,* Jews were closely associated with the voyages of discovery of the fifteenth and sixteenth centuries, so that there would be no departure from tradition even in this. (It is enough to mention the Marrano explorer, Pedro Texeira, who explored the overland route between Europe and the Far East.) Columbus, as a sailor of fortune and amateur corsair in his early days, has his parallel in the Portuguese, Sir Edward Brampton, who made his way to England during the Wars of the Roses, was converted, received several naval and military commands from Edward IV, and primed Perkin Warbeck with the information which qualified him for his bid for the throne a little later on. The art of weaving, which Columbus' family followed, was traditionally associated with the Jews in the Mediterranean world, and in 1391 the *conversos* of Majorca were specifically authorized to learn and practise it. And, if Christopher himself at one time resorted to book-selling in order to earn a livelihood, that calling was followed by at least one Jewish contemporary of his, whose accounts (dealing exclusively with non-Hebrew works) have recently been discovered in the Bodleian Library, as well as by many Marranos arraigned from time to time by the Inquisition.

V

It has been pointed out that the natural Spanish counterpart of the name "Colombo" is not "Colón," which the explorer adopted, but the Catalan "Colóm" (he was never,
of course, called "Columbus"). Why, then, should the former form have prevailed? Madariaga explains the fact by
suggesting that the Colombo family were Catalan Jews,
among whom the surname "Colóm" was by no means un-
common, that this was in fact the transitional form between
the two names, and that Columbus abandoned it precisely
because of its suspicious Jewish associations. This is hypothetical. But it is an extraordinary fact that among Italian
Jews the transition from "Colon" to "Colombo" and *vice
versa*, which needs so much explanation, was not only possible but invariable. The surname "Colombo" is even today
frequently found in Italy. Sometimes it is simply the Italian
translation of the Hebrew name "Jonah," or Dove—the
name borne, for example, by the cabalistic rabbi of Venice,
Abraham Jonah, reported by legend to have saved the Ghetto
from destruction in 1797 by means of the amulets he affixed
to the gates. It may generally be assumed that persons belonging to this family are of comparatively recent Levantine
origin. But there were very old-established Italian Jews,
too, who bore the name, particularly in Piedmont and the
northern provinces. In their case, the Hebrew equivalent
(or rather original) was in fact "Colon" (קולון). I do not
mean by this that there was some accidental connection.
I mean that a man who signed his Hebrew letters "Colon"
was *invariably* known in the outside world by the name
"Colombo," which was the easiest approximation that a
liquid-voiced Italian would reach. Here, then, we have the
transition between the two forms.

On the basis of this, we may advance a stage further. The name "Colon" is met with only, it seems, among persons of French origin. The earliest example on record is found in an Old French elegy on the martyrs of Troyes of 1288, where it is used as the equivalent of the Hebrew "Jonah"; and in my collection I have a superb prayer-book according to the rite of the communities of North Italy that followed the French rite, written for Solomon Jedidiah Hayim Colon. The most illustrious member of the family, it happens, was a contemporary of Christopher Columbus—the eminent, quarrelsome Rabbi Joseph ben Solomon Colon, an exile from Chambéry in Savoy, who died at Padua in 1480 after having been summarily expelled from Mantua as a result of an intermittent dispute with another Jewish scholar. Now, the route of the exiles from France who arrived in Italy is well known. On coming over the Alps, they settled down in Piedmont, where the three communities of Asti, Fossano and Moncalvo followed the old French tradition. It was with this part of Italy, in the hinterland of Genoa, that the Jewish ColonColombo family was associated. That Colombus may have come into contact with some of them is therefore far from improbable; it may even be that he knew of the existence of Joseph Colon (whom Italians would have called Giuseppe Colombo) , the most eminent Italian rabbi of the age.

I may add at this point that I have now discovered a Rabbi Perex Colombo, who was spiritual leader of the Jewish community of Safed in Palestine immediately after the Expulsion, from 1496 onwards; and a Jew from Tortosa in Spain, named "Columbus," who was living at Genoa in 1274. Pure coincidence, of course, but what a curious one!

The reader must not jump at conclusions. This is not meant to imply that Columbus belonged to the Jewish family of Colon. But what may be stated quite definitely is that, while other persons named "Colombo" would normally have contracted their name into "Colóm" if they wished to make it seem Spanish, only a Jew or someone acquainted with the Jewish tradition would naturally and automatically have considered it to be the equivalent of "Colón" and rendered it in this manner. The fact that Columbus not only did this, but also harped on the fact so insistently and with such mystical reiteration, conjuring his children never on any account to vary it, certainly seems to corroborate the theory of his Jewish assocations.

vi

It is well known that Columbus regarded his discovery of America as something almost incidental to the glorious object of a Crusade, led by the Catholic sovereigns, which would finally recover the Holy Land and Jerusalem for Christendom. Considering that at this time Turkey was the great haven of refuge for the Jews, and Spain their arch-persecutor, this would seem to militate against the theory of his Jewish origin, for nothing was more calculated to prejudice the Jewish position in those few countries where tranquillity still obtained. Consideration of the background, however, presents the matter in a different light. Recent discoveries in the records of the Inquisition have revealed the fact that in the middle of the fifteenth century the Marranos considered that their tribulations were the prelude to the "pangs of the Messiah"; that the advance of the Turk in the East and the overthrow of the Byzantine Empire were the first signs of the approaching deliverance; and that the outcome of these wars between the Cross and the Crescent would be the restoration of their people to Jerusalem, to which they confidently looked forward in the immediate future. (Whole ship-loads of them, indeed, left Spain at this time for the

Near East in order to participate in the Messianic deliverance.) Translate this obsession, on the part of New Christians with Jewish sympathies, into the mentality of a New Christian with Christian sympathies, and you get the idea that these wars were to culminate in a great Crusade with the divine benediction, which would plant the Cross in Jerusalem and lead the remnant of Israel to realize at last the verities of Chrstianity—precisely, in fact what the explorer professed to wish.

His obsession with matters Jewish (it is hardly less) sometimes led Columbus into unexpected excursions into Hebraic lore. Some of these almost seem to indicate a study of Jewish literature at first hand. He refers to Jerusalem, for example, as the world's navel—a curious phrase, which however is used by the rabbis of the Talmud in a familiar passage. But the most extraordinary of these indications is in a note of Columbus' on the *Historia rerum ubikue gestarum* of Pope Pius II. In this he reckoned the age of the world "according to the Jews," coming down to the year 1481, which was 5241 *anno mundi*. This was quite accurate, and not very difficult to ascertain. But let us examine the note more carefully: *y desde la destruccion de la 2a casa segundo los judios fasta agora sciendo el año del nacimiento de nuestro Señor de 1481 son 1413 años.* That is: "And from the destruction of the Second House according to the Jews to the present day, being the year of the birth of Our Lord 1481, are 1413 ycars." By "the Second House" Columbus means the Second Temple in Jerusalem: the words are a literal translation of the Hebrew phrase always used—Gentiles spoke of "the Destruction of Jerusalem." Jerusalem was destroyed in the year 70. But according to the Jewish tradition (quite inaccurate, it may be added), universally used in Jewish lore and chronology, that tragic event took place two years earlier, in the year 68—the precise year that is indicated in this passage (1481 *minus* 1413 equals 68, not 70).

Thus, in an all-important point of Jewish chronology, Christopher Columbus followed the inaccurate Jewish, not the accurate Gentile, tradition. This is assuredly something that must be taken into account in a final summing-up of the problem. I told Señor de Madariaga about it when I met him one day in the Bodleian Library. "That clinches it," he said.

It is of the utmost importance to bear in mind the date of the entry in question. It was written in 1481, three years before Columbus came to Spain. It it not therefore a by-product of the explorer's intimacy with Don Isaac Abrabanel or Abraham Senior or Zacuto, the great astronomer whose works he is known to have used. It is part of the intellectual equipment of his early years, passed so far as we know in an ostensibly non-Jewish environment. It is not easy to explain this except on the assumption that his was a semi-Jewish family. How could one explain it today if someone arrived from a remote village in Central China and spoke a language akin to Yiddish, bore a quasi-Jewish name, insisted for reasons of his own on some sort of observance of the Ninth of Ab, and showed a disconcerting knowledge of certain minutiae of Jewish life? The parallel is by no means remote.

Columbus' theories and computations were to a large extent based upon the Apocryhal *Book of Esdras*. To this, for some unknown reason, he attached an immense importance, which it is not easy to explain on rational or on ordinary theological grounds. But here, again, one can discern if one wishes a Marrano parallel. To the Jew the Apocrypha carried no weight, and was indeed at that time almost unknown. But the Marranos, finding it in the Latin Bible, and realizing its essentially Jewish quality, studied it with avidity and made a remarkably ample use of it. Indeed, the Marrano theology rested largely on the interpretation of a passage in the Apocryphal *Epistle of Baruch,* and the characteristic Marrano prayer was found in the Apocryphal additions to *Esther.* For a person of Marrano extraction to have laid particular stress on the Apocryphal *Book of Esdras* was thus precisely what one might have anticipated.

vii

It is now necessary to turn for a moment to the theories of a somewhat pathetic American enthusiast, Maurice David, in his little work, *Who Was Columbus?* (New York, 1933), in which he considered that he had settled the question once for all. His evidence was purely documentary. At the top left-hand corner of all but one of the letters addressed by Columbus to his son Diego, there is a marking in which it is possible for the eye of faith to read the Hebrew letters ב"ה standing for *beEzrath haShem* (that is, "With the help of God"—not *Baruch haShem,* or "Blessed be God," as the author of the theory believed). No letters addressed to other persons bear this sign; and the solitary one addressed to Diego which does not bear it (as has already been suggested) had to be shown to the King and Queen.

Personally, I am skeptical. In fact, this may be nothing more than a library sign; for all the letters bearing it come from the Veragua collection, and the exception is from that of Alba. Nevertheless, I must point out that the theory is not quite so fantastic as might appear at the first impression. For it was certainly usual among the Marranos for old religious customs to persist in an atrophied, meaningless form. For example, until the nineteenth century it was customary for some of the older men among the crypto-Jews, who still maintain their existence in Northern Portugal, to cover their shoulders with a white cloth when praying. This is obviously a reminiscence of the traditional Jewish prayer-vestment, the *Tallith*. It had lost its form; it had lost its meaning; its biblical associations had been forgotten; but memory was tenacious enough to retain a vague approximation to the outward form. In much the same way, a Marrano of the fifteenth century may have remembered how his father, when writing in Hebrew, used to make a certain mark on the top of the letter, which invoked the Divine benediction. It would not have been altogether unnatural had he and his sons continued the habit mechanically, long after the letters had lost appreciable similarity to their original form, and long after they themselves had ceased to remember the true significance.

A word now regarding Columbus' curious signature, the use of which he enjoined in the most rigorous terms on "Don Diego, my son, or anyone who may inherit this entail." Its form was thus:

.S.

.S . A . S.

X M Y

A good many interpretations of this mystical hotch-potch have been given. Maurice David devised one based on the Hebrew, but unfortunately it makes no sense. (To this, of course, it would be possible to reply that an accurate use of the Holy Tongue on the explorer's part is hardly to be anticipated!) Professor Amzalak, of Lisbon, has put forward a more satisfactory, but over-elaborate, conjecture. I do not propose to join in this particular contest. There is one point, however, that I wish to make. I do not think that any Marrano would have had any doubt as to the significance of the first part of the formula. Down to the present day they continue to use the Hebrew *Adonai* for the

Divine Name, and in all the old Spanish prayer-books and Bibles (for example, the Ferrara and Amsterdam editions) as well as in manuscripts of the pre-Columbus age, this is regularly contracted, whether from religious scruple or for economy of space, into the single letter .A. *with a full stop before and after.* Hence the formula

.S.

.S . A . S.

would almost certainly have meant: SANCTUS, SANCTUS, SANCTUS ADONAI—"Holy, Holy, Holy is the Lord" [*i.e.,* "of Hosts"]—the traditional Hebrew *Kedusha,* based on Isaiah 6, 3, and quite unexceptionable even in the most orthodox Christian eyes because of its Trinitarian interpretation.

If this interpretation were correct, the X in the next line would presumably stand for *Christus,* in its very common Greek form *Xristos,* and the M for *Maria;* and there would be nothing left for the Y except to represent the corresponding Greek letter. Hence the line would stand for the pidgin-Greek formula, ΧΡΙΣΤΟΣ ΜΑΡΙΗΣ ΥΙΟΣ—"Christ, son of Mary"—which would form an admirable pendant to the Trinitarian declaration: "Holy, Holy, Holy, is *Adonai.*" [2] I don't want readers to misunderstand me and think that I am putting this forward dogmatically, or that I am unaware of the orthodox Christian interpretation: *Servus Supplex Altissimi Salvatoris.* I most definitely maintain, however, that if Columbus were of Jewish extraction and conscious of the fact, though a convinced Christian, this is the sort of mystical jumble in which he might have indulged.

---

[2] The alternative *Christus, Maria, Joseph,* seems to me unsatisfactory. Why Joseph? And, if Joseph, why the Y instead of J or I? Incidentally, the *trishagion* could also be read into Columbus's acrostic down and across— *Sanctus Adonai Sebaoth, Sanctus Adonai Sebaoth, Sanctus Adonai Sebaoth.*

We now approach the crux of the whole problem. If the thesis is correct, if Christopher Columbus was indeed descended from Spanish Jews converted to Christianity, to what family did he actually belong? What, in fact, was Christopher Columbus' real, his Jewish name?

On the basis of the data we have, interpreted in the light of Jewish literature, it is possible to make a suggestion—and, I may add, a suggestion which is not wholly fantastic. But, in a world which, for all I know to the contrary, may be on the point of collapse, it is not to be expected of me to put forward my thesis here. I prefer to retain it in reserve as my stock-in-trade should I ever join the rest of the Occident as a refugee in Columbus' happy land of Cipango.

14. THE JEWISH ANCESTRY OF MICHEL DE MONTAIGNE[1]

i

IT HAS been noted long since that while Michel de Montaigne is exquisitely garrulous about most personal matters, does not neglect his own family, and speaks at adequate length about his father, he only mentions his mother incidentally, as having been passably versed in the Latin tongue.[2] Were it not for a casual contemporary note, elaborated by painstaking research in the nineteenth century, her very name would be forgotten today; we would not even know, as we do, that she was called Antoinette Louppes, or Lopès, and that she belonged to a Spanish family established at Bordeaux. Recent enquiries have carried our knowledge a little further, showing us the manner of woman she was and identifying her father and other members of the family, who played an honored, even illustrious, part in mercantile life at Bordeaux and Toulouse. There, however, notwithstanding the minute research that has been devoted to the problem, the matter rests. What was the con-

---

1 *Revue des Cours et Conférences*, 1937; (and *Bulletin de la société des amis de Montaigne*, 1937) ; where extremely detailed references are given. My thesis is adopted in F. Strowski's standard work, *Montaigne, la vie publique et privé* (Paris, 1938). Attention was drawn to the new material almost simultaneously by the Abbé Maturin Dréano, who writes to me that he first had cognizance of it in December, 1929, and embodied it in his thesis, *La Pensée religieuse de Montaigne*, which was presented at the Sorbonne at the end of 1935 and received the imprimatur on February 6, 1936, but was not published until March, 1937. By this time, I had called public attention to the material for the first time in a letter published in the London *Times Literary Supplement* in April, 1936. I mention these data both to establish the priorities and to illustrate the minor pitfalls of scholarship.

2 *Essays*, I. xxv: "Mon père et ma mère y apprindrent assez de Latin pour l'entendre, et en acquirent à suffisance pour s'en servir à la necessité."

dition of her family prior to its arrival in France from Spain, what was its history, what its antecedents—all this is still wrapped in the most complete obscurity.

Two indications of fundamental importance have not, however, been utilized hitherto; and when followed up they lead, as will be seen, to conclusions which may almost be qualified as sensational. In the first place, the family of Montaigne's mother was described in the legal documents concerning them as Lopez *dict. de Villeneuve* (the phrase is of constant recurrence). This agnomen was generally assumed —and naturally so—to refer to one of the innumerable Villeneuves in France; though the indefatigable Malvezin was inclined to look for it in Spain, in a village in the neighborhood of Toledo. The other point, revealed only in the most recent researches, is the precise place of origin of the family, who have been established, by a casual reference in a notarial deed, as hailing from Saragossa. This indicates an immediate line of enquiry. Let us look for the family Louppes de Villeneuve, in its original Spanish form, in the Saragossan records; and, since so many of the *émigrés* from Spain to France at this period were of Jewish origin (as Montaigne's mother was suspected to be, though hitherto without any definite proof), let us look for them among the Marranos or "New Christians" of that city, converted not long since from Judaism to an uneasy Christianity. (A reconstruction of the Montaigne family tree will be found on page 234 of this volume.)

ii

In 1507, when the pestilence was raging in Aragon, a certain jurist of Saragossa named Juan de Anchias, Assessor of the Holy Inquisition, occupied his enforced leisure, in a highly malicious fashion, by drawing up detailed genealogical lists which demonstrated the precise Jewish antecedents of a very large proportion of the contemporary local notables. It is this work—the notorious "Green Book of Aragon," or *Libro Verde de Aragon*—which should naturally be consulted first of all with the object which we have in view. The search will not be in vain.

At the time of the massacres in Spain at the close of the fourteenth and beginning of the fifteenth centuries, large numbers of Jews, particularly of the wealthier classes, became converted nominally to Christianity in order to escape death. It is with these, who were in most cases suspected of remaining faithful at heart to their former faith, that the *Libro Verde de Aragon* especially deals. Among them, we are informed by the garrulous author, was the Paçagon (Pazagon, Patagon) family of Calatayud—a family which, as will be seen later, had played a prominent part in local Jewish life for the previous century or more. At its head, at this time, was Moses Paçagon, a ragman (*trapero*). On his conversion,[3] he called himself (no doubt after some aristocrat who had condescended to stand his sponsor at baptism) Garcia Lopez—contracted into Garcilopez. Since the family resided and had property in that portion of Calatayud known as Villanueva, or New-Town (an important distinction, since the Jewish quarter lay *inside* the oldest line of fortifications), he was known as Garcia Lopez *de Villanueva*. This appelation was shared by all of his family who followed or accompanied him into the bosom of the Church. Ultimately, he removed from Calatayud to Saragossa, a busier commercial center, occupying a house here

---

[3] The actual date of the conversions is not easily to be ascertained. It is improbable however that it was at the outset of the persecutions, in 1391: for Calatayud does not seem to have suffered particularly in that year, and on the other hand we find some members of the family professing Judaism a good deal later. There were other waves of forced conversion in 1411 and 1413-4, Calatayud being particularly affected in the latter years. Failing any indication to the contrary, it may be assumed that the Paçagon family (or a large part of it) embraced Christianity on this occasion.

in the Plaza de San Gil. The rest of the family followed him in the end to his new home. Thus it became associated exclusively with Saragossa, the place of origin of Montaigne's forebears. It cannot be doubted for a moment that this is the family in which we are interested and to which the great French essayist's mother belonged.

Moses Paçagon had two sons, who followed him (though not, as it seems, immediately or simultaneously) into Christianity. One, a merchant, became known on his conversion as Ramón. He had a brother, Abraham, who though more steadfast than he, and remaining a professing Jew for some years longer, had no objection to maintaining relations with his errant kinsman; indeed, in 1459 we find them engaged in business dealings together. Ultimately, the attractions, or the pressure, of the dominant faith became too great for Abraham to bear, and he too was converted, assuming the name Gabriel Lopez de Villanueva. But in point of fact, Ramon himself was very little of a Christian at heart, and, when the Inquisition was introduced into Aragon, he was one of its early victims, being penanced on May 15, 1491, and subsequently burned.

His brother Abraham was in very close relationship with the family of Luis de Santangel, the Marrano jurist, but for whose enthusiastic support the first voyage of Christopher Columbus would never have taken place. The Santangel family, like the Lopez, originated at Calatayud. On the death of Pedro Martinez de Santangel, his heirs sold Abraham Paçagon their house in Villanueva, reserving, however, the right (which they subsequently exercised) to excavate in the cellars for the treasure which they suspected their father to have concealed there.[4] Subsequently, after his conversion, Abraham's son, Don Angel de Villanueva, married

---

[4] Kayserling, *Christopher Columbus*, p. 53, erroneously considered that it was the famous *escribano de ración* who was conducting the treasure-hunt.

Luisa de Santangel, daughter of Columbus' patron, receiving a magnificent wedding-present from King Ferdinand himself. Don Angel ultimately became, in 1515, *baile* of Cerdagne. Another grandson of the rag-man of Calatayud was, probably, Garcia Lopez the merchant (*Garcilopez mercader*), who was burned in effigy by the Inquisition in 1486. He owed his life presumably to the fact that he had sought refuge in flight, and is in all probability to be identified with the Garcia Lopez de Villanueva who established himself in Provence, where he founded a well-known family.[5] His wife, Eleanora Perez, had been less fortunate, meeting her death like more than one of her kinsfolk at an Inquisitorial pyre.

iii

Moses Paçagon, the rag-man of Calatayud, had a close kinsman (*pariente muy propinquo*) —probably then his first cousin—Mayer Paçagon. He, too, became a titular Christian at about the same time, under the name Juan Lopez de Villanueva. According to the author of the *Libro Verde de Aragon,* he had two sons, Juan Fernando and Martin Pablo, both of whom founded large families.

We may dismiss the first of these, Juan Fernando, at once. He, too, was a Judaizer at heart, ultimately suffering at the stake for his secret attachment to his ancestral faith, like so many of his kinsmen. By his marriage with a member of the well-known Çapata family, he had three sons. The eldest, Luis, was father of Prospero Lopez, who married a Buendia and in turn begat Petronilla, Montalegre, and Maria Lopez. The second son of Juan Fernando was Juan,

---

5 It is stated that Garcia Lopez left Spain about 1440 in order to take refuge in France. This date is highly improbable, as the general flight from Spain began only half a century later, after the establishment of the Inquisition.

father of Hernando, Juan, and a daughter named Juana. The third, 'Micer' Fernando, was more distinguished than either of his brothers; for he embraced the profession of law and prospered so greatly that he was able to repurchase the ancestral home from the Rector. He married Maria de Santa Cruz, daughter of Diego de Santa Cruz of Saragossa, and had by her no fewer than eight children—Juan, Jeronimo, Diego, Luis, Francisco, and Bartholomé, as well as two daughters who became nuns. This fact was not, indeed, a sign of orthodoxy; for Micer Fernando Lopez, like his father, was a Jew at heart and like him perished at the stake, while his wife similarly appeared at an auto-de-fé, though suffering less drastic punishment. Notwithstanding this, their son Jeronimo became an official of the archbishop, Don Fernando de Aragon, while Bartholomé studied law and married an "Old Christian" named Maria de Ciria. It is worth while to note all these seemingly unimportant details; for it is with Michel de Montaigne's cousins and contemporaries that we are dealing!

Martin Pablo Lopez, Mayer Paçagon's second son, similarly left a numerous progeny. We are not informed about them, unfortunately, in quite such detail as hitherto, and it is necessary to exercise some ingenuity in order to straighten out the genealogical tangle. One of his sons was the lawyer, Micer Pablo Lopez, penanced by the Inquisition on May 15, 1491, on the same day as his kinsman Ramón. He in turn was father of Dr. Pablo Lopez, Prior of the Cathedral Church of Sancta Maria del Pilar in Saragossa. But this celibate cleric was not Micer Pablo's only descendant; for the *Libro Verde* plainly informs us that the latter, with his brother Juan Fernando, was the ancestor of those Lopez who were living at Saragossa in 1507. Elsewhere, we learn that a brother of Juan Fernando Lopez (*i.e.*, Micer Pablo Lopez—his only non-celibate brother) was grandfather of Antonio and Juan Lopez—well-known characters, presumably, at the time of writing. This is the first time that the name Antonio, subsequently so common in the French branch both in its male and female form (Antoinette) enters into the Lopez family tree.

Now, our records at this period are tolerably complete; yet only two brothers of the Lopez de Villanueva family, who were named Antonio and Juan respectively, are to be found. Recent research has established the fact that Pedro Lopez of Toulouse, Michel de Montaigne's grandfather, was son of one Antonio Lopez of Saragossa. The latter had (in addition to brother Jacob and six sisters) *a brother named Juan* settled at Toulouse (where he died in 1497 or 1498 [6]) —the pioneer, as it seems, of the French branch of the family. Here, obviously, we have the Antonio and Juan, the grandchildren of Martin Pablo Lopez who are referred to in the contemporary record.

A further piece of evidence may be adduced to confirm this inference. Among the brothers of Pedro Lopez, Montaigne's grandfather, was a Martin Lopez, who lived at Antwerp.[7] It may be assumed that he perpetuated, as was usual, a family name—presumably, therefore, that of Martin Pablo Lopez from whom he was descended. No document gives

---

[6] Another Juan Lopes died in London, intestate, in 1501 (Probate Registry Office, Somerset House, P.C.C.). He may also have belonged to the family, for we know the Lopes of Bordeaux to have had mercantile dealings with England, and even to have established one of their brothers there as agent. Pedro (Pierre) Lopez also seems to have begun his commercial career in London.

[7] The chronological feasibility of the line of the descent here suggested should perhaps be demonstrated.

Mayor Paçagon, baptized at the beginning of the fourteenth century, may have been born any time between 1330 and 1360. His son, Martin Lopez de Villanueva, was perhaps born about 1390. Micer Pablo Lopez, his son, can have been born in 1425, and was thus between sixty and seventy when he was "penanced" by the Inquisition in 1491. Martin, his son, can have been born in 1445: Antonio in 1470: Pedro in 1490, being thus between twenty and thirty when Antoinette (Montaigne's mother) was born, and a little over fifty at the time of his death in 1542-3.

the name which is necessary to complete this family chain—
that of the son of Micer Pablo Lopez of Saragossa and father
of Antonio Lopez. It is, however, to be imagined that he
was named Martin after his grandfather (the name was conceivably a Latinization of the Hebrew Mayer), transmitting the appellation after him in the regular fashion to
the grandson who settled in Flanders. Research in the
notarial archives in Saragossa and Calatayud would be necessary to confirm this conjecture finally. Whether it is correct or not, what has been said above is sufficient to demonstrate that *Michel de Montaigne was a direct descendant in
the seventh generation of Mayer Paçagon, Jew of Calatayud,
converted to Christianity about the beginning of the fifteenth
century under the name Juan Lopez de Villanueva.*

iv

Why did the Lopez family, or so many of its members,
leave Spain? It may be assumed, not exclusively for business
reasons; that would explain a partial but not a wholesale
emigration on the part of the tribe. It is far from improbable
that the reason is to be sought in some of the facts reported
above. The Inquisition was at this time at the height of its
power in Aragon. The somewhat insensate conspiracy of
the Marranos against its introduction, which had resulted in
the assassination of Pedro Arbues, had strengthened its
hands. Now, there was no part of Spain where it was working so steadily and so remorselessly. The great New Christian families of the region were marked out above all for
suspicion; and suspicion could soon translate itself into
action, arrest, condemnation, and finally the most agonizing
of deaths.

Among the suspected families was that of Lopez. Already
on June 25, 1486, at the eleventh auto-de-fé held in Sara-

gossa, one of those sentenced (as has been indicated before) had been Garcia Lopez, the merchant, "who, being a Christian, performed Jewish ceremonies and gave charity to the *cedaza* [*i.e., Cedakah (Zedakal) or poor fund*], and possessed a book of hours (*i.e., prayer-book*) and Bible in Hebrew, and never confessed or communicated." The culprit had anticipated execution by flight, and was, as it seems, the forerunner of the Lopes de Villanueva family in France. His wife was condemned in 1487 "for observing Jewish ceremonies, fasts, and food." Gil Lopez was relaxed in effigy on September 18, 1492; Juan Lopez, merchant (possibly Montaigne's great-great-uncle of Toulouse, where he is first encountered in 1491), was penanced on November 28, 1490; Micer Pablo Lopez and Ramón Lopez on May 15, 1491; Garcia Lopez, the physician, on May 15, 1502; Fernando Lopez, his son Micer Fernando and Micer Pablo, all were burned, as well as others mentioned above.

In France, renegades from Christianity were not indeed safe, but the members of suspected families were tolerably certain of security, providing that they maintained a reasonable degree of circumspection. One may therefore decide that so many members of the Lopez family left Spain, almost in a body, at the beginning of the sixteenth century or shortly before, in order to seek a refuge from the operations of the Inquisition. Whether they had much of an inclination towards Judaism is another matter. Certainly, they tended to preserve a great degree of family solidarity. On the other hand, it is known that they contributed various staunch paladins of Christianity, both in its Catholic and its Reformed forms. Moreover, Antoinette Lopez's father, Pedro Lopez, married an "Old Christian" woman, Giraulde de Puy, member of an old-established Bordeaux family. One may assume from this that his Jewish sympathies, though perhaps not entirely submerged, were certainly not dominant. His famous grandson therefore could afford to look upon Jewish matters with the ostensible detachment of an outsider.[8]

v

The documents at our disposal give us a good deal of information with regard to the Paçagon (Pazagon, Patagon) family, from which the Lopez de Villanueva—and hence Michel de Montaigne—descended. This appears to have been most prominent in Aragon, though an isolated offshoot is found in Portugal, where in 1395 one Isaac Passacom [9] led the community of Coimbra in its temerarious refusal to pay the Prior of the Church of St. James his customary tribute of eggs, on the ground that they were not his parishioners and that he had no authority over them. The earliest mention of the family dates back over half a century before this date, to 1333, when Isaac (Açach) Paçagon of Saragossa nominated his brother, Moses Paçagon, as his procurator. It is not easy to differentiate these from the Calatayud branch. At this place, Don Joseph (Juce) Paçagon *el mayor,* Isaac (Açach) Paçagon, and Juce Paçagon, *el menor,* appear in 1356 among the leaders of the community, and in 1414, Samuel and Samuel ben Abraham Paçagon were included among its official lay heads.

Notwithstanding the loss of some of the most notable of its members through conversion, others remained steadfast to their Judaism. In 1436, we encounter a second Isaac (Açach) Paçagon as one of the heads of the community of Calatayud, representing the poorer classes. He had a name-

---

8 He refers in his *Voyage en Italie* to the Jewish "palio" at Rome and to the forced sermons, but without any noticeable feeling of sympathy; and one would hardly imagine from his more famous account of the Forced Conversion in Portugal in 1497 that he was speaking of his own kinsfolk.

9 Kayserling, ingeniously but improbably suggested that the name may be derived from the Hebrew *Paskan,* i.e., Decisor.

sake in Saragossa, a second Açach Paçagon, whose wife's name was Sol, and who may or may not have been connected with Junez (Jonas?) Paçagon (1458) and with Abraham Paçagon (1466). The last-named, married to Struga, daughter of Zevi, we know to have been a staunch supporter of the synagogue in the Barrio Nuevo of Saragossa, and in 1425 was with Janto (Shem-Tob?) Paçagon among the founders of a new charitable society in the *juderia*. On the very eve of the Expulsion from Spain, one encounters at Calatayud one Jaco (Jacob) Paçagon (1489), and a litigious kinsman, Samuel, son of the late Abraham Paçagon.

To link all these up with the converted branch of the family is difficult; but it is by no means improbable that the Moses Paçagon mentioned above, who flourished in 1333, may have been the grandfather of the first converts—Moses, *alias* Garcilopez, and Mayer, the ancestor of Michel de Montaigne. Moses' father, like his son, was perhaps named Abraham; Mayer's may have been that Samuel Paçagon mentioned in our documents. And, considering that the name Abraham Paçagon recurs constantly in the small Jewish community of Calatayud down to the close of the fifteenth century, it certainly seems as though there were living in Montaigne's own day, in the Jewish quarter of some fetid city of the Levant, members of the family who could, had they desired, have traced their relationship with him.

vi

Reference has been made above to Montaigne's greatuncle, Martin Lopez, who is mentioned in various documents of the period as being resident in Antwerp. With the aid of another collection of material which is now available, though not hitherto utilized in this connection, the story of this branch of the family may also be followed up, and yet further light shed upon the enquiring spirit which Montaigne inherited from his mother's family. Let it be said at once that the Antwerp records speak specifically of Martin Lopez *de Villanueva* (or *de Villeneuve*), thus placing the possibility of a mistaken identity out of the question.

Martin Lopez, then (we are informed), arrived in Flanders no later than 1520, probably via London. Settling at Antwerp, he accumulated a considerable fortune in the spice-trade. One of his daughters, Eleanora (d. 1602), married a prominent merchant named Antonio del Rio, very active in public life; they were the parents of Martin del Rio (1551-1608), the famous Jesuit scholar. Another child of Martin Lopez was Ursula (born 1537, married 1555) who became the wife of Marco Perez, head of the Spanish mercantile colony at Antwerp, subsequently the leader of the Calvinist movement in that city and in the Low Countries generally; after her husband's death, in 1580, a medal was struck in her honor.[10] Martin Lopez also had a son, named Martin like himself, who played a very prominent part in local political and religious life. He worked in close association with his brother-in-law, Marco Perez; and his commercial position was strengthened by the fact that the Spanish branch of his family lent money to Philip II of Spain, and that he had a cousin, Pedro, high in the service of the government of the Low Countries in Brussels.[11] In conjunction with Perez, he was one of the first to adhere to the protest of the nobles in favor of religious liberty and to support their movement; and he

10 It is impossible to follow in detail the descendants of Ursula Lopez, who bore her husband twelve children in their comparatively brief married life.

11 Pierre Lopez, Montaigne's grandfather, had another brother in Flanders, besides Martin: Pedro Lopes was no doubt his son.

assisted him in financing the confederate forces in the field. He, too, was a staunch Calvinist: preached in the church; played a prominent role in communal affairs; and was reckoned one of the pillars of Reform in the Netherlands. In 1568, therefore, when the rigors of the law were at last enforced against the religious Reformers in the Low Country, he fled for his life, and his goods were confiscated. Some of his family, however, remained; in particular a daughter, Sarah (named after his wife, Sarah de Landas), who married Jacob Sweerts and was the mother of Johannes Antonides van der Linden (1609-1644), Professor of Medicine at Leyden and a close friend of Menasseh ben Israel, whose portrait was engraved by Rembrandt—a hitherto overlooked Jewish contact of the painter.[12]

Generally, genealogical researches such as the present one have little more than sentimental interest. In the present instance, the author may venture to suggest that this is not the case. In the first place, we are introduced to a whole brood of Michel de Montaigne's kinsfolk—merchants and financiers, lawyers and scholars, Catholic clerics and Protestant enthusiasts—of whose existence he can hardly have been unaware and with some of whom he was very likely in personal touch. In the second place, it is now possible to prove what was hitherto only conjectured— that he was on his mother's side of Jewish descent, being the great-great-great-great-great-grandson of Mayer Paçagon, a converted member of a distinguished Jewish family of Calatayud. Possibly, some of his ironic, skeptical mentality may have been due to this fact; for had not more than one of his kinsmen been burned by the Inquisition not long before his own day, and was not one of his cousins a leader of the Calvinistic party in the Low Countries? It may well

---

12 Another Flemish member of the family was Eleanora Lopez de Villanueva, who married Juan de la Palma de St. Fuentes.

be, indeed, that this was the reason why, in his writings, he refrained from mentioning his mother—a silence which, long considered inexplicable, was perhaps merely discreet.[13]

Finally, there is one other consideration, to which recent events in Europe have given a special significance. The enquiry shows us clearly, with fullest documentation, how in the veins of the most exquisitely French of all French writers there flows a non-Gallic current; and how that genius which came to maturity on French soil was nourished and diversified by an alien—so-called Semitic—strain, thereby becoming more powerful and more versatile, without being made any the less French.

---

[13] It is impossible to go here into the vexed question, whether Montaigne's mother, Antoinette de Lopes, judaised or no. From the information collected above, it is obvious that the family as a whole lost its interest in Judaism at an early date.

15. THE ORIGIN OF GHETTO[1]

GHETTO (ge.to) . 1611. [It.,? abbrev. of *borghetto,* dim. of *borgo* BOROUGH.] The quarter in a city, chiefly in Italy, to which the Jews were restricted.

(Shorter Oxford Dictionary, I, 790) .

i

A RECENT erudite publication has once more brought to the fore the vexed question of the origin of the word *"Ghetto,"* which, originating almost without a doubt in Italy, has become acclimatized in every language of Europe. The present writer published not long ago a detailed history of the Ghetto of Venice—the oldest and most famous of all. In the course of his investigations, much new material bearing upon the institution was inevitably brought to light. He ventures to sum up here the conclusion at which he has arrived, on the basis of his researches, which he believes to place the whole problem at last beyond the sphere of conjecture.

It will be as well to begin by giving a summary of the theories which have hitherto been put forward. The most salient of the origins suggested are the following.

1. The Italian *Borghetto,* diminutive of *Borgo,* with the first syllable elided.

This derivation, which has the support of the *Oxford Dictionary,* is preeminently plausible. In support of this

---

[1] Originally published in *Romania,* vol. LX (1934) , pp. 67-76. The writing of the essay had been prompted by the monograph of R. Giacomelli, "Ghetto," in *Archivum Romanicum,* vol. XVI, no. 4 (Oct.-Dec. 1932) , with an appendix, *ibid.,* XVII (1933) , referred to in an Additional Note to my original article.

theory, it was possible to point to the existence at Civita-vecchia, where no Jewish settlement ever existed (in the Ghetto period at least) of a suburb, or *borgo,* still known as *Ghetto,* its inhabitants being called *ghettaroli.* It has now, however, been discovered that, though this was indeed never a Jewish quarter, it was actually prepared as the place or residence of a colony of Jews whom Innocent XI proposed to settle in the city in 1692, as an integral part of his policy of developing the port. While therefore there is no over-whelming objection to this derivation (excepting for the somewhat unusual elision of the first syllable) no positive evidence can be adduced in its support.

2. Hebrew גט (*ghēt*), or Divorce.

This etymology appears to have been first put forward by the great historian Ludovico Antonio Muratori in his *Dissertazione sopra le antichità italiane,* XXXIII a. Its ro-mantic simplicity gave it a wide appeal, and even today it is perhaps the most current hypothesis. It has the weighty support of Gregorovius (*Figuren-Geschichte:* ... *Der Ghetto und die Juden in Rom*) and of numerous later authorities. The latest paladin of this theory is R. Giacomelli, who in a learned article in the *Archivum Romanicum* in 1932 points out that in certain places in Italy (in Rome itself, for ex-ample) the institution was actually known among the Jews themselves by the name of *Ghet* (pronounced *gghętte*). He adduces, moreover, a Papal Bull of Pius IV., of February 27, 1562, which authorized the Jews to open shops *extra ghectum seu septum hebraicum.* This proves plainly, according to him, that at this period the term *ghetto* at Rome did not sig-nify the Jewish quarter, but the barrier by which it was en-closed. First applied by the unfortunate Jews of the Eternal City to designate the wall constructed to separate them from the outside world, it became officially adopted in the Papal

Latin, through the medium of which it ultimately passed into general usage.

The objections to this theory, plausible though it is, are very strong. In the first place (as will be seen below) the use of the term to designate the specific quarter inhabited by the Jews considerably antedates the year 1555, when such an institution was established in Rome. (Giacomelli himself admits this fact, though a little mysteriously, he fails to attach any importance to it). Secondly, the Hebrew *get* does not properly signify the "act" of divorce, but the formal "legal instrument" drawn up for that purpose: it is occasionally used, indeed, to designate other types of legal documents. It would appear out of the question that a term bearing this narrow signification could have been applied to the place designated for the Jewish separation. Moreover (and this is perhaps more important) the Ghetto was never officially known among the Italian Jewish communities by any homophonous equivalent, but always as חצר *Hazer* (Court), מגרש *Migrash* (place), מסילה *Mesillah* (Street), and the like.[2] In most places, indeed, these terms prevailed in popular usage as well. On the other hand, it is not to be excluded that the pronunciation current at Rome was affected (half jocularly, perhaps, in the first instance) by the well-known Hebrew word.

3. The Tuscan dialectical *Guitto,* or Modenese *Ghitto,* signifying "sordid."

This was the original view put forward by Muratori, subsequently discarded; and under the circumstances it is hardly right to discuss it seriously. It may, however, be

---

2 *Mesillah* (locally pronounced, by the curious phonetic vagary characteristic there, as *Mefillah!*) was the term universally used among the Jews of Avignon and the Comtat Venaissin, amongst themselves, to designate the "*carrière des juifs.*"

observed, firstly, that dirt was no *distinctive* characteristic of the Italian Ghetto of the sixteenth century; and, secondly, that its early history has nothing to do with those regions where the dialectical terms in question were current.

4. The Latin *Judaica,* through *Giudaca* or *Giudecca,* the term often applied to the Jewish Quarter from the tenth century onwards.

This theory is cited by S. Kahn in *Jewish Encyclopaedia,* V., 652. In criticism of it, it is enough to observe that phonetic similarity is virtually absent.

5. The Yiddish, or Judaeo-German, *ghectus,* from the German *Gehecktes Ort,* or Hedged Place.

(Joffe in the *Jubilee Volume* of the Yiddish Scientific Institute in Vilna in honor of Dr. Alfred Landau).

6. The Latin *Aegyptus,* through the Italian *Egitto.*

(W. Meyer-Lübke in *Romanisches Etymologisches Wörterbuch,* 1911).

7. The Greek γειτων, γειτσνιχ (neighborhood, vicinity).

(Marco Mortara in *Revue des Etudes Juives,* X (1884), 306 n.i.).

8. The Hebrew עידה ('Edah) (community) (Israel Abrahams, *Jewish Life in the Middle Ages,* p. 78), a suggestion which would appear more plausible were the similarity of pronunciation between the two words closer. Others suggest the kindred Syriac word עטה ('Etah). But it is difficult to understand why Syriac should become current in Venice.

9. The Gothic *gatvo* (Anglo-Saxon *gete,* High German *Gasse*).

(*Monatschrift für Geschichte und Wissenschaft des Judenthums,* III. 438. Cf. Cassuto in *Encyclopaedia Italiana, s.v.* GHETTO).

These last hypotheses do credit to the ingenuity of the persons who have invented them. None, in point of fact, seems particularly plausible. The origin of a term essentially Italian in usage must be looked for in Italy, and it cannot be discussed seriously without reference to the history of the institution to which it applies. This, then, is now necessary.

ii

The first place in the world in which the name *Ghetto* was associated with the Jewish quarter was Venice. The Jewish community of this city, numerous and illustrious though it was afterwards to become, was not by any means of ancient establishment. The fierce commercial (rather than religious) intolerance of the early Republic effectively prevented the formation of any Jewish settlement. For a long time they were excluded even from Venetian shipping. In the twelfth century, indeed, Levantine merchants were permitted to come to the city for the purpose of trade. They were not, as yet, permitted to reside in the heart of the city and had to deposit their merchandise and conduct their affairs on the island of Spinalunga. In the course of time, this became known after them as the *Giudecca,* a title which it still bears.[3]

These transients were unable to establish any settled community. In 1366, indeed, a small body of Jewish moneylenders was invited over from the *terra ferma* in order to

---

[3] This is the most probable, but not the only, derivation suggested for the name. It goes back, however, to the sixteenth century (Archivio di Stato di Venezia, *Santo Uffizio,* busta 24).

open loan-banks for the benefit of the poor. After less than thirty years, in 1394, the Republic refused to renew their *condotta,* and they retired back to the mainland. For the next century, the Jews were represented in Venice only by transients, who were sedulously prevented from making a long stay.

In 1508, however, the Venetian territories on the *terra ferma* (where numerous Jewish communities, some of very ancient establishment, had continued to exist) were invaded by the forces of the piratical League of Cambrai, formed by the Pope, France, Spain, and the majority of the Italian powers with the laudable object of partitioning the Venetian dominions. The progress of the armies was rapid, and hordes of fugitives poured across the Lagoon from all parts. Under circumstances such as these, it was contrary to all standards even of sixteenth-century morality (as well as of policy) to exclude even Jews, and large numbers of them were permitted to come to Venice without any obstacle being put in their way. After the enemy forces retired, many places (especially Mestre, whence a large contingent of the refugees had come) still lay in ruins, and the Jews had an excellent pretext for remaining. Preachers inveighed against them from the pulpit, and statesmen in the Senate; but it proved impossible to rid the city of this leaven of unbelief. Thus, notwithstanding the wide-spread antipathy, Venice found itself confronted with the presence of a numerous Jewish community, under the adroit leadership of the wealthy Anselmo del Banco, formerly of Mestre. There was a growing feeling that, since the city could not rid itself of them, they should at least be put under control.

On April 22, 1515, the first step was taken, when at a meeting of the *Pregadi,* Zorzi Emo suggested that the Jews should be sent to live on the *Giudecca*—the island where, according to report, the Levantine Jewish merchants had established themselves centuries before. This proposal was defeated owing to the exertions of Anselmo del Banco and his colleagues. In the following year, however (as usual, towards Easter-tide), the question was raised again. At a meeting of the *Collegio* on March 26, 1516 (reported by the indefatigable Sanuto in his *Diaries*), Zacaria Dolfin, one of the *savi*, arose and complained about the Jews, who, he said, should not have been allowed in the city. It was essential that they should be segregated and thus prevented from contaminating Christian burghers by their pernicious influence. Accordingly, he considered it to be desirable to send them to live in the New Foundry, which was like a castle and could be cut off completely by draw-bridge (*"il mandarli tuti a star in Geto nuovo ch'è come un castelo per far ponti levatori et serar di nuovo"*). Notwithstanding the continued opposition of Del Banco and his associates, this advice was adopted. On April 10, 1516, the Jews, hitherto scattered about the city, were compelled to transfer themselves *en masse* to their new abode.

The district assigned to them, the *Geto Nuovo*, or *Corte delle Calli*, was, in form, an island, cut off entirely from the rest of the city by the ubiquitous canals. The walls and gates with which it was provided completed the segregation. The population which it could hold was, however, strictly limited. It had been instituted (as we have seen) for the native Italian Jews, and German immigrants, who had been driven from the *terra ferma*. The Levantine merchants visiting the city, always privileged, were in a special category and were for the moment still permitted to live wherever they pleased, without disturbance. After some time, however, it was determined that these also should be segregated. They were not sent to join their Occidental coreligionists in the *Geto Nuovo*, but were installed in the so-called "Old" Foundry, or *Geto Vecchio*—a narrow area between the former and the

Fondamenta della Pescaria.[4] For a long time these two areas
were under different administrations, their inhabitants being
carefully distinguished as "Germans" and "Levantines" respectively; but ultimately the two became merged. In 1633,
owing to the continued immigration, which made the total
population approach 5,000, a further small extension was
authorized to the northeast of the Jewish quarter. This was
called *Ghetto Nuovissimo*—a title given to it in all probability only when it became associated with the Jewish settlement. With the *Ghetto* or *Geto Vecchio* and the *Ghetto
Nuovo*, however, the case was different. The area in question was known by these names even before it had any
Jewish associations. Moreover, the original Jewish quarter
was (contrary to what would naturally be supposed) not the
"Old" Ghetto but the *"New"* Ghetto, the former being a
later extension! This fact alone is sufficient to make it plain,
beyond all shadow of a doubt, that the origin of the word
is to be looked for in Venetian, not in Jewish, antiquities,
and that its Jewish associations are purely accidental.

iii

The enquiry addressed to Venetian antiquities elicits a
ready and unquestionable response. In the north of Venice,
there had been from time immemorial two islands, subsequently joined by a bridge. The one, towards the Canareggio, had become habitable quite early and had been used

---

4 A map of the Venetian Ghetto, showing its historical development and
the situation of its characteristic institutions, may be found at the close of
my *History of the Jews in Venice.*

It appears that the use of the term *geto* to denote the Jewish quarter,
without any strictly topographical indication, began at Venice at an early
date. Cf. Sanuto, *Diarii*, for March 4, 1531: *In questa sera in Geto fu fato tra
Zudei una bellissima Comedia nè vi potè intrar alchuno christian. . . .* The
foundry was disused after the first half of the fifteenth century. David
Reubeni in his Diary refers to "the Ghetto, the place of the Jews," in Venice
in 1524.

as a foundry (*geto*) ; this name being given to it by reason of the operation of casting metals (*gettare*) which was carried on in it. In the fifteenth century, the other island was reclaimed and adapted for the same purpose. This accordingly became known as the *Getto Nuovo*, while the other was called the *Getto Vecchio*. The name *Getto*, as applied to this area, dates back at least as far as the fourteenth century, while the word is found in Venetian terminology as early as 1306.[5]

The Jewish quarter of Venice was the oldest of its sort in Italy, if not in the world. It was here that the example was set of instituting a special area for Jewish residence, surrounded on all sides with walls or other impassable barriers, provided with gates which were closed at nightfall, and made to serve as the principal instrument for the utter segregation of its unfortunate denizens from ordinary social intercourse. Outside this precinct, no Jew was allowed to live: within it, no Christian was permitted to remain once night had fallen and the prison-gates were closed.

This institution served as model for all those which were established in the rest of Italy in consequence of the Catholic Reaction. The injunction was given as far as Rome was concerned in the Bull *Cum Nimis Absurdum* of July 12, 1555: the Jewish quarter formally came into being on July 26, and it was walled on October 3. The example was followed in Florence and Tuscany in 1571, in Verona in 1599, in Padua in 1602, and so on. It is not by any means remark-

---

[5] There is a Venetian reference of 1306 to Nicholas Aymus *qui est officialis ad gettum* (Romanin, *Storia documentata di Venezia*, II, 378). The spelling, in view of later developments, is noteworthy. Cf. also Tassini, *Curiosità Veneziane, sub voce* (4th ed. pp. 319-321), with the reference to Temanza there given.

It can only be a coincidence that the Jewish quarter of Mestre (the parent-colony of Venice, so far as the Jewish settlement was concerned) was known as *Piraghetto*. (*Notizie storiche del castello di Mestre* [Venice, 1839], I, 119). It is possible that the consonantal transformation of the Venetian Jewish quarter was influenced by this extraordinary, but surely accidental, similarity.

able that the name of the original Venetian institution should have been applied also to these successive imitations. This, no doubt, was responsible for its first hesitant use in Pius IV.'s Bull of 1562, and ultimately for the official adoption of the term in all other parts of Italy. Hence, in an analogous manner, it spread into other European languages, though with the looser sense of a quarter inhabited in great part by Jews, without any legal connotation.

One difficulty only arises—that of the transition of *geto* (*ǧẹto*) to *ghetto* (*ǧẹto*). It has already been pointed out that there is in fact nothing insuperable in this. We have the examples of similar words, such as *traghetto* and *conghiettura*, in which the *g* has hardened. Moreover, the Italian *ghetta* (an old term for a Foundry) provides a precise feminine equivalent for the consonantal structure of the word; while the influence of the German *Giessen* may also have had some influence on its development.[6] It seems very probable that the G hardened at a comparatively early date— possibly, through the influence of the Jews themselves. It is significant, in any case, that in the Responsa of Rabbi Moses Isserles, in the middle of the sixteenth century, an important document containing much historical information refers repeatedly to the *Ghetto* (גיטו) *Nuovo* and *Ghetto Vecchio*.[7] But the final proof is to be found in the living tradition of the City of the Lagoons; for there can be no doubt that the area spoken of by Dolfin and others in 1516 as the *Geto* is identical with that which is now universally, and officially, known as the *Ghetto*—a name it has borne for many generations.

The derivation here under discussion was championed

---

[6] Spitzer, *Wörter und Sachen*, VI, 204.

[7] Responsum 51 (the Italian words have been phenomenally mutilated in later editions). Cf. also the various contemporary Hebrew pamphlets on the Tamari-Venturozzo divorce case (Venice and Mantua, 1565-6). In these, the form *Ghet* (גט) is used.

in 1869 by L. Stern and supported by numerous later authorities. But, as a matter of fact, it goes back two and a half centuries further, to a period when the history of the area in question was still fresh in human memory. The editor of Sansovino's *Venetia Città Nobilissima*—less than a hundred years after the foundation of the institution—discussed the origin of the name and had no hesitation in declaring that it derived from the foundry which formerly existed on this spot.[8] In his day, moreover, there was visible proof of this hypothesis: for, over the main gateway of the Ghetto, towards the Canareggio, there was to be seen a painted cannon-ball— a plain indication of its former use and of the real origin of the name.[9] Against this concrete fact, coupled with unbroken Venetian tradition and the undisputed historical facts, there does not seem to be any possibility of appeal.

---

[8] Ed. 1604, p. 256. The passage in question is not to be found in the original edition of 1581. It is a striking instance of how the literary discoveries of the nineteenth and twentieth centuries were anticipated two or three hundred years before.

[9] While correcting the proofs of this volume, the idea has occurred to me that conceivably this may have been the origin of the pawnbroker's characteristic sign of the Three Balls, never I think adequately explained.

16. THE BACKGROUND OF SHYLOCK[1]

THAT Shylock was a sheer figment of Shakespeare's imagination, there has never been any doubt. Yet this figment
has acquired an objective reality more vital than that of
most creatures of flesh and blood. His actions are still a by-
word, his name is a reproach, and his unfortunate coreligionists are taxed sometimes with his reputed misdeeds. It
was therefore natural that critics of the past generation—
men of the calibre of Heine, Elze, or Brandes—persisted in
regarding him as a real personality, paying homage to Shakespeare's genius when they were in Venice by visits as literary
pilgrims to the Rialto and the Ghetto. Today, on the basis
of fuller information, it is not altogether futile to fill out
the details of Shylock's background and to attempt to show
what manner of man he must have been had he actually
lived, granted the general truth of the fictional incidents
in which he figures.

For that they are fictional does not admit of any doubt.
In his *Merchant of Venice,* Shakespeare as usual adapted
an old story to suit his dramatic requirements. The somewhat
puerile episode of the "Pound of Flesh" dates back to the
thirteenth century, if not earlier. A Jew is not always the
villain of the piece, however, and in one memorable instance
he actually figures as the victim. In Leti's *Vita di Sisto
Quinto* we are told that in 1585, when the news reached
Rome that Drake had captured San Domingo, a Christian
merchant named Paolo Maria Secchi wagered a thousand
ducats against a pound of flesh with a Jew, Sansone Ceneda,
that it was not true. The latter lost: the Christian demanded
repayment; and it was only the sapience of the Pope, who

---
1 Originally published in *Review of English Studies,* vol. IX (1933).

anticipated Portia's decision, which brought the matter to a conclusion.

The tale was, indeed, first chronicled late in the seventeenth century; but it is not absolutely out of the question that it embodies some popular legend current contemporaneously, which may have reached Shakespeare's ears in a more or less garbled form. It may be added that the name Ceneda is a characteristically Jewish one in Italy, though not notoriously or exaggeratedly so—a fact which makes the story all the more credible. Strangely enough, the other great Elizabethan drama in which a Jew figures has likewise an inverted parallel in history. Marlowe's *Jew of Malta* attempted to betray the island to the Turk. It was long alleged that no Jews lived there at the period, the verisimilitude of the tale thus entirely disappearing. Recent research has shown that this is not the case. But the only conspiracy known to local history in which a Jew was implicated, on whatever side, was the Turkish Plot of 1749, which was frustrated solely through the assistance given by the neophyte, Joseph Antonio Cohen.

Even the name Shylock is obscure in its Jewish connection. It is conceivable that Shakespeare derived it from "Shiloch the Babylonian" mentioned in the apocryphal chronicle of Joseph ben Gorion, which was so popular in his day. On the other hand, it has been pointed out that all the Jewish names which occur in the *Merchant of Venice*—Shylock (Shelah), Jessica (Jesca), Chus (Cush) and Tubal —are closely paralleled in two successive chapters of the Book of Genesis (10. 2, 6, 24; 11. 14-5, 29). There is on record, moreover, a contemporary pamphlet, *Caleb Shillocke, his Prophecie, or the Jewes Prediction,* first published in 1606. (There was another edition in the following year.) It is not, however, quite certain whether the nomenclature was borrowed from Shakespeare, or whether an earlier edition, as yet unrecorded, served as the latter's inspiration. In any case, as far as the Ghetto was concerned, the name Shylock was absolutely unknown; and nothing approaching it is to be found in Venetian sources, printed or manuscript. This may be stated without equivocation.[2]

The question of nomenclature aside, it is not difficult in our present state of knowledge to reconstruct Shylock's actual background and to depict, without leaving much margin for error, those details which Shakespeare relegated to the imagination. Israel Zangwill pictured him as a Spanish Jew who had fled from the persecutions of the Inquisition with his mind filled with hatred against Christianity. Hunter, in 1845, asserted that he was a Levantine. As a matter of fact, both conjectures happen to be out of the question, on the author's own showing. Venetian Jewry, in Shakespeare's day and long after, was divided into three "nations," which were accorded absolutely different treatment one from another and maintained their own separate institutions. Among these, there were, indeed, "Ponentines," comprising refugees from Spain and Portugal, and "Levantines," consisting of Turkish subjects from the Near East. More prominent than these, about the streets of the city and on the Rialto, was the *Nazione Tedesca*, or German nation. This was the oldest of all in establishment, dating from the beginning of the sixteenth century, or even earlier. Though the least wealthy of the three, it was by far the most

---

2 It is a curious coincidence that Shakespeare happens to give both of Antonio's closest friends names which have a strong Jewish flavor. The nearest actual parallel to Bassanio is Bassano, which, in modern Italy, is considered characteristic. Similarly, Gratiano, under the form Graziano, happens to be a typically Italian Jewish name. A certain Lazzaro di Graziano Levi had collaborated in 1558 with the poet Solomon Usque in writing a play on Esther. This was produced more than once in Venice in the second half of the sixteenth century, and may conceivably have been published (as a *rifacimento* of it by Leone da Modena certainly was in 1612). It would be an extraordinary flight of fact if the name of one of Shakespeare's typical Venetian Christians were actually suggested to him, in some subconscious manner, by that of a contemporary Venetian Jew and fellow-playwright!

numerous, supporting a majority of the synagogues and easily surpassing all other local elements combined. (It may be mentioned, *en passant,* that old Gobbo's inquiry for the house of "master Jew," in sixteenth-century Venice, would have been somewhat lacking in precision; and it was fortunate that he found his son to guide him.)

Now, there can be no doubt whatsoever that Shylock, had he existed, would have belonged to this "nation." The proof is very simple. He was by profession a moneylender— the whole of Shakespeare's story, indeed, turns upon this fact. But, as it happens, it was only the *Nazione Tedesca* which was allowed to practice this occupation. Both the Levantines and the Ponentines were rigorously restricted, by law, to commerce, and they controlled a great part of the maritime trade of Venice—particularly that with the Levant, which owed its prosperity to them. The so-called "Germans," on the other hand, were tolerated in Venice solely on condition of maintaining the essential moneylending establishments in which the tender conscience of the Serenissima would not allow any Christian to engage. They were not permitted to dabble in trade, however much they desired to do so; and the only occupation legally open to them beside that of moneylending was dealing in second-hand clothes. The other two categories, on the other hand, were specifically prohibited, in their periodical *condotte,* or licences, from engaging in either of these two callings. This very strong legal differentiation between the two classes continued until the close of the seventeenth century. Hence, by the fact of his engaging in the profession of financier, and of making Antonio a loan, it is perfectly obvious that Shylock must have belonged to the *Nazione Tedesca*—the German nation.

The variety of pledges which Venetian Jews accumulated in their hands in the course of business was bewildering. All the treasures of palaces along the Grand Canal, from roof to cellar, sometimes succumbed to the magnet of the Ghetto. They were well known to have in their possession a splendid assortment of gems and jewelry, so much so that sumptuary laws were necessary to put a check on the amount worn. Shakespeare's picture of the nature and extent of Jessica's depredations in her father's house is absolutely true to life in this respect. And it would be far from unlikely that a rich Jewish moneylender would have "in readiness" among his unredeemed pledges a "page's suit," in which his errant daughter might disguise herself for the purpose of flight.[3] In this, as in other respects, Shakespeare's intuition has enabled him to sketch in trivial details with such remarkable fidelity as to render it quite conceivable that (as has been conjectured) he knew Italy at first hand from a visit with the English players in 1593.

The fact that Shylock belonged to the German "nation" does not imply that he was of German birth, or even of immediate German origin; though his relations with Frankfort, where he had bought the ring stolen by Jessica, render this hypothesis possible. The *Nazione Tedesca,* as we have seen, was the oldest in establishment of all sections of the Jewish community in Venice, dating back by Shakespeare's day for a full century. From the very beginning it had comprised, not only immigrants from across the Alps, but also native, semi-autochthonous, Italian elements: and by now it was fully assimilated to the dominant culture of the country and of the city. Indeed, whereas the Levantines and Ponentines spoke Spanish or Portuguese amongst themselves, car-

---

3 Similarly, Ben Jonson's Sir Politick Would-Be, within the first week of his landing at Venice:

"I had read Contarene, took me a house,
Dealt with my Jews to furnish it with movables"—

a characteristic profession of theirs in Venice, facilitated by their accumulations of second-hand commodities and unredeemed pledges. For a case in point, see the contemporary *Travels of Peter Wendy,* p. 92.

rying on a great part of their communal business in those languages, the *Nazione Tedesca* had, for the most part, completely abandoned the last relic of their ancestral German and used Italian for all ordinary purposes. There were, of course, some arrivals of more recent date, but the latter followed willy-nilly the fashion predominant in the Ghetto. Shylock was therefore, in all probability, a native. It is obvious, indeed, that Shakespeare did not consider him a foreigner; had he done so, the temptation of making him speak a broken English, like Dr. Caius in *The Merry Wives of Windsor,* would have been irresistible.

It is true, on the other hand, that Shylock is not a citizen. Shakespeare makes this fact absolutely plain:

> It is enacted in the laws of Venice
> If it be proved against an alien,
> That, by direct or indirect attempts,
> He seek the life of any citizen . . .

With reference to this crucial passage, it must be borne in mind that the Jew of the Ghetto period was considered something less than a native of the country, even if he were born there. It is remarkable, and it is perhaps something more than a coincidence, that this was nowhere given such precise juridical expression as it was in Venice. The attempts made there so consistently to exclude the Jews from economic life were based upon the assumption that the Jews were, in fact, aliens, however long they and their fathers before them had resided under the protection of the Lion of St. Marco. Indeed, as late as the last decades of the eighteenth century, it was expressly laid down in their recurrent *condotte* that "the Jews of Venice, and of the State, or any other Jew, cannot claim nor enjoy any right of Citizenship." Juridically, Shylock was therefore an alien, whether born in Venice or no.

ii

Having thus decided upon his ancestry, it is possible to go even a little further and to state the precise situation of "the next turning of all, on the left," where he lived. The Ghetto at Venice was a commodious area, capable of giving accommodation (with an unconscionable degree of over-crowding) to as many as five thousand souls. It consisted of streets, and alleys and squares, leading all the way from the Canarregio to the Rio S. Girolamo. But, in Shakespeare's day, it was rigorously divided off into districts. The "Ponen-tines" and the "Levantines" were supposed to live in the Ghetto Vecchio, or Old Foundry, which had been set aside as an exclusive place of residence for them in 1514. The *Nazione Tedesca* were confined to the *Ghetto Nuovo*—that same area, surrounded on all sides by water and thus easily cut off from the outside world, to which they had been first relegated in 1516 (the *Ghetto Nuovissimo,* the last exten-sion, had not yet come into existence). It is true that the two areas were contiguous; but the two ethnic elements which inhabited them remained quite distinct. Thus, for example, when in 1586 a tide of migration set in from the crowded *Ghetto Nuovo* to the more ample Levantine quar-ter, the local authorities (who were responsible for seeing that the rents of all the houses, occupied or unoccupied, were punctually paid) intervened with a menace of excom-munication to stop the movement; and in 1609 the assistance of the civil authorities was invoked to force the "German" Jews back into their own overcrowded district. There can be no doubt, accordingly, that Shylock, as a moneylender and therefore one of the *Nazione Tedesca,* lived in the *Ghetto Nuovo*—a broad square, with ramshackle houses seek-ing vertically the expansion which they were unable to ob-tain laterally. It should be added that, owing to the oppressive restrictions which continued to prevail until the Napoleonic era, Shylock would have got into severe trouble had he actually left the Ghetto at night to have supper with Bassanio; while Launcelot Gobbo was wise in quitting his service before his misdemeanor was known to the authorities, who sternly prohibited the employment of Christians by Jews in a subordinate capacity, under whatever pretext.

iii

Even as to dress, it is possible to speak with a certain degree of confidence. Shakespeare presumably knew of the institution of the Jewish badge, intended to mark off the Jew for contumely from all other men. It was, indeed, all but universal in Europe in his day; and contemporary visitors to Germany or Italy or the South of France brought back detailed descriptions of it, as one of the most characteristic features of the Jewish Quarter.

One of the nineteenth-century stage Shylocks wore it in the shape of the two tables of stone. This, however, was a purely English invention, enforced in the reign of Henry III and Edward I prior to the expulsion of 1290. Other producers have preferred a yellow circle attached to the cloak, such as we see in contemporary German prints. But, in Venice (as in other Italian cities) the Jewish badge had its own history and its own tradition. At the beginning it had indeed been in the universal form of a circle of yellow cloth the size of a small loaf, which had to be sewn on the breast of the outer garment. This was not considered sufficiently prominent. Hence, at a later period, every Jew had to wear a yellow bonnet, or one covered with material of that color. But ultimately, at the close of the sixteenth century, the statutory hue was changed to red—a convention which continued to prevail until the fall of the Serenissima. For the Levantine merchants, indeed, who were under a different control, the distinctive badge remained as before, and they could be distinguished by the yellow turbans which they wore. Shylock, however, was a *Tedesco* by nation, as we have seen. By Shakespeare's time the change of hue had already come about, as far as they were concerned. A traveller of the following century describes the "badge" as a hat covered with crimson cloth, lined and edged with black; while the poor used a waxed material instead. Shylock certainly did not belong to the poorer classes; and it is a headgear of the former description which he must have worn. It will be remembered how, according to Evelyn's account (certainly not *vero,* but admirably *ben trovato*), the same color prevailed for the purpose in Rome, until one day a short-sighted cardinal mistook a red-hatted stranger for a fellow prince of the Church, and saluted him accordingly.

As for the rest of the costume, it is not easy to be quite so precise. What, exactly, was the "Jewish gaberdine" on which Messer Antonio spat? One cannot be over-definite on this point: unless Shakespeare had some vague idea of the *Tallith* or "praying-shawl," which is, however, worn only during prayer. The Levantine merchants are known to have continued to wear their flowing Oriental robes. The "Ponentines," for the most part polished refugees from Spain and Portugal, were probably dressed in full contemporary fashion, excepting for the fact that they were not permitted to bear swords. The rest of the population were a little less fashionable. Their clothing was not outlandish, however, nor did they wear any special garments. One may imagine them, probably, dressed for the most part in the style of the day before yesterday, but not, on the whole, in such a way as to attract special attention. Generally, though not (contrary to the ordinary impression) universally, they would be bearded. Shylock was notoriously so;

indeed, it was on his beard that Antonio had "voided his rheum," thereby arousing his rancor in the first instance.[4] Nevertheless, the inhabitants of the Venetian Ghetto were not by any means unprepossessing: Thomas Coryat, only a few years after, was surprised at the number of "elegant and sweet-featured" persons whom he found there. As for Jessica, she may well have been dressed in the height of contemporary female elegance. Coryat spoke of the Ghetto belles, "some as beautiful as I ever I saw," who excelled English countesses for the splendor of their raiment and had serving-wenches to hold up their trains. However, if she ever went outside the Ghetto, she would have had to cover her head with a kerchief of the same crimson hue as her father's hat.

iv

"Go, Tubal, and meet me at our Synagogue." It is not difficult to say what synagogue is intended. Obviously, it is not the Spanish Synagogue, at present the show-place of the Venetian Ghetto, in which sentimental tourists think of Shylock and of Jessica. This, indeed, dates back in its present form to the period subsequent to Shakespeare's death, having been remodelled in 1635 by Longhena, architect of Santa Maria della Salute. In any case, Shylock, as a "German" Jew, would not have frequented it. He would have attended one of the "Ashkenazi" Synagogues, where the service was carried out according to his ancestral tradition. Of these, those two which were in existence in his day are still standing, though no longer regularly opened for service;

---

4 From the context, it appears to be fully within the bounds of possibility that it was Shylock's beard which Shakespeare had in mind as the "Jewish gaberdine."

"You . . . spit upon my Jewish gaberdine . . .
You, that did void your rheum upon my beard. . . ."

the *Scuola Grande Tedesca,* founded in 1529, and the *Scuola Canton,* founded in 1532, side by side in a corner of the *Ghetto Nuovo.* It was in one of these that Shylock must have worshipped, and in which, if anywhere, his restless spirit must be sought today.

With this architectural detail, we may finish the picture of the historic Shylock. We are to imagine a bearded figure, soberly dressed save for his crimson hat, living in the *Ghetto Nuovo* at Venice. By ancestry, he was a German, though probably belonging to a family which had long been resident under the protection of the Lion of St. Marco. It is hardly to be doubted that he spoke excellent Italian, though possibly with a slightly guttural accent and with a few peculiar turns of phrase. Professionally he was a moneylender, his activities being regulated by the terms of the periodical *condotte* of his "nation," renewed every ten years. Incidentally, he sometimes came into possession of a variety of second-hand wares, as well as precious stones, though traffic in them was not his main activity. As, according to legend, Pope remarked, with reference to Macklin's production, in the most execrable couplet in English literature:

> "This is the Jew
> That Shakespeare drew."

17. SUMPTUARY LAWS[1]

i

THE problem of the Marriage Magnificent, the Barmitzvah Beautiful, and the Berith Bounteous, is not by
any means new or an essentially Occidental one. In every
age and in every clime, some Jews have tended to indulge
themselves at times, on occasions of domestic rejoicing, in
a manner which the more sensitive and more sensible regarded as tactless, and which, besides, invariably led to the
investment of a disproportionate amount of their savings in
jewelry and adornments for their women-folk. But there
was one great difference between former times and these.
Once upon a time (it seems strangely remote nowadays), a
Jewish community signified more than an institution for
supervising burials and public worship, and the Jewish
communal authorities wielded a power which was little less
than absolute. At that time, they were not disposed to sit
with folded arms while a minority of their coreligionists, by
their ostentatious mode of living, brought jealousy and perhaps danger upon the whole body. There was, however, one
remedy.

The Sumptuary Law, in limitation of personal extravagance, was among the commonplaces of medieval legislation. It was natural for the Jews (fortified, indeed, by
talmudic example) to imitate their neighbors in this, as
in much else. From ancient Palestine down to modern

---

1 Originally published in *Jewish Chronicle Supplement*, April, 1934. The
basis for this study was my article, "Sumptuary Laws of the Community of
Carpentras" (from Ms. material in the Library of Columbia University,
N. Y.), which I published in the *Jewish Quarterly Review*, N. S., XVIII
(1928), pp. 357-383, and an exceptionally rich collection of Italian *Prag-
matiche* which I have since amassed in my own library.

Europe, accordingly, the story is almost continuous of how the Jewish authorities endeavored to check extravagance among their coreligionists, both for the living and for the dead. The persecuted communities of the Rhineland were at one in this respect with their remote descendants in Poland and Lithuania and their happier brethren in Italy. The Jews of Spain submitted to such restrictions in the days of their prosperity, before the shadow of persecution had fallen athwart the Peninsula; and their grandchildren imitated them in their far-flung havens of refuge from Salonika to Hamburg. At the close of the seventeenth century, inspired perhaps by the example of Louis XIV, in his later days of piety and obscurantism, the Community of Metz laid down, in a series of no less than five enactments, new regulations to be observed by its members. The regulations were so minute that they led to the bringing of a lawsuit by certain recalcitrants, and so little understood that even the benevolent Abbé Grégoire could say that individuals had been threatened with unheard-of penalties for the crime of desiring to be clean, or of wearing a little powder on their hair. In the Community of Nice (which one hardly associates to-day with restriction of extravagance, but which was then a relatively unimportant port in the Kingdom of Sardinia), a similar code was derisively called the *Takkanah di biscottini,* because it went so far as to limit the quantity of biscuits which might be offered on the occasion of any domestic celebration.

This, however, missed the whole point of the regulations, which is illustrated, in language that would apply equally well even at the present day, in the preamble to the Sumptuary Code enacted at Carpentras (one of the Four Communities under Papal rule, not far from Avignon) in 1712:

"Seeing the efforts of heads of families to procure their sustenance and to earn the wherewithal to pay the taxes and impositions incident upon each one; seeing moreover how, when occasion arises for any religious festivity which is incumbent upon them (such as a circumcision or a wedding), they indulge in expenditure greater than they can afford, so that there is trembling in place of joy by reason of the drain of their money, making them limit their household expenditure and their payments for (communal) dues . . ."

On another occasion, the preface is even more explicit:-

"We, undersigned, the representatives and Wardens of the Community (may the Lord protect it!), seeing the envy of each man for his neighbor and how each one endeavors to show his superiority over his neighbor, so that there is no distinction between rich and poor, all desiring to appear men of eminence and of wealth in their apparel and the adornments of their womenfolk, without being able to sustain the expense; in consequence whereof they are brought low and borrow needlessly from Gentiles, and become impoverished . . ."

Moreover, it was impossible to overlook

". . . the envy and hatred of the Gentiles, who fix their gaze upon us . . . and their anger does not cease, when they see the children of Israel going forth each one in his raiment, according to the good hand of the Lord upon him . . ."

An obvious question which arises is, how these codes could be enforced. Ghetto society, however, knew sanctions of which our sophisticated age is innocent. Simultaneously with the enactment of these regulations, a sentence of excommunication was promulgated against those who should deliberately contravene them. No one might visit the recalcitrant or speak to him or do business with him; he could not attend synagogue, have his children initiated into the Covenant of Abraham, or even be buried in consecrated ground if he should die. In the narrow atmosphere of the Ghetto these penalties were sufficiently formidable to bring the most headstrong to his senses. Sometimes, too, the civil authorities took a hand and inflicted condign punishment upon transgressors.

ii

Nowhere, of course, was Jewish life more elaborately organized than in Italy. Here, the Sumptuary Law was a commonplace. Almost every community had its own code or *Pragmatica* which was periodically revised and occasionally published. The community of Mantua, for example (where apparently the standard of education was high), issued Hebrew broadsides every seven years, which were affixed to the walls of the synagogues and other public places, and gave the housewife detailed instructions as to what she might or might not wear, or provide at table on special occasions during the ensuing period. Other communities (Rome, Ancona, Reggio, Modena, etc.) issued their regulations in Italian, in pamphlet form. Venice, curiously enough, never printed anything of the sort; but every now and again the leaders of the community issued their ukase, intimating what they had decided in view of the latest aberrations of fashion. Thus, by the Sumptuary Laws of 1696-7, it was forbidden for any person to wear brocade or lace of gold, whether at the neck or wrists, on any ordinary occasion. No one was to wear more than two rings at a time. The amount which a man might expend on his periwig was limited to twelve ducats; while a woman might not exceed four ducats for a fan, or five for a muff. (Special provision was made, however, for masquerades, when persons went out wearing fancy dress!) On occasions of domestic cele-bration, a maximum of two ducats might be spent on fresh flowers, whether for wearing in the head-dress or for adorning the house; and a total of twenty guests might be invited, exclusive of relatives who had come expressly from other cities. In Carpentras, restriction went further. Only twelve guests might be invited to the banquet on the occasion of a *Berith*,[1] and no more than sixteen exclusive of the Reader, the Preacher and the Best Man) to that on the occasion of a wedding; while the last bachelor party, or *collation*, which the bridegroom had hitherto been accustomed to give to signalize his loss of freedom, was henceforth forbidden entirely.

iii

To give a better idea of the scope and detail of some of these Sumptuary Codes, a selection of the chapter-headings of the *Pragmatica* enacted by the Rome community in 1726 is here appended:—

I. Dancing and similar recreations are prohibited.

II. Occasions when such pastimes are permitted.

III. Prohibition of entertainments, &c., and what is allowed.

IV. What may be given to guests on the day of a Circumcision. . . .

VI. Whom the Godmothers may take with them, and how they must conduct themselves when they go in their carriage.

VII. Prohibition of gifts on this occasion, and what may be spent for the Cradle Gift.

VIII. Limitation of gifts on the occasion of betrothals.

IX. What the bride may present to the bridegroom [only the *Arba Kanforth*, a skull-cap and *Tallith*-bag—the whole not to exceed ten ducats in value.]

X. What may be given on the occasion of weddings.

---

[1] Circumcision, literally, "covenant."

XI. Limitation of the expenditure on and value of the *Tallith* . . .

XV. Entertainments which are permitted, and the persons who may be invited to them on the occasion of betrothals and marriages.

XVI. Who may be invited to the feast on the occasion of a Circumcision.

XVII. Viands which are permitted on such occasions.

XVIII. Entertainment permitted to the *Hatan Torah* and *Hatan Bereshith,* and the method to be followed on such occasions.

XIX. Regulation regarding the clothing and head-dress of women . . .

XXI. Limitation of the value of such articles of costume as are permitted.

XXIII. The times when any sort of costume is allowed [e.g. when worn by the bride and bridegroom on the occasion of their wedding, &c.].

XXIV. Fans with silver handles, and prayer-books with solid silver covers are prohibited.

XXV. Limitation of the jewelry permitted to women.

XXVI. Reform of the clothing, &c., of men.

XXVII. Prohibition for women to go with the breast uncovered, or to attend comedies and parties [excepting in the company of their husbands or close relatives].

XXVIII. Prohibition of gambling, and definition of the days on which it is permitted [Hanukkah, Purim, &c.].

XXIX. Limitation of expenses on the occasion of a death.

From these terse headings, it is possible to see how minutely the whole of daily existence was covered by these regulations, and what a vast amount of light they throw upon the social life of the Ghetto. The *Pragmatica* of Ancona, of 1766, goes sometimes into even more picturesque detail, specifying the number of torches which might accompany the bridegroom when he went to visit his bride; the amount of money which might be spent on his present of flowers or on the illumination of the marriage-contract; what the masqueraders might wear on Purim; and forbidding sweets or coins to be thrown down from the windows on the bridal *cortège*.

iv

It will be noted that nothing has been said hitherto with regard to the Barmitzvah festivities. The reason is very obvious—that this ceremony was then regarded as being of very minor importance, no special celebrations being associated with it. There is, however, a fugitive reference to it in the Ancona code referred to just above. It is perhaps worth while quoting the entire passage, so as to give a more precise idea of the system as a whole. The clause relating to the unrestricted entertainment of the poor, printed here in italics, is especially worthy of attention.

XXXII. *Regarding the Banquets or Entertainments permitted on various functions, and of the sweetmeats to be given on them and on the entry of boys into their fourteenth year [known as Bar Mitzvah].*

It is forbidden to make more than one entertainment or banquet, whether in the ceremony of betrothal or of circumcision (called *Milah*) or of the Redemption of the First-Born; similarly in that before the bride leaves her father's house. At weddings, two only shall be permitted. In all of these entertainments, only eighteen persons may be invited, men and women included. However, this number need not comprise the family of the house in which the entertainment takes place—father, mother, children-in-law, grandparents, step-father and mother, brothers and sisters.

In such entertainments, it shall not be permitted to serve more than two sweets or syrups, besides marzipan cakes and confetti (sugar-almonds), as above specified. *However, on the occasion of a betrothal it shall be permitted to arrange a feast for the poor who do not contribute to the communal taxation, without limitation of number,* in addition to the two mentioned above. On other occasions, and on the eve of the betrothal, the guests may number only two, in addition to the relations above-mentioned; children below thirteen years, visitors from other cities, and six servants (other than those belonging to the household), not being included in this number.

On the occasion when boys enter their fourteenth year (known as *Barmitzvah*), no entertainment may be given. All that is permitted is to serve coffee and a biscuit to those who go to present their congratulations at the house."

It all seems very petty, no doubt, to our enlightened age. Yet our fathers were wiser than their supercilious descendants give them credit for being. They were aware of the ruinous consequences which sometimes followed in the train of competitive magnificence. They knew very well the discredit, and even danger, which the ostentation of a small group of Jews might bring upon the mass of their coreligionists. The Ghetto no doubt had its failures; but, in that preeminently bourgeois environment, they knew how to cope with bourgeois weaknesses which are today certainly no less rampant than they were three centuries ago. The study of the old methods and the old ideals may well be useful even after this interval of time.

18. FORCED BAPTISMS[1]

A Contribution to the History of Jewish Persecution

i

ON the night of Tuesday, December 9, 1783, the Roman ghetto was wrapped in its usual outward calm. There was indeed, a semi-festive air abroad, for the day just past had been the New Moon of Kislev 5544 according to the Jewish reckoning. The stillness was broken by an unwonted noise. The Gate of Severus, the principal of those which segregated the ghetto from the outer world, was thrown open by its keepers and a coach attended by an ample escort rumbled in over the cobbled streets. At this unusual disturbance windows and doors were thrown open and people came out into the streets, hastily putting on their heads the yellow hats of shame which by a recent ordinance they had to wear even in the privacy of their own quarter. The coach came to a halt and its occupants, a judge and a notary of the Vicariate, gave a brusque order for the rabbis and lay heads of the community to be brought before them.

By this time the nature of their errand had been imagined. These were the darkest days of the Roman Jewry. Pius VI (1775-1799), the occupant of the Papal throne, had outdone any of his predecessors in his treatment of the Jews,

---

[1] This is a combination of two articles: "The Forced Baptisms of 1783 at Rome and the Community of London," which appeared originally in the *Jewish Quarterly Review*, N.S., vol. XVI (1925), pp. 105-116; and "Forced Baptisms in Italy: A Contribution to the History of Jewish Persecution," *ibid.*, vol. XXVIII (1936), pp. 117-136. These are rounded off by additional material collected in the course of the controversy with the Roman Catholic Father Day referred to at the close of this essay, which was published in the London *Jewish Guardian* early in 1930.

and his *Editto sopra gli Ebrei,* published in the year of his accession, had marked for them the depths of degradation. All the oppressions and indignities suffered under former rulers were now confirmed and accentuated. Greatest and most inhuman of all was the practice of forced baptisms, first systematized and given full legal authority by Benedict XIV as recently as 1747. The pretexts for it were so flimsy as to be almost negligible.

There were then in the ghetto two orphans of good family, brother and sister, aged eleven and seven years respectively, living peacefully in the house of their maternal grandmother. Many years before, a great aunt (sister of their father's father) had become converted to Christianity and had married a Gentile. Her son, now a grown man, had suddenly developed great concern for the spiritual welfare of his little kinsmen and had expressed the desire that they should be brought into the Christian fold for the salvation of their souls. The principal of the House of Catechumens accordingly demanded the immediate surrender of the children in the name of the Pope; and his present representatives were furnished with written authority to that effect, peremptorily ordering their submission without giving any reason. This was an innovation. The very existence of the apostate and her son had been forgotten in the ghetto, and no pretext for the demand could be thought of. The leaders of the community pointed out that no one outside the ghetto could have any conceivable claim to authority over the children, who still had living not only their grandmother but also two maternal aunts and a first cousin on their father's side. They pleaded that the orphans should be left untouched, as had been the case on former occasions, until the matter had been fully enquired into; and they offered themselves as surety, in their persons and property, that the children would be forthcoming if the decision went against them. When this was refused, they begged that they should at least be given time to communicate with the principal of the House of Catechumens in order to ascertain his reasons.

The two emissaries remained obdurate and ordered their victims to be surrendered immediately. By now, they were no longer to be found. Their relatives and friends, on hearing of the fate in store for them, which to them was worse than death, had hastened to hide them. This was of no avail, as the emissaries instructed those of their escort to seize as hostages any children whom they could find. The order was carried out ruthlessly, and it seemed that scores would be sacrificed in order to save the two. Nothing was left but to give the unfortunate orphans up to their fate. The carriage lumbered out again with its prey through the prison gate to the freer air of the outer world amidst the tears and lamentations of the inhabitants. The Jews of Rome were less than human if menaces and perhaps even stones were not intermingled with the groanings which saluted the loss of their dear ones.

No time was lost in reporting at the House of Catechumens the nature of the reception which the mission had received and the reason for the delay in its return. On the next day an armed force entered the ghetto and arrested the ringleaders of the evening before. No fewer than sixty young men were dragged off to prison, where they were put in chains and treated with the utmost cruelty. Some were redeemed by their families by the payment of large sums of money. Those for whom this was impossible were left in their dungeons, suffering from increasing ill-treatment, until the community as a whole was able to arrange for their collective ransom at a heavy price. It was not until the eve of Passover, four and a half months later, that they were released. The two children were submitted to the usual cruel temptations in the House of Catechumens until, seventeen days later, they were baptized. The official report was that this had been of their own free will; but it was rumored that the elder of the two had said that he could never believe in a faith for the propagation of which such methods had to be used.

The tragedy was at an end; but the matter could not be allowed to rest there. Hitherto forced baptism of this sort had been possible only if the person making the request could be presumed to have some especial claim to authority over the victim. In the present case that pretext could hardly be used, as the relationship was distant and several nearer relatives were still living. If this were allowed to pass without protest, there was no knowing where the affair would end. If it is true that from 1634 to 1790 no less than 2430 Jews had been baptized in Rome, there was hardly a person in the ghetto who did not have some relative in the bosom of the Catholic Church, and no one could consider his children safe. The leaders of the community consulted a number of well-known lawyers upon the question. They replied unanimously that the seizure of the two orphans had been absolutely illegal even according to the harsh practice which had previously obtained and the ordinances of preceding Popes. It was too late, indeed, to get the children restored. Once they had been baptized, whether by fair means or foul, the Catholic Church would not renounce its hold. But nevertheless, they were of the opinion that immediate steps should be taken to prevent this from becoming a precedent for future occasions. Other prominent Roman citizens friendly toward the Jews were in agreement with this view. They advised that a petition should be presented to the Pope, showing him how the present case was against all precedent and contrary to the decisions of his predecessors. If possible, he should be persuaded to have an inquiry made into the question through the medium of the Inquisition, to which

should be referred any doubtful instances which might arise
in the future. Above all, the persons claimed should be
suffered to remain in the shelter of the ghetto until their case
was determined. Thus some sort of restraint would be put
on the nefarious zeal of the principal of the House of Catechumens. The Pope was petitioned in the sense suggested;
and the community took advantage of the opportunity to
give utterance to their other grievances—the insanitary and
exiguous place of abode assigned to them, the prohibition
to engage in the liberal professions, their material and moral
degradation. This led to the appointment of a commission
to examine into their condition. A memorial was subsequently presented to it by twelve friendly Christian advocates
(comprising no doubt those consulted by the community
in its trouble), in which the grievances of the Jews were
more amply exposed and suggestions were made for the
amelioration of their position. Nothing, however, ensued;
and above all the major injustice which had given rise to
the petition remained untouched. Though such a blatant
piece of tyranny was perhaps never repeated, the forced baptisms continued at intervals for nearly a century, until the
last days of Papal Rome.

ii

The repercussions of these events were not confined to
the banks of the Tiber. The news-letters in the various
Italian cities reported the case as a triumph for the faith;
and the intelligence was not confined to Italy alone. The
story has hitherto been repeated with many inaccuracies
(even as regards the date!) upon the strength of a report
in a contemporary German periodical. The present account
is based, excepting for a few minor details, upon the more
reliable authority of a Hebrew document of Italian proven-

ance in the possession of the writer—a closely written quarto sheet in which the event is described in detail. No place or names are given, but it is obvious from the date and other details to what it refers. Though the language is not flawless, it is on the whole a fine and graphic piece of historical composition and deserves preservation if on that score alone. It is apparently an excerpt from the letter of appeal which is known to have been sent all over Europe, written, as it seems, some time in the second half of 1784. We know one to have reached the community of Berlin.

That one should have been sent to the Sephardic congregation in London is only to be expected. Apparently it was not only moral support which was asked for, but also some assistance in bearing the heavy financial burden entailed in the release of the unfortunates who had been imprisoned for their opposition to the kidnapping, as well as for the payment of the lawyers and the expenses incidental upon the petition to the Pope. The London community, however, though lavish enough in their sympathy, could promise nothing more. The siege of Gibraltar had only recently ended, and the fugitives from that place who had arrived in England in complete destitution monopolized the charitable activities of the congregation. Moreover (and this may have been a more cogent reason), the previous relations with Italy had not augured well, since a heavy loan made to the perennially needy community of Venice half a century before had not been repaid, as it has not to the present day. The reply to Rome was accordingly couched in a polite but firm negative.

Nevertheless, this correspondence was not wholly lacking in result. It was the first direct intercourse between the two communities; and it led to advances of a more ambitious nature. On June 2, 1787, the Jews of Rome presented a petition to the Pope complaining of the impossibility of bearing up under the weight of the financial burden to which they were subjected, and making various suggestions for its alleviation. They must have met on this occasion, as on so many others, with a rebuff. It seems, as though in consequence of this, the presidents of the community, Tranquillo del Monte and Salamone Ambron, had the venturesome idea of arranging a wholesale immigration to some place where they could obtain more favorable treatment. They wrote accordingly to London, asking what privileges were enjoyed by their English co-religionists. The ultimate idea seems to have been to apply to the King, whom they considered in the light of some petty Italian ruler, asking for definite concessions, in guarantee of their settlement, no doubt in return for a monetary payment. As may be imagined, the reply was this time cold in the extreme. The Romans were told that they should not judge England by the criterion of other places, since its government was a limited monarchy in which the benevolence of Parliament as well as of the King would be necessary, and that the Jews enjoyed in the country no privileges beyond those possessed by other foreigners—the right of property and the free exercise of their religion.

iii

The episode of 1783 which has been described in the foregoing pages was only one, and perhaps not even the most objectionable, of an entire series of such outrages which continued down to a period almost within living memory. For, of the abuses from which the Jews of Italy, and of the Papal States in particular, suffered during the dark period which was ushered in for them by the Counter-Reformation, none weighed more harshly than the practice of forced baptisms. This had indeed been condemned on frequent occasions by successive Popes of a more enlightened age, but with increasing reserves. When, in 1543, at the instigation of Ignatius Loyola, Pope Paul III instituted the House of Catechumens at Rome, he thus laid the foundation of what was afterwards to develop into an intolerable abuse. Henceforth, any Jew over whom the Church could devise the slightest semblance of claim could be carried off to this place (maintained, by a refinement of cruelty, out of a special levy laid upon the various synagogues), where he was made to appreciate the spiritual advantages of the dominant faith. Consent was indeed necessary before the baptism of an adult: but a few days or weeks of incarceration in the House of Catechumens was sufficient to break all but the strongest wills. By the eighteenth century, the system received semi-official sanction: and thereafter the abuses continued in an unending succession down to the last days of the temporal rule of the Popes. The merest caricature of a ceremony performed with ditch-water by some drunken ruffian or superstitious servant-girl, or the wish of a converted relative with the slightest claim to authority over the victim, was sufficient to cause children to be torn from their parents' arms, and some even who were no longer children to be dragged to the font by brute force.

A few examples will best illustrate the outrages which occurred. In 1602, one Baruch Ambron was seized by a certain priest and handed over to a person who endeavored to persuade him to be baptized. Three days later, in his desperation, he threw himself out of a window, but escaped with his life. Transferred to another instructor, he managed to flee back into the Ghetto, but was brought back. At last, after another fortnight of persuasion, Faith was at last triumphant and he consented to receive baptism. Two years later, the four children of Rabbi Joshua Ascarelli became converted, after withstanding persuasion with a fortitude remarkable for their age. One day, some time later, in friendly conversation with a Dominican friar, a Roman Jew had jokingly offered to have one of his children baptized if the Pope himself would act as godfather. His foolish pleasantry cost him, not one, but two of his children, of whom the younger was seized out of her cradle. This was more than even the downtrodden Roman Jews could bear, and brought about a veritable insurrection in the Ghetto. One evening, at the beginning of 1762, the son of a Carpentras rabbi was leaving the synagogue when he was pounced upon by a recent neophyte of infamous reputation who summarily performed over him a parody of the ceremony of initiation into the Christian faith. This sufficed to have the child dragged away from his home and brought up as a Christian. On this occasion, the Papal Curia itself condemned the action on receiving an appeal, and the culprit was summarily punished. So far as the victim was concerned, however, nothing was done, it being held that the sacrament of baptism was inviolable even when conferred under such circumstances: and he was brought up in the Christian faith. Local legend still recounts how he died many years afterwards in Rome as a Cardinal—a sort of psychological compensatory which not infrequently figures in Jewish folklore in such cases. (The best-known instance is the famous legend of the kidnapped Elhanan, "The Jewish Pope.")

The instances that now follow are all based on manuscript or record sources found by or in the collection of the present writer.

iv

At Ferrara a House of Neophytes was established by the Bishop, Palolo Leoni, in 1584—very shortly before the beginning of the papal régime. It was noteworthy for the magnificent Hebrew library with which it was shortly afterwards endowed. In the eighteenth century, it reached the height of its influence, as is shown by the contemporary pamphlet containing its regulations. This, approved by the Cardinal Archbishop, Marcello Crescenzi, carefully laid down the conditions regarding the Congregation, the Prior, the Under Prior, the Visitors, the Chancellors, the Minister or Agent, the Custodian, etc. One of the duties of the last-mentioned functionary was to see that the denizens prayed for the conversion of their former brethren in disbelief, and that no Jew passed in the neighborhood while any person was under instruction. The Catechumens, on the other hand, were not to send or to receive letters, or to look out of the windows. In case any of them expressed the desire to return to the ghetto, he should be retained for at least forty days afterwards, in order to see whether he could be prevailed upon to change his mind. In the meanwhile, he was not to be allowed to receive his food from his fellow-Jews, but had to eat whatever was given to him: the expense, of course, being defrayed by his former co-religionists. Detailed regulations were laid down governing the "offering" by the Catechumens of their children or some other person over whom they had some claim to authority, who could thereupon be kidnapped from the ghetto. This vexed question had, as a matter of fact, very recently been the subject of a formal declaration at Rome by Pope Benedict XIV, in consequence of a recent case in Rome, when an apostate grandmother had "claimed" her grandchildren for baptism. It was this Pope who, four years previously, had first systematized this abuse and given it legal authority.

Another shameful episode took place at Ancona in 1735. The Lenten Sermons here were delivered that year by Dr. Paolo Medici, a not unscholarly convert, author of many books and an energetic proselytizer. Advantage was taken of his presence to designate him to preach, Sabbath by Sabbath, the conversionist sermons prescribed by Pope Gregory VIII in 1577-84; and the Jews were compelled to come to hear him. Among them was a young man, aged about thirty, bearing the somewhat improbable name of Sabbato Nachamù, who had formerly been in the employment of the community of Corfu, had studied in Jerusalem, and laid claim to the title of Rabbi. The latter took advantage of the fact that on Fridays the rabbis did not have the usual discussion in their "Academy" to put himself in touch with the preacher.

The result was seen on the following day, when, immediately after Medici's sermon to the Jews, Nachamù arose and made public profession of Christianity. There is no call to question his sincerity; it is the sequel which revolts every feeling of decency and humanity. Nachamù was married —he alleged that he had come to Ancona to fetch his family to Jerusalem, where he had some expectation of receiving a salaried appointment. Accordingly, he took the first opportunity to "offer" to the Church, not only a son of his of three and a half years, but also the child which his wife was shortly expected to bear.

A force was immediately despatched into the ghetto, where, after a little difficulty, the boy was discovered, hidden away in the house of one of the synagogue beadles. Whereas the father was sent to Rome, to be baptized in state, the child was admitted to the Christian faith immediately "lest he should perish without having received Holy Baptism, as a result of being set to travel at such tender years." Meanwhile, the expectant mother was torn away from her own family and co-religionists, and placed in a Christian hospital. She resolutely refused to follow her husband's example. However, immediately her child was born, it was taken out of her arms and baptized forthwith. Henceforth, she had no claim nor share in it. Medici wrote an account of the episode (translated also into foreign languages), using it with singular obtuseness and lack of imagination to demonstrate "how great is the mercy of our most pitiful God."

The same year witnessed another episode of a similar nature at Cento, not far from Ferrara. There had just returned to this place a woman named Mazal-tob Olivetti, daughter of a local Jewish householder named Jacob Olivetti, and wife of one Samuel Ascoli, of Urbino, a recent neophyte living in the House of Catechumens at Rome. The authorities here learned from Ascoli that he had left his wife pregnant, and instigated him to "claim" the child that was to be born. After a vain search at Urbino and Pesaro, she was at last traced in her native town, whither she had made her way afoot, pregnant as she was. The authorities at Cento were more humane than at Ancona and allowed her to remain with her family in the ghetto, though under constant supervision. When her hour came, a Christian midwife was sent to be present and supervise. Immediately the child was born, the latter rushed it out of the ghetto and to the Church of S. Biagio, where it was baptized forthwith by the *arciprete,* the well-known littérateur, Girolamo Baruffaldi.

The problem which now arose was how the child could be nursed. This was soon solved: the mother, too, was dragged out of the ghetto and into the House of Catechumens, so that her intentions with regard to baptism might be sounded! This inhumanity might have been spared; for on the following night the baby died—partly, without doubt, in consequence of what it had already been through in its short, unhappy life. That its soul had been saved was, on the other hand, considered a reason for general rejoicing; and the body was given a stately, choral funeral, the procession going out of its way to pass the gates and windows of the ghetto. The mother, not yet in a condition to go home and broken by her sufferings, ultimately consented to submit to baptism, her example being followed in the end, and not without persuasion, by a favorite sister. The ceremony was conducted with the greatest pomp, duly described in contemporary brochures, the officiating priest being Prospero Lambertini, Cardinal Archbishop of Bologna, subsequently Pope Benedict XIV.

Another rare publication, which has hitherto escaped attention, reveals a whole tragi-comedy of the sort in detail. Early in the second half of the eighteenth century (the date must have been approximately 1760), a six-year-old girl living in Padua, named Francesca Vandelli, saw a surgeon summarily baptize a dying infant, saying that this would enable it to enter Paradise. Little Francesca had a Jewish playmate, Regina Salomoni, aged at this time only three. On the next occasion when they met, Francesca informed the other, gravely, that she would not be able to enter Paradise, since she was not baptized. Regina's tears may be imagined. To comfort her, Francesca added that it would be easy enough to remedy matters, and told her how it could be done. The six-year-old then made the three-year-old repeat the Mystery of the Holy Trinity, afterwards taking some water and pouring it over her head, muttering the baptismal formula the whilst. On feeling her hair and face all wet, the infant neophyte began to cry. The other dried her as best she could with a handkerchief, and adjured her not to say a word about this to anybody.

Many years passed. By 1785, both children were grown up and married—Francesca to Francesco Negrini, secretary of the *monte* of Ferrara, and Regina to Leone Bianchini, one of the richest and best known Jews in the ghetto of the same city. Can it be that the two met, and quarreled? However that may be, in November 1785, the former sud-

denly made known (for the quiet of her soul, as she said)
the full story of this infantile episode. The Archbishop of
Ferrara at that time was Cardinal Alessandro Mattei, who
(the city being under the rule of the Holy See) was omni-
potent in matters temporal as well as spiritual. Accordingly,
on the night of November 24th, he summoned Regina
Bianchini and her husband to his palace. The latter was
dismissed almost immediately. The unfortunate wife, on
the other hand, was detained almost as a prisoner, notwithstanding her advanced state of pregnancy.

On the next day, the two women were examined in detail
and a full *compte rendu* was drawn up for submission to
the Pope. Meanwhile, a counter-report was prepared by
Bianchini's advisers in the ghetto and sent to Rome by
express messenger. The juridical points under discussion
narrowed themselves down to the following:

1) Should the deposition of the denunciant be accepted?
2) Was the baptism valid?
3) If the baptism was valid, should its object be
   invited, or forced, to remain a Christian?

At Rome, the discussions were long but inconclusive.
At a special session on December 6, 1785, the Holy Office
examined the question in all its aspects. Though prepared
to accept the denunciant's evidence, it was unable to come
to any decision with regard to the second point—viz., the
validity of the baptism. Accordingly, there was no alternative but to allow the unfortunate Regina Bianchini to return home, though only after giving surety that she would
present herself again if called for. Before dismissal, however,
she was to be "mildly admonished." It is not difficult to
imagine what form these mild admonishments took, or what
pressure was put upon the unfortunate Jewess, during her

weeks of detention, to make her abjure her faith. Fortunately, it is unlikely that the experiment was repeated, since the whole episode was set on record, in all its details, in a little pamphlet published immediately afterwards.[2] The fact that the matter was seriously considered is nevertheless enough to demonstrate the depths of the degradation and persecution to which the Jews of the Papal States could be subjected.

Very similar to this was another Ferrara episode which took place shortly after the restoration of the old régime, in 1817. On February 22nd of that year, an armed force was sent by order of the Archbishop's tribunal to the house of Angelo Ancona, where his infant daughter, Alessandra, aged between five and six years, was seized. The pretext for this was that five years previously, when the child was only two months old, she had been baptized clandestinely by her nurse, Maria Facchini (subsequently dismissed for dishonesty). Her excuse for this action was that her charge appeared to be dying; but the family physician, a non-Jew, affirmed that she had never been in the remotest danger of her life. The community sent a deputation to Rome to wait upon the Pope and protest against this outrage, and the Holy Office was instructed to examine the question. Whatever the outcome, the episode caused something like a reign of terror in the Ferrara ghetto. No family could now feel safe. It was impossible to tell when, and after what interval of years, some person who had once been left alone in the house for a few minutes might present himself and levy the most atrocious form of blackmail, to be satisfied only at the price of a beloved child. So abject was the terror that it became necessary for parents to obtain a sworn statement from a nurse or maid-servant, who had been in their em-

---

2 The episode aroused a good deal of attention abroad, being reported at some length even in the English press (e.g., *The World*, a London periodical of the period).

ployment, to the effect that she had never performed an action which might give the Catholic Church the slightest manner of claim on any of their children.

iv

A further category of source-material from which a good deal of information may be derived is the broadside poem which was so often published in honor of the fresh victory gained by the Holy Church. Of these—unknown hitherto to bibliographers, and neglected by historians—there are several in the collection of the present writer: curious relics of a past unhappy age.[3]

As a matter of fact, these triumphant publications sometimes reveal how utterly insubstantial was the victory, and how unscrupulous the means chosen to achieve it. Thus, more than one of them shows that the new soul acquired by the Catholic Church had been "claimed"—virtually kidnaped, that is—by some relative who had previously apostatized. In 1838, for example (according to a Ms. note on the foot of one of these broadsides), a certain Michael Forli had been baptized in Ferrara, assuming the name of Tommaso Calcaleoni. Ultimately, he embraced the ecclesiastical career, being trained for the priesthood in the Archiepiscopal Seminary. In the ghetto (still an established institution at Ferrara), he had a small brother, to whom he laid claim (notwithstanding the fact that their parents, Joseph and Anna Forli, were still living). The poor child was dragged away from home and baptized with great pomp under the name Paolo Calcaleoni. This triumph induced Monseigneur Agostino Peruzzi to compose a couple of sonnets, in which he blandly called attention to the fact that in the ghetto

---

[3] A good many of them are listed and described in the article in the *Jewish Quarterly Review*, vol. xxvii (1936), pp. 117-136, on which the present study is based; the curious reader is recommended to refer to this for further details.

there were two distraught parents, in anguish for their loss (*Iva una coppia in doglia, E forse d'ira in lagrime, smarrita*). The President of the House of Catechumens actually published these effusions, dedicating them to the godfather!

A penciled note at the foot of another poem of 1831 explains the circumstances of the episode. A brother of this neophyte, a boy member of the Ancona family, had fallen very ill. A maid-servant of his parents, who were living in the ghetto of Ferrara, imagined that he was in danger of death and baptized him secretly (obviously, without the use of Holy Water, or recourse to the aid of a priest). Subsequently, the child recovered. Some time afterwards, the maid-servant told the whole story to her confessor. The latter obliged her to give full particulars to the *curia* of the Archbishop, who was at that time Cardinal Odescalchi. The latter's decision was precisely what might have been expected. He ordered the child to be seized from his parents' house, taken away from the ghetto, and handed over to a Christian family to be brought up. It can have been little comfort to the parents that he himself, the Cardinal Archbishop, adopted the child as his son, and before resigning his high office assigned him a certain amount for his upkeep. Some time later, a sister of this unfortunate youth (named Scalchi after his "benefactor"), was herself baptized. The circumstances seem suspicious. It can hardly be doubted that pressure had been put upon her, her brother having perhaps "claimed" her to be kidnaped as he himself had been and introduced willy-nilly to the Christian faith.[4]

---

[4] The subsequent history of Luigi Carlo Scalchi (formerly Angelo Vita Ancona) is interesting. He became a prominent figure in Italian journalism of the age of the *Risorgimento*, editing first *Il Nemico del Diavolo Zoppo* and then (from 1848) *L'Imparziale*, of Rome. He had been baptized at the age of four.

It is not without its significance that the Cardinal Odescalchi took the precaution of foreshortening his surname before bestowing it on this infant proselyte; he was plainly taking precautions against any possibility of confusion with his own family!

V

These last episodes bring us well on towards the second half of the nineteenth century, when, in 1858, the whole of Europe was shocked by the notorious Mortara case.[5] This was the most famous incident of its sort. Edgardo Mortara was child of a well-to-do Jewish family living at Bologna. As a baby, he had suffered (it was afterwards reported) from a serious illness. Fearing that he might die, and his soul suffer eternal damnation, the superstitious servant girl who was acting as his nurse baptized him by stealth with the most ridiculous travesty of the proper ceremony. Four years later, she confessed to a priest what she had done. He reported the matter to Rome, where the Congregation of the Inquisition ordered action to be taken. On June 23, 1858, a force of soldiers went to the house of the Mortara family at ten o'clock at night, and tore the child out of his parents' arms to be brought up in the faith into which he had been so informally received: he was at this time six or seven years of age. A storm of protest swept through Europe; but all availed nothing, excepting to secure the parents one last interview with their child. Modern apologists endeavoured to justify what occurred by calling attention to the breach of the law committed by the Mortara family in having a Christian servant in their employment at all, and by pointing out that on the capture of Rome twelve years later, after having been sedulously kept away from all Jewish influence

---

5 The latest contribution to the literature on this subject is *The Mortara Mystery*, by Father A. F. Day ("Published for the Catholic Guild of Israel by the Catholic Truth Society"), 1930. This little work is the amplification of an article in *The Month* for June 1929, which in turn was occasioned by a controversy with the present writer which began at a public lecture in London and was continued in the columns of *The Jewish Guardian* and elsewhere. When my *Short History of the Jewish People* was published in 1935, Father Day wrote to me indignantly protesting against my statement that Edgardo Mortara was "kidnapped": he was removed from his parents' custody by process of the law!

during the most impressionable years of his life, Edgardo Mortara neglected the opportunity to return to his ancestral faith.†

This was, as has been mentioned, the most famous case of the sort; but it was by no means isolated, even at this late period. A few years previously, a drunken ruffian threw some dirty water upon a Jewish lad whom he met in a wine shop with the words: "You are baptized": and this sufficed to have him carried off. One day in 1864, a priest enticed a boy of ten to the House of Catechumens on the pretext of giving him a pair of shoes to take to his master to repair. Before long, the Catholic Church received a new adherent. The boy's sister died as a result of the shock, his mother became mad, and his father had to leave Rome: while a fellow-Jew was thrown into prison because he had dared to glance at the new convert one day as he was looking out of one of the windows of the House of Catechumens. Such cases out of the period almost within living memory can be multiplied.

The present writer is never tired of accentuating the fact that the Jew is under a distinct debt of gratitude towards the Popes, almost his solitary protector, and frequently his patron, in a barbaric age. The later period of persecution was induced by external circumstances, and should not blind our eyes to the long tradition of tolerance which lay behind it. Nevertheless, this should not make us altogether oblivious of this most subtle of all forms of persecution which martyred not the Jewish body, but that parental affection which is the most delicate part of the Jewish soul.

---

† Father Mortara died as recently as 1940 in Belgium, at the period of the German invasion, in advanced old age: an extraordinary link with past history.

19. ROMANCE AT URBINO[1]

i

THE ponderous tomes of the rabbinic literature, as it is popularly conceived, would be the last place to which one would turn to find material of human interest. But law must of necessity deal with life; and fact, in spite of the fatuous proverb, is sometimes stranger than fiction. Accordingly, in the arid wastes of talmudic casuistry one may occasionally find concealed some green oasis to comfort and refresh the weary heart of the studious pilgrim. Of these, none can surely surpass for sheer dramatic interest—and also, incidentally, for the light it throws upon Jewish social life in bygone times—one story unfolded in the *Pahad Isaac* [2] (the great Talmudic encyclopaedia of Isaac Lampronti, a Ferrarese Rabbi of the eighteenth century), under the heading *Safek*—"Doubt," dealing with an instance of a disputed marriage. Over ninety pages of the work are devoted to the reproduction of correspondence, responsa and other documents concerning this case, which roused so much interest in its day. In the account which follows no attempt has been made to enter, on the one hand, into the intricacies of the casuistic discussion, nor, on the other, to improve the story by the addition or alteration of a single fact. The tale is told as far as possible just as it is recorded in the crabbed rabbinic account.

---

[1] Originally published in the *Jewish Chronicle Supplement*, May 1925; and *Opinion*, April 1936.

[2] The publication of the first of the thirteen volumes of this stupendous work—a mine of information on the social history as well as the legal institutions of the Jews in Italy—took place at Venice in 1750; of the last, at Berlin. 137 years later.

The scene is laid in the old-world city of Urbino. Here a considerable nucleus of Jews had gathered when, as the capital of an independent duchy, it was a center of enlightenment and tolerance; and they remained, though sadly reduced in numbers and in wealth, when, owing to the extinction of the ruling house, the territory fell under the sway of the Holy See. In the ghetto of this place, in the early years of the eighteenth century, there lived an orphan girl, Consola Moscato, of considerable beauty, if contemporary accounts are to be believed, and much sought after by the youth of the city. But her choice fell upon her cousin, young Solomon Vita Castello—even in the ghetto, Nature would have its way!—and a match was arranged between them. The wedding was not to take place at once, and meanwhile (the girl's father being dead, and the mother remarried) the young couple were living under the same roof, in the house of an aunt. Economic conditions, however, were unfavorable. The year stipulated for the marriage passed, and then another, and still nothing was done. Not until three years later were active steps taken. One Thursday at the end of June 1727, Castello purchased from an itinerant Jewish merchant a dress for the bride to wear on her wedding day—"a chamber-habit and skirt of crimson cloth with flowers of gold-colored silk," with stomacher to match, for which he paid no less than twelve zecchins; and we are given a glimpse of the delighted bride going to the tailor with her mother, Signora Diana, to try on the dress.

Just after, the bridegroom fell ill, and his mind became affected. One day he escaped from control and threw himself down a well. Help came so quickly that he was saved; and he was henceforth kept bound hand and foot to prevent another attempt against himself. Thereafter, his madness took another turn. At intervals of lucidity, indeed (or what it was convenient to consider lucidity), he promised to divide his property between the synagogue of his native place and the charities of the Holy Land. But in his relapses he commenced to call upon the Saints to come to his help— a not unnatural thing to do, seeing that this was the every-day vocabulary of those with whom he was accustomed to mix. In horror, his kinsfolk stopped his mouth and told him to say the *Shema*. He replied with blasphemies.

Before long, the details became known generally, and priests, avid for another soul to save, were sent by the ecclesiastical authorities to listen to his ravings. This caused serious preoccupation, and not on behalf of the young man alone. Cases were frequent enough in which persons had been seized from the ghetto and forced to the baptismal font in fulfilment of the supposed wish of a converted relative with some sort of moral claim, however flimsy, to authority over them. Were the young man taken to the House of Catechumens, there was every danger that his promised bride would be carried off after him by force. In terror, she fled back to her mother's house. This, however, was not a sufficient guarantee for her safety. There seemed to be only one way by which she could be adequately protected—by taking steps to supersede, if not annul, her former engagement. Accordingly, with her full consent, she hastily went through the ceremony of betrothal to a third party, Moses Samuel Guglielmi on Friday, October 17, 1727. In the hurry there was no time to procure the usual plain gold ring, and one inset with jewels was used. She was immediately dressed, and treated, as a betrothed woman. Guglielmi himself certainly took the matter seriously, and set about kissing and fondling the maiden to an extent which shocked the prim eyewitnesses. Thus it was considered that, even if things came to the worst, she could no longer be presumed under the authority of Castello, with whom no formal ceremony of betrothal had as yet taken place.

ii

It was not long before the latter recovered his health and senses. He found to his horror that during his illness his property and his bride had alike been alienated. On the other side matters were no better, and a visitor once found the girl and her mother absolutely distraught, smiting their heads and unable to eat, in remorse at what had happened. Natural affection reasserted itself. Consola expressed her desire to cancel all that had happened and to return to the man of her choice; and the two families supported her intention. They neglected, however, the formal act of betrothal which had intervened. The Council of the community, appealed to by the rabbi (a stern upholder of law and what he considered to be morality), warned them repeatedly, but in vain, that what they were proposing was illegal. The rabbi, Judah Vita Guglielmi, was presumably a relative of the rival claimant, and his impartiality was not above question. The young couple were brought together one day, and in the greatest secrecy, behind closed doors, the full marriage ceremony was performed. To justify their action, they appealed, firstly, to the anterior contract that had existed between them, which made the intervening betrothal invalid; secondly, to the fact that the bride had been misled at the time of that ceremony into believing that Castello's illness was incurable; and, thirdly, to the technical irregularity of the use in the function of a jewelled ring, of which, indeed, it was noticed that the bride, womanlike, had taken particular notice. Yet another plea was whispered, more in keeping with the place and age, and sworn witnesses were ultimately forthcoming to substantiate it. It was alleged that Guglielmi, hopelessly enamoured with Consola, had recourse to enchantment to break the bond of love which attached her to Castello. Two Jews and—horror of horrors! —a Gentile sorceress had been employed to exercise the black art on his behalf, ultimately with success. The other side had been driven to follow suit, and through the magical powers of a priest of Cesena, aided by the repetition of six Psalms, the spell had been broken, so that the young couple returned to their pristine love. The time of this happy consummation is given with most circumstantial accuracy as being about two o'clock in the afternoon on Thursday, November 12, 1727. It was only after this that they had taken the drastic step.

The rabbi of Urbino, seeing his authority flouted, had only one course before him: he appealed to the spiritual head of the neighboring community of Pesaro, Jacob Israel Bemporad, informing him that he had looked into the writings of Christian theologians as well as Jewish before coming to a decision. This in itself was enough to rouse the opposition of the other, who gave it as his opinion that the original contract had sufficient binding force to invalidate the intervening ceremony of betrothal. He submitted his views for approbation to Samson Morpurgo, rabbi of Ancona, the nearest great community, whose fame was known far and wide. The latter hesitated to decide at once upon so tangled a question and advised his correspondent to wait to hear the opinions of the talmudic authorities of other major centers of learning throughout Italy before acting upon his opinion. The other, however, neglected his advice. Upon the following Sabbath, Bemporad and his coadjutor, Isaac d'Urbino, had it proclaimed in the synagogue that the intermediate ceremony had no validity, and that the match between the young couple was beyond all question legal. Henceforth the two lived together as man and wife.

iii

Thereupon the storm broke. Guglielmi, thus branded publicly (as he had been without any equivocation, privately) as an ignoramus, appealed far and near against what he regarded as this open immorality. All the rabbinic authorities in Italy were involved in the dispute which centered round the love idyll in the obscure ghetto of Urbino. It was feared that by their high-handed action the rabbis of Pesaro had run the risk of contaminating the pure seed of Israel with the taint of illegitimacy. Even the indulgent Morpurgo declared that the ceremony of marriage should be gone through again, after a formal divorce from the rival claimant. Other authorities were less sympathetic to the claims of love in its conflict with law. But certain points of fact were still in doubt, Morpurgo being charged by his colleagues to inquire into them while passing through Pesaro on his way home after a visit to Ferrara; and the matter was complicated by scarcely veiled threats of violence or even bloodshed from the one side or the other if the result were unfavorable. Worst of all, the secular authorities had taken cognizance of the dispute, which was one in which they could not unreasonably claim the right of decision. Tranquillo Vita Corcos, chief rabbi of Rome, succeeded, however, in inducing the Papal representative to abstain from intervention; though, but for his years and infirmities, he would have undertaken the arduous journey in order to inquire into the matter in person.

Bemporad, startled at the opposition which his action had aroused and at the intervention of the revered figure of a rabbi from Jerusalem who happened to be in the neighborhood collecting funds for the Holy Land, succeeded in inducing the young couple to separate until the final decision was reached, and thus to avoid the penalties of excommuni-

cation menaced on all sides. The verdict was now not long
delayed, all concurring unanimously in a long and closely
argued decision arrived at by Solomon David del Vecchio,
scion of a famous family of sages and rabbi at Sinigaglia. It
was decided that the bride must be formally divorced by both
of the rival claimants for her hand, neither of whom could
be legally considered her husband.

The episode was not yet ended. Fiction would here enter
upon an account of a lifelong fidelity or of broken hearts.
The legalist, while not excluding such romantic possibilities, is satisfied to present only the sordid actuality. Guglielmi, contented with worsting his rival, apparently did what
was required of him without demur. Castello, however, was
less compliant. He had fought hard for his bride, he had
gone to considerable expense on her behalf, and was now to
be deprived of all without compensation. Accordingly, he
demanded a preliminary reimbursement of all the expenditure which he had undergone for Consola since the day of
their first acquaintance. Until he received this he refused
to grant her freedom, so that she would be condemned to
live indefinitely in a state of perpetual grass-widowhood.
The news of this mean action was soon reported abroad and
aroused general indignation. Gone now was the forbear-
ance which had previously characterized the dispute, and
the anonymity with which the identity of the principals had
hitherto been discreetly veiled. The rabbis of Ancona ful-
minated the excommunication against the recalcitrant, now
for the first time mentioned by name. None might have
dealings with him, none do him any favor, none instruct
him, none even help in his burial, unless he conceded to
his unfortunate bride the treatment which authority and
equity alike imposed. To this the rabbis of Rome, Leghorn,
Florence, Ferrara, Mantua, Reggio, Modena, Casale, and
Alessandria all subscribed—nearly all who had taken part

in the earlier dispute, and a few more. No doubt he at last yielded and the excommunication was withdrawn. But history should be less indulgent in relaxing the ban. Castello's offence against her was gravest of all; for what misdemeanor could be worse than introducing so sordid an ending to the most delicate and dramatic love-idyll that ever delighted the mind of the student or graced the pages of a rabbinic law-book?

20. "WHEN WE REMEMBERED ZION":[1]

The Musical Academy of the Venetian Ghetto

i

WHAT does Music say to the Gentiles? Assuredly, *'I have been stolen from the land of the Hebrews'* [Genesis 40.15]." Thus wrote the sarcastic Immanuel of Rome, imitator if not friend of Dante, at the beginning of the fourteenth century. It is today clear that the theft was incomplete, or else that the recovery has been extraordinarily rapid. If this is so, it is in no small measure due to Italian Jewry.

The Jewish community of old time did not signify merely an association for the performance of certain religious rites. Social activities, from the dowering of the bride to the visiting of the sick, were comprised no less among its activities; and the amenities of life were not by any means forgotten. As far as the Arts went, painting and sculpture were almost excluded by the over-rigid interpretation of the Ten Commandments—though, indeed, by no means so absolutely as is generally imagined. Humanistic interests were therefore concentrated all the more in music, against which no similar objection could be raised. Hence, in any general consideration of the history of Italy at the period of the Renaissance, it is impossible to overlook the part which the Jews played in this important sphere of activity. Even to ecclesiastical melody they made their contribution; though

[1] Originally published in the *Jewish Chronicle Supplement*, December 1931, and in Italian in *La Rassegna Mensile di Israel*, vol. III, pp. 161-2, where the documents are printed in their original language.

those who did so could naturally not maintain formal allegiance to their ancestral faith. Most noteworthy was one
Giovanni Maria, who, despite his Italian name, was a German musician of Jewish origin. He, being exiled from Florence through a sentence of death passed against him by
reason of homicide, betook himself, after a short stay in
Venice, to Rome, where he attained considerable reputation
as a flutist and composer, was raised by Pope Leo X to the
dignity of Count and was enfeoffed with the castle of Ver-
rochio. Another protégé of this same Pope, notorious for
his benevolence towards the Jews, was Jacopo di Sansecondo,
who was equally famous for his personal beauty and his
ability as a violinist, and served as model for Raphael's
"Apollo del Parnasso"—as Giovanni Maria was said to have
done to Sebastian del Piombo for his "Violinist." A contemporary of theirs was Elia Vannini, who offered his contributions to sacred song from the seclusion of a Carmelite monastery and is said to have been of Jewish birth. Infidelity to
the religion of their fathers was not, however, an invariable
characteristic of these Jewish artists, even when their interests were wholly secular, such as "Guglielmo ebreo Pesarese,"
who was attached to the Court of Lorenzo de' Medici and
there composed his famous *Trattato dell' arte del Ballo*—
the earliest scientific treatise on the art of dancing now extant; or his contemporary Giuseppe Ebreo, author of one
of the compositions which the other included in his work.

The center of this activity was the Court of Mantua,
under the patronage of the house of Gonzaga. Here, Jewish
artists were able to figure definitely in their Jewish capacity.
The art of the theater had not yet become a profession; and,
whenever the Court desired to witness a dramatic repre-
sentation, it was natural for it to be imposed (like other
burdens) upon that section of the population which was
supposed to have the means to afford it and which had per-

haps already shown, in its Purim comedies centered around the story of Esther, a notable histrionic sense. Hence, during the entire period from 1525 to 1605, whenever it was wished to have a comedy presented for the delectation of the Court, the duty—and the expenses—often fell upon the Jews. It is on record how, on Fridays, the spectacle had to begin earlier, so that it could be finished before the Sabbath: and how on feast-days it had to be postponed, or else shorn of its most attractive details.

The interest of the Jews was not confined to acting, Leone de' Sommi Portaleone, by profession a *sopher* or scribe, by hobby a Hebrew poet, and founder of a synagogue which long continued to exist in his native city, may be considered the first impresario of modern times. He was a prolific versifier and wrote comedies in Italian, upon specifically non-Hebraic themes. The poet Manfredi entrusted to him the presentation of one of his plays. But he is specially remembered as author of a volume of *Dialogues upon the Representative Art*—the first work of the kind—in which he displays an intuition of the minutiae of theatercraft so advanced for his age as to be almost incredible. It is not to be wondered at, if the Accademia degl' Invaghiti, not being able to admit him as a full member by reason of his religion and of the knightly dignity which was entailed, conferred upon him the title of *scrittore accademico*.

As far as music is concerned, it would have been possible to organize in Mantua at that period a concert-party of remarkable ability composed exclusively of Jews. Abramo dell' Arpa and his nephew Abramino indicate clearly by their name the instrument at which they excelled. Isacchino Massarano (another delightful diminutive!) played the lute, sang soprano, and taught music and dancing. David Civita was a composer of some merit, who dedicated his *Premitie Armoniche* (Venice, 1616) to Ferdinando Gonzaga. A contemporary, and probably fellow-townsman, of his was Allegro Porto, who published at least three volumes of original compositions, one of which was dedicated to the Emperor Ferdinand II.

But there was one Mantuan family which distinguished itself peculiarly at this period. Salamone dé Rossi was a prolific composer. He published, besides a number of non-Jewish works, the first volumes of synagogal music extant. His merits were so generally recognized that, like Leone de' Sommi before him, he was exempted from the obligation of wearing the badge of shame imposed upon the Jews by law. His sister, called by the operatic professional name of Madame Europa, was a celebrated singer; her son, Anselmo, was known both as an instrumentalist and as a composer. The array of Jewish artists at the Court of Mantua at this period was not limited to those mentioned above. Any deficiencies in the abilities of the others could be remedied by Simone Basilea, a ventriloquist, who enjoyed the same exemption as de' Rossi and is said to have been able to act an entire comedy by himself, without any assistance.

ii

The prototype of the Italian ghetto was that of Venice, which, thanks to its position, its population and its culture, was among the most important in the Peninsula. Naturally, it was not inferior to the others in this field. Nevertheless, two tendencies were to be discerned here—the hyper-orthodox, and a trifle Philistine, especially represented by recent immigrants from beyond the Alps; and the less uncompromising and more aesthetic, which was more specifically Italian. The outstanding representative of the latter was, naturally, Leone da Modena, that strange prodigy, the despair and delight of his age, who perhaps more than any other represented Judaism to the outside world. He is said to have had a good tenor voice. In his youth he studied music and dancing, and he taught the former art among the twenty-six professions which he unsuccessfully practiced in manhood. In the city in which he exercised his influence it is not to be wondered that the Jews played a notable part in artistic life.

This was, indeed, no innovation. As early as 1443 the Senate, alarmed at the success and the close social relations with the general population engendered by the schools of singing and music maintained by the Jews, ordered that they should be closed down, and forbade any Jew henceforth to teach these subjects under pain of six months' imprisonment and a heavy fine. The prejudice continued apparently in governing circles without any alteration. "This night," wrote Marin Sanuto, on March 4th, 1531 (it was the day, though he did not know it, of the feast of Purim), "there was acted in the ghetto amongst the Jews a splendid comedy, though no Christian was able to be present by order of the Dieci. They finished it at 10 o'clock at night." Nevertheless, in 1559, and again in 1592, a play on Esther by the illustrious Marrano writer, Solomon Usque, was presented publicly before a select company of nobility and gentry.

There was thus ample precedent for the outburst of activity in this same sphere which took place at Venice at the opening of the seventeenth century. In 1609 a singer named Rachel was a familiar figure in the salons of the Venetian patricians. Leone da Modena (whom we find on another occasion writing to a friend requesting him to secure him a good place for the regatta!), not content with adapting from the Spanish Usque's drama, *Esther,* composed an original pastoral comedy, *Rachel and Jacob,* of which we know, since on one occasion he was compelled to pledge his only copy to a friend. Perhaps it was in this that his brother-in-law, Moses, acted on that occasion when his young son Mordecai somewhat impiously quoted: *Then sang Moses*—in an intermezzo. It was one of his pupils, Benedetto Luzzatto, who published at Venice in 1631 a pastoral fable in five acts entitled *L'Amor Possente,* which he dedicated to Don Foresto d'Este, while in 1611 Modena edited a similar work. *I Trionfi,* by his friend Angelo Alatino. In the midst of all this activity it is not remarkable that (to the disgust of pietists like Azariah Picho and Samuel Aboab) a regular theater was instituted in the ghetto—apparently with Leone da Modena's approval, if not at his incitement—to which men and women of every class thronged promiscuously.[2]

Thus far, the puritans of the ghetto had to stifle their annoyance, for social life only was in question. Once, however, the synagogue was entered and an attempt was made to introduce a more decorous employment of melody in religious functions, they immediately arose in arms, for was not this a patent imitation of the Gentiles—*hukkat haGoy?* The apostate Giulio Morosini (who, in his youth when he had been known as Samuel Nahmias, had been a disciple of Leone da Modena) gives in his scurrilous polemic, *Via della Fede,* a graphic description of the scenes in the synagogue at that period during the Rejoicing of the Law, which shows plainly how informally—not to say ludicrously—his one-time co-religionists endeavored to give expression to their passion for music:

In the cities in which the Jews have a ghetto, the synagogues are kept open all day and all night. . . . Similarly in many places,

---

[2] It may be mentioned that the histrionic interests of Italian Jewry were by no means confined to the seventeenth century. In Siena, on March 31, 1793, Leone Forti was accorded permission to present a *tragedia sacra* during the forthcoming Passover, though men and women were seated separately, and it was planned to have one special presentation for the tender sex! In Venice, at the time of the Siege of 1848, the Jewish dramatic society gave a special performance to raise money for patriotic causes.

and in particular at Venice, a sort of half-carnival is held on this evening: for many maidens and brides mask themselves, so as not to be recognized, and go to visit all of the synagogues. The synagogues are similarly thronged at this period by Christian ladies and gentlemen, out of curiosity, more than at any other feast, to see the preparations. . . . There are present all nations: Spaniards, Levantines, Portuguese, Germans, Greeks, Italians and others, and each sings according to his own usage. Since they do not use instruments, some clap their hands above the head, some smite their thighs, some imitate the castanets with their fingers, some pretend to play the guitar by scraping their doublets. In short, they so act with these noises, jumpings and dancings, with strange contortions of their faces, their mouths, their arms and all their other members, that it appears to be Carnival mimicry. . . .

From this description may be deduced how urgent was the necessity of introducing greater discipline in the synagogal service. One festal night in 1605, therefore, the congregation in one of the Ferrara synagogues had the agreeable surprise of hearing a choir of half a dozen youths repeat certain hymns with all the artificial graces which can be acquired only by prolonged practice. The pietists immediately arose in protest against so un-Jewish an innovation. Modena, with some of his colleagues, retorted in a formal rabbinic responsum, in which he convincingly demonstrated that no conceivable legal objection could exist to prevent any person who possessed a beautiful voice from exercising it as best he could, to the glory of God. Seventeen years later this was printed by way of preface to the *Shir haShirim* of Salamone de' Rossi mentioned above, together with an approbation in which he insisted, perhaps a trifle optimistically, that the words would not suffer by reason of the musical rendering. In another responsum he discussed the question whether it was permissible to repeat the name of God in the musical setting to a hymn. And when a new Scroll of the Law was consecrated at Modena, he composed, at the request of a friend, a special poem "to be recited to music" in celebration of the event.

iii

Hitherto musical interests in the ghetto at Venice had been merely sporadic. Some years later, however, political conditions afforded the opportunity for a more organized activity. In 1628, the House of Gonzaga, which ruled Mantua, became extinct, leaving no heir more direct than Charles de Rethel, Duke of Nevers. The Spaniards, however, were unwilling to see a French prince established so near to the Milanese; and, at their instigation, the Emperor Ferdinand sent an army across the Alps to dispossess the new Duke. The Jews of Mantua, assured of the latter's favor, worked manfully on his behalf, taking part in the work for the fortification of the city, even at the expense of the sanctity of the Sabbath. After its capture, therefore, they were subjected to a persecution of the most severe nature, their sufferings being described by Abraham Massarano, son of the musician Isacchino, in his work, *"HaGaluth vehaPeduth"* (Venice, 1634). A good number of the members of the community had fled to Venice before the siege began. Among these, there must have been several of the musicians who flourished about the Ducal Court, and of whom mention has been made above. It was to their ability and experience that there must be attributed the foundation for the first time in the Venetian ghetto of a regularly organized musical society. Again, we must allow the renegade, Giulio Morosini, to use his own words:—

I well remember what happened at Venice in my times, about 1628, if I am not mistaken, when many of the Jews fled from Mantua through the war and came to Venice. Since every sort of study then flourished at Mantua, the Jews had similarly applied themselves to music and to playing. When these arrived at Venice, there was formed in the ghetto of that city a Musical Academy, which met generally twice a week, in the evenings. It was frequented only by some of the principal and richest members of the community, who supported it, of whom I was one: and my master, Leo da Modena, was *maestro di cappella*. That year there served as Bridegrooms in this feast (the Rejoicing in the Law), as described above, two wealthy and splendid persons, one of whom was a member of this same Academy. They accordingly introduced into the Spanish *Scuola* (very richly prepared, and adorned with a great quantity of silver and precious stones) two choirs with music, after our custom. The two evenings, that is, on the Eighth Day of the Feast and on the Rejoicing in the Law, part of the evening service was chanted according to a musical setting in Hebrew, as well as different Psalms: and the *Minha*, that is, Vespers, on the last day similarly with solemn music, which lasted for some hours into the night. There were present many members of the nobility, both gentlemen and ladies, who greatly applauded; so that it was necessary to station at the door many captains and officers, so that it could pass off quietly. Among the instruments an organ was also taken into the synagogue, but the rabbis would not allow it to be played, it being an instrument which is ordinarily played in our churches. But what! All this was a blaze of straw. The Academy lasted little, and the Music returned to its former state. . . .

Morosino goes on to insinuate that the reason for the failure of the attempt lay in the fact that the Jews were no longer a fit receptacle for the divine gift of song. In this he displays all of the spitefulness of the renegade, which renders him suspect also in the other more discreditable particulars which he gives. In part, the decline of musical interest is to be attributed to the gradual restriction brought about by the effect of the slavery of the ghetto upon the free Jewish spirit. But the immediate cause of the failure of the attempt, as of its origin, is to be sought in external events.

iv

In 1630 there raged throughout Italy that terrible pestilence which Mazzoni has immortalized in his famous romance, *I Promessi Sposi*. In Venice alone, in a period of sixteen months, there perished nearly 50,000 persons out of a total population of less than 150,000. The Jews suffered similarly, though not in the same proportions as their fellow-townsmen. The first victims were struck down in the Ghetto Vecchio in the autumn of 1630, during the days of Penitence. From that date the infection spread rapidly, so that within two months no less than 170 persons perished. Many of the wealthy Spanish merchants fled, especially to the Levant and to Verona. (No doubt it was because of this, and not, as local legend asserts, through the deliberate spite of the general population, that the community of this city lost two-thirds of its members, and was compelled to add another layer of earth in its cemetery to accommodate the victims). Leone da Modena, with characteristic fatalism, remained at Venice without being attacked; though his was the only family in the house in which he lived that had no victim to lament. Only in the winter of 1631 could the infection be considered at an end, and in all the synagogues of Venice services of thanksgiving were held, preceded by a penitential fast, on the New Moon of Kislev.

Among the victims there were, it seems, many of the members of the musical circle. This led to the suspension of the regular activity of the Academy, which henceforth continued a truncated existence, meeting only on rare occasions.

Nevertheless, it survived for at least nine years, contrary to Morosini's spiteful assertions. This is proved by a letter of Leone da Modena himself, of which a rough draft is preserved with that of other of his correspondence. It is written in an execrable hand, and replete with alterations and scratchings out, so that the text and the sense cannot be restored with any degree of certainty. The general significance can, however, be recovered without too much difficulty. It appears that a non-Jewish amateur recently arrived in the city had founded a new musical society. Having heard of the similar institution which existed in the ghetto, he wrote suggesting some sort of collaboration between the two societies—especially, it would seem, the interchange of original compositions. It fell to Leone da Modena, as *maestro di cappella* and a noted stylist, to compose the reply. The following is a translation, as far as it can be reconstructed, of the letter which he wrote:

Most Magnificent and Excellent Signore,

Once our musical gathering rightly had the name of Academy, because it numbered some musicians, both vocal and instrumental, not unworthy of the title. The enterprise . . . received the motto *Dum recordaremur Sion,* out of Psalm cxxxvii, *Super flumina Babilonii,* and its name was Degli Imperiti—all in allusion to the unhappy state of our captivity, which prevents the perfection of any virtuous action. But, by reason of the disaster in the year of the Plague, when we lost the best members that we had, our company remained so solitary that it indeed deserved the name; for, no longer an academy, we meet together seldom and practice only imperfectly. Whatever it may be, it truly appreciates the goodwill that your honor shows it by yours of the 28th of the past month, and promises hearty reciprocation. It grieves us more than you not to be able to profit ourselves of your settled abode in this city, which we are sure would give fullness of harmony to our poor attempts. We would willingly avail ourselves of your courtesy if you will communicate to us the mature fruits which will be produced in the new Academy which you announce: henceforth, we can offer nothing, having no fertile store of Composers. Nevertheless, you will always be loved, esteemed, and remembered worthily by us, as we hope to be remembered by you: and we augur you all felicity from the Lord.

Your Magnificent and Excellent Honor's always most affectionate,

THE MUSICAL COMPANY OF THE GHETTO OF VENICE.

The importance of this document is considerable. It is the only Jewish source thus far known which confirms the existence of this semi-legendary Academy and of the part which Leone da Modena played in it. It demonstrates clearly the excellent relations which the institution (and, hence, the ghetto as a whole) still maintained with the outside world, before the policy of repression became effective. We are informed for the first time of the real reason for the failure of the experiment—the result of a great general disaster, not merely of internal apathy; and we see that, nevertheless, it was able to protract its existence for at least another nine years. Interesting above all is the fact that we are told the real title of the institution. It was known to the outside world by the name "The Company of Musicians of the Ghetto at Venice," though it called itself, with mock modesty, "The Academy of the Unskilled." But every association in the ghetto had an additional name taken from some biblical verse: from the *Hebrath Hesed veEmet,* which emulated towards the dead the last "kindness and truth" that Joseph swore to his father, down to the *Shomerim laBoker*— "Watchers for the Morning," in the Psalmist's phrase—who saluted the dawn with prayers and hymns. The musical society drew its inspiration from that most beautiful and most moving of all the Hebrew poems (Psalm cxxxvii) :

"By the rivers of Babylon, there we sat down, yea, we wept, when we remembered Zion. We hanged our harps upon the willows in the midst thereof. For there they that carried us away captive required of us a song: and they that wasted us required of us mirth, saying, Sing us one of the songs of Zion. How shall we sing the Lord's song in a strange land? . . ."

From the last words of the first verse, the short-lived Musical Academy of the Venetian ghetto took its name: "When we remembered Zion"—*Dum recordaremur Sion.*

21. THE AMAZING ABRAHAM COLORNI[1]

i

IT IS notorious to students that Jews have been responsible for all manner of inventions, ranging from Esperanto to penicillin, and from the handkerchief to the automobile. Hitherto, however, it has been insufficiently realized that it was a Jew who invented card tricks. The career of this unsung hero is extraordinary enough to merit, if not a monument, at least a cursory sketch.

Abraham Colorni was born in Mantua, about the year 1540. Nothing, or somewhat less than nothing, is known as to his antecedents; though the name is frequently used as the secular equivalent to the Hebrew *Saba,* or *Sebag,* and apparently indicates that the family once distinguished itself in the profession of dyeing. (Colorno is a small place in the Duchy of Parma and Piacenza, where a diminutive Jewish community once existed.)

The young Abraham struck out on a fresh line for himself. True, for a Jew, the choice of profession was strictly limited; but, in Renaissance Italy, no check was imposed on ingenuity and mechanical skill. Already at the beginning of the fifteenth century the Venetian Senate had employed a Jewish hydraulic engineer named Solomon, who, it was understood had a perfect mastery and expertness in the matter of levelling the waters: and the instance was not an isolated one. Accordingly, Colorni took up the profession of engineer:

---

[1] Originally published in the *American Hebrew*, May 4, 1934, and *La Rassegna Mensile di Israel*, vol. IX, pp. 147-58, where various Italian documents are given.

and, when he emerged from obscurity in the last quarter of the sixteenth century, he had already established a considerable reputation in this capacity. Of his previous life we know only that he had received a comprehensive education and had studied fencing under the best masters.

In 1578, we find him in the service of Don Alfonso II, d'Este, Duke of Ferrara. He appears to have had something to do with the construction of the sumptuous hunting lodge known as the Palazzo della Mesola, and was actively concerned with the renovation of the fortifications of the city— at that time, one of the wonders of Europe. For his specialty was military engineering. He invented all manner of ingenious appliances to facilitate the art of warfare. Some of these sound astonishingly modern—pontoons which could be thrown across streams or moats in a few moments, and rendered the strongest fortress vulnerable; collapsible boats, which could be contracted into a very small space and were invaluable for night attacks; folding ladders, equally useful for assaulting bastions or extinguishing fires, and similar contraptions. He boasted that he could bring a besieged army into safety out of a beleaguered position by means of concealed trenches. In addition, he devised improvements in the manufacture of gunpowder, artillery-shot, and mines; and described with gusto a series of musical instruments which could serve as military weapons in case of need. On one occasion, he offered to the Venetian Government a new, though expensive plan by which crowds of persons could be exterminated at banquets or at Church, without any suspicion being aroused, together with an antidote which he was prepared to sell with it.

But his most extraordinary invention was a primitive machine-gun, which anticipated by many generations the quick-firers of the nineteenth century. The Duke of Ferrara actually ordered from him 2,000 arquebuses which could fire ten shots in succession with a single priming: and, though it is not on record whether they were delivered or no, it is suggestive that the latter shortly after offered some similar engines of war to His Holiness the Pope.

ii

It appears that Colorni's bellicosity was not confined to the laboratory. For, thanks to his early training, he was an expert swordsman and, more than once, distinguished himself in duels fought (as he indicates) to defend his honor. In the civil sphere, he was an expert in the difficult art of stucco-working; he devised an instrument for measuring distances; he constructed an improved clock and sun-dial; and he invented the earliest-known taximeter applied to carriages.

He must have been an amusing companion, this versatile Italian Jew, and there is little wonder that he had a large circle of Gentile admirers, who gladly penned commendations, in prose or verse, to his works. He was in correspondence with the prolific Canon Tomaso Garzoni of Bagnocavallo, who admired his attainments, commended his works, longed for his conversion, and described his various inventions eulogistically in that astounding sixteenth-century potpourri, *La Piazza Universale di tutte le professioni del mondo*. In the preliminary matter to certain editions of this famous work, there is a dedicatory letter describing his accomplishments, enumerating his achievements, and expressing heartfelt regret that so exceptional a person should remain enveloped in the error of Judaism.

Colorni had an entrée even to Courts. In that of Mantua, we obtain a glimpse of him on one occasion reading the palm of His Highness, Duke Vicenzo himself—though he was

frank enough to confess that he did not have the slightest
belief in the science. Sometimes, no doubt, he made his
appearance with an enticing work of ancient art, recently
discovered, acquired, or manufactured. For his studio of
antiques at Ferrara was famous.

On the long winter nights, he must have been an especially welcome visitor. He was an expert at conjuring and
sleight-of-hand. One of his tricks was to offer the assembled
company a plate of nuts, inviting all present to help themselves at random. Inside, each one would find the gem which
he most desired (even if it happened to be a polished dia-
mond) ; while the other nuts, left on the plate, would be
empty. He boasted that he could escape from any prison,
however strong, without using sorcery on the one hand
or special instruments on the other; and, no doubt, he gave
demonstrations to his friends. It was amazing, almost miraculous. "Work of the demon," contemporaries called it; and
he added to their sense of mystification by assuring them
gravely that his achievements were due to certain occult
natural qualities inherent in his person.

But, above all, Colorni was an expert in card tricks—
the first, perhaps, on record. Garzoni gives us some idea of
how he could keep the company amused:—

"Messer Abraham Colorni, the famous engineer of His Highness, the Duke of Ferrara, is acquainted with numerous rare and
delightful games with playing cards. For example, he sometimes
will change the cards in somebody else's hand for others completely different; or, again, he puts the pack face downwards in
the middle of the table, and tells those round to take whichever
they desire, without his seeing; but by his manipulations, it
always turns out to be just the one he says.

"Sometimes he will do the following experiment, viz., he
makes someone take two cards, and tells him to imagine that
one of the two is changed into the other, which punctually takes

place! Again, stripping off the surface of a card, he will show written beneath in minuscular writing the very thoughts of the person who was holding it, or had it concealed in his bosom. At other times, he makes any card named by one of the company at will come out of the pack. He knows also a thousand other tricks of the sort, which by his kindness I have seen with my own eyes, together with more than ten other friends, who have all been equally amazed."

This interest in cards is not, indeed, to be wondered at: for Jews are found smuggling cards into Florence when at the height of the Savonarolan reaction such inventions of the devil were forbidden in that city; while in Germany the beadle of at least one synagogue manufactured them in his spare time.

iii

With his pen, Colorni was no less active than with his brain. In 1580, he obtained permission to publish his *Euthimetria,* which described a new contrivance for measuring distances, though for some obscure reason, it never saw the light. According to his Jewish contemporary, Raphael Mirami, an expert in the application and mis-application of mirrors, and author of the *Specularia* (Ferrara, 1582), the idea was based upon the use of reflectors.

Other works of his included a volume of mathematical tables and a treatise, entitled *Chiriofisonomia,* against the "superstitions" of physiognomy and chiromancy, which, according to another admirer, should have been sufficient to make his glory flourish eternally. This was composed at the express request of Vicenzo Gonzaga, Duke of Mantua, to whom it is dedicated. Both of these works, long reputed lost, are preserved in manuscript in the former Ducal Library at Wolfenbüttel. Another volume extant only in manuscript is an Italian translation of the magical "Key of King Solomon." The only one of his works to be printed is the ingenious *Scotographia,* or art of writing secretly and safely in any language (Prague, 1593).

"The dignity and splendor of your name is now celebrated throughout Italy," Garzoni had written to Colorni in 1589. It was the universality of the latter's fame which brought about his ultimate downfall. For a couple of decades he passed his time cheerfully between the courts of Mantua and Ferrara. In 1589, Alfonso d'Este lent him to his warlike brother-in-law who ruled Savoy. It is hard to speculate what superb military machine he was expected to perfect at the court of Moncalieri. But his genius was no less useful for the arts of peace than for those of war. The Duke of Savoy was crippled with gout; and the versatile engineer constructed him a new carriage—a sort of horse-drawn invalid chair—in which he could be conveyed without cause for blasphemy or apprehension. At the same time, he seized the opportunity to dispose of a couple of medallions with which he had provided himself before leaving home.

It was not long before the reputation of the ingenious Hebrew crossed the Alps. It happened that at this time the Archduke Maximilian, brother of the Emperor Rudolph II, and claimant to the Polish throne, was captured by Zamojski, Chancellor of the kingdom over which he aspired to rule. Since January 1588, he had been a prisoner. One of the Emperor's servants, a certain Funech, had passed some time at the court of Ferrara and recalled having met there a certain Jew who, like love, laughed at locksmiths and boasted that he could escape from any prison. What more natural than that application should be made for this paragon to be sent to the Court of Prague to see whether he could help in the present juncture?

It was all the more so, indeed, since the Emperor had a penchant for studies of the sort in which Colorni was interested. His court was a paradise of alchemists, astrologers, and magicians. Tycho Brahe was there wearing a silver nose, to replace the aquiline original lost in an argument, and was beset on all sides by an incongruous crowd of lesser fry. The State apartments were furnished in the style of a quack's study, stuffed crocodiles hanging from the ceiling, cabalistic symbols adorning the walls, and human skulls littering the table. At night, the skies above the city were lit up with the reflection from the furnace of Gold Alley, where the alchemists foregathered. True, the position of Jews in the Imperial entourage was a trifle precarious: for a certain Bernard Topfler maintained that gold could literally be distilled from their bodies, at the rate of six ounces per Jew per year. However, the favor shown by the Emperor to a Polish Hebrew named Mordecai of Nelle, who acted as official historiographer for matters alchemical, proved that there was no immediate peril.

Colorni, on his arrival, must have felt in an awkward quandary. With consummate tact, he fell ill, with the result that it was only some months later that he was received in audience. By this time, the question of the Archduke's release had ceased to be pressing. In any case, Colorni was adroit enough to turn the conversation to more practical matters—card-tricks, quick-firing arquebuses, and a new invention of his which seems to have anticipated the cinema with the additional advantage that the spectators saw what they, and not the operator, desired.

His success was instantaneous. Rudolph assigned him a house, paid him a pension, accepted the dedication of the *Scotographia* and (notwithstanding his preoccupations concerning the education of his sons and the betrothal of his daughter, already "over-mature"), kept him at court for some eight years.

By this time, other rulers had heard of Colorni's fulminous abilities, and wished to have the advantage of his presence. Even Zsigmond Báthory, Prince of Transylvania, was desirous of borrowing his services. But his request arrived too late, as Colorni had already obtained permission from the Duke of Ferrara to accede to the invitation of Frederick, Duke of Württemberg, to come to visit him for six weeks at Stuttgart. Here, as usual, he began to flaunt his marvelous inventions: how he could extract saltpeter (that indispensable ingredient of gunpowder) from the most unpromising soil by an improved method; how he had invented a light cannon of unprecedented efficaciousness; how he had a device for seeing at night; how he could send a letter into a besieged fortress with perfect safety, even if the bearer were stripped naked and searched, and himself desired to give up the secret.

The Duke, more practical than the Emperor, took him very seriously, and ordered him to get to work on the first-mentioned project. The inventor hedged, pleading first that the season was unpropitious, and secondly, that he had never undertaken to do anything of the sort. Nevertheless, the Duke insisted, ultimately, giving orders for his guest to be kept under strict surveillance and restricted to the most meager fare until he fulfilled his undertaking. The six weeks lengthened into months, and the months into years. Colorni claimed that the money advanced for his experiments was too little, while the Duke demanded that, in the absence of any satisfactory result, the full sum expended should be returned. At Mantua, Simon Colorni, Abraham's son, besieged the Duke with petitions to secure his father's release, and was actually sent to Württemberg with a formal request to that effect. But his powers of persuasion were inadequate.

iv

In the end, early in 1599, a little more than two years after his first arrival on a six-weeks' visit, the unfortunate inventor was forced to put one of his numerous devices to the test. It was not, however, that which the sordid German princeling had endeavored to elicit. One morning, his gaolers found his room empty. The prison may not have been one of great strength; but, even so, Colorni had not disdained to exercise his occult powers upon it, having escaped overnight. Making his way via Modena to Mantua, he threw himself on the mercy of the Duke. The latter and his Duchess received their errant servant benignantly.

A minor diplomatic crisis ensued. From Stuttgart a steady flow of letters demanded the fugitive's imprisonment or, at least, full pecuniary satisfaction for all claims upon him. Notwithstanding the bait of support in its claim on the township of Castelgoffredo, the court of Mantua continued to resist. An impasse had been reached when Colorni, true to his invariable tact and consideration, shuffled off this involved mortal coil. After protracted and despairing attempts to lay hands upon the dead man's son or brother-in-law, the Duke of Württemberg allowed the question to lapse.

With Colorni, the majority of his secrets perished. The world had to wait until the nineteenth century for a satisfactory quick-firing gun: modern taximeters are sometimes fallible; and, even in America, no adequate method of escaping from prison has yet been perfected. These, indeed, are not necessities for the ordinary man.

But Colorni's ingenuity was not generally so sordid as its objectives, and the loss to mankind is not to be measured by this standard. Who knows, for example, what sublime card-tricks have perished by reason of his untimely demise?

22. THE MADONNA OF THE SCROLL[1]

i

WHEN you visit Sienna, you will, of course, go to inspect the synagogue. It lies in the very center of the town, just behind the magnificent old Palazzo Pubblico, in a narrow mediaeval street. Not much imagination is needed to see in this the ancient ghetto. It is not long since those courts, now almost abandoned, were throbbing with an intense Jewish life. Around the well—adorned with a statue, until certain Polish pietists raised objections to this breach of the second commandment—the women sat and gossiped, while the men prayed, and studied, and worked, and quarrelled, and sometimes even came to blows. Surprising, indeed, this last. We have for it, though, the authority of Giuseppe da Modena; and who should know better than that semi-illiterate seventeenth-century huckster, foremost in every quarrel which took place in the ghetto, who had the inspiration of writing an account of them afterwards? The synagogue itself, you will be told by experts, dates back almost to the foundation of the community, to the fourteenth century; but it was restored about 1770, when half the poetasters in Italy combined in a volume of hymns to be recited on the occasion of its re-dedication. The interior is a trifle ornate, though not without a certain dignity. Unquestionably the most interesting feature is the Ark of the Law, with its heavily-ornamented bronze doors overlaid with gilt. This slender veneer is quite insufficient to conceal the fact that at some period in their history they

1 Originally published in the *Menorah Journal*, vol. XV (1928), pp. 358-62.

had been very badly treated. The whole surface is covered with dents and gashes, obviously the marks of axes which had been used at some time or other to break into the sanctuary. So ruthlessly were they employed that perfect restoration has become impossible: and the eye of credulity can even see a few bullet-holes amongst the ancient scars. If you ask your cicerone, and if he likes you, he will inform you how it all came about; and it may be that he will add the tale of the Madonna of the Scroll.

ii

The progress of the French Revolution was hailed by the Jewish communities in Italy with a not unnatural joy. Up to the close of the eighteenth century they had been treated throughout the peninsula with a more than mediaeval intolerance. From this, the armies of the Revolution, as they poured over the Alps, brought instantaneous deliverance. In every place to which they penetrated the Rights of Man were proclaimed, the gates of the ghetto were broken down, and the inmates were summoned forth at last to enjoy the free air of the outer world. Small wonder that the Jews enthusiastically espoused the principles of the Revolution and became amongst the most zealous supporters of the new regime. They entered eagerly into civic life. They enrolled themselves in the Revolutionary Guard. And, when the reaction came, they suffered correspondingly. In a brilliant campaign in 1796-7, Citizen Bonaparte had reduced the whole of Northern Italy. The generals whom he left in charge during his absence in Egypt were, however, unable to make headway against the coalition which was formed against them. In the spring of 1799, the French armies were driven back towards the Alps, and the Cisalpine Republic was overthrown. Everywhere counter-revolutionary principles triumphed. In the Romagna the Jewish communities were terrorized; and while Pesaro and Urbino had occasion to institute the local Purims to celebrate their deliverance, a veritable pogrom took place at Senigallia, where thirteen persons perished, the rest of the community fleeing to Ancona. On the other side of the Apennines the reverses of the French encouraged the people of the fervently catholic and reactionary city of Arezzo to rise and expel their garrison. Emboldened by this success they set out, in the name of the Church and the ancient political absolutism, to free the rest of the Province from the yoke of the new ideas introduced by the oppressor. That the Jews were in a special measure their bugbear, goes without saying. At Arezzo itself, there was only the merest handful, and they escaped without great hurt. At Pitigliano one Jew was killed and eighteen more thrown into gaol. Further outbreaks took place at Florence and Leghorn. The community of the little township of Monte San Savino, whose houses were sacked, anticipated the danger by abandoning their homes and taking refuge in the neighboring city of Sienna; and it was never again properly re-established. Amongst the refugees was Salamone Fiorentino, the famous poet, whose admirers compared him to Petrarch himself. The choice of a refuge was not a wise one; for at Sienna itself excesses took place which have left an indelible impression in the minds of the Jews of Italy and the people of Tuscany as a whole.

The relief experienced by the community of Sienna during the brief period of French domination had been so great that the ghetto itself had been impregnated by its principles. The Jews had taken a prominent share in setting up the inevitable "Tree of Liberty," on which, it was said, they had the intention of hanging all loyal Christians. Domestically, the spiritual and lay heads of the community were actually designated as the "Citizen" Rabbi and the "Citizen" wardens. There was accordingly all the more pretext for identifying them with all that was objectionable in the past regime. Moreover, the anti-religious campaign in which the French had indulged had invested the present reaction with something of the nature of a crusade; and in any crusade those who had persistently refused the Cross were inevitably marked out for attack. It was in the morning of Friday, June 28, 1799, that the Aretine detachments entered Sienna, having forced the French garrison to capitulate. Those who had been known to favor the revolutionary Government were immediately hounded down. A considerable detachment of the invaders, joined by some of the worst elements among the population of the city, made its way to the ghetto.

Here scenes of indescribable horror took place. The houses were broken into and sacked, and whatever could be found was carried off. Account books and notes of hand were destroyed indiscriminately by prudent debtors. For the zeal of the people had not been entirely political or religious in origin. "Burn those damned books," one involved patrician, who had gone to the Jews for assistance, had been heard to call as he joined the mob. Several persons were killed and many others wounded. The experience of the Gallichi family was terrible, but it was more fortunate than that of the generality. "They broke down the door of our house," one of them wrote, "and forced their way in, with the intention of killing us; and they carried off six hundred ducats' worth of silver and linen as well as three watches, one of which was gold. Five times did they return, always with their weapons girt on and cudgels raised and pistols pointed at our chests. It is impossible to describe how we felt, for we were reduced to the end of our lives. The said . . . (the word here used is intranscribeable) tried to break into our shop, but, praised be God, we were miraculously saved. . . ." Not all, however, were so fortunate. More than one person was murdered in his own house. Michael Valech, returning home, was killed in the sight of his young wife, already six months advanced in pregnancy. She threw herself sobbing across his body, her body racked with premature labor, and shared his fate. To the day of his death the person responsible for this double crime (a servant in a monastery near Lucignano) was known as "the beast." It was popularly believed—and not by the Jews alone—that every one of those responsible for these outrages perished miserably.

The butchery continued throughout the city. Two Jews caught abroad were hounded to death in the Piazza. Another, who had taken refuge in a church, was chased out by the verger and barbarously put to death on the threshold. Meanwhile, the Tree of Liberty in front of the Palazzo Pubblico had been torn down and burned. Drunk with passion, the mob rushed into the neighboring ghetto and returned dragging the bodies of several of the Jews, which they threw into the flames. Some were not quite dead and made terrible efforts to escape their agony. Those who succeeded in getting clear of the flames were ruthlessly cast back with pitchforks. The stench of the burning bodies was terrible. In all thirteen persons were killed, including four of the refugees from Monte San Savino, and a couple of women. Of the number of those wounded no record was kept.

A few of the priests, more humane than the rest, begged the Archbishop to do the duty of a Christian, and to bear the sacrament into the ghetto in order to check the crimes which were being perpetrated in the name of Christ. *Furor Populi, furor Dei,* replied the Prince of the Church coldly. Only when the worst was over did he allow himself to be persuaded to go out and address the mob, at some little distance from the actual scene of the outrage. On the other hand, an abbé, named Carlo Bellanti, who had sheltered one of the Jews in his house until the riots were over, was long remembered with gratitude.

The synagogue was meanwhile crowded with fugitives, trusting in the solidity or the sanctity of the building, and praying for the miracle which might save them at the last moment. It did not, however, come about. . The building was broken into by the infuriated mob. Four persons at least were killed here and many more wounded. The floor of the building ran with human blood. At the far end of the building stood the Ark of the Law, austere and mysterious. This attracted the attention of the invaders above all. Assuredly, they thought, this was the sanctuary, in which the Jews kept their treasures. The doors were massive and new: but they could not long withstand a determined assault with axes, the marks of which are still to be seen. The interior, when the doors were at last forced open, appeared somewhat disappointing. There was nothing within but the row of Scrolls of the Law, some of them with their silver bells and ornaments. These soon disappeared (the charity boxes at the entrance had become casualties much earlier). As for the Scrolls themselves, their sanctity was recognized sufficiently for them to be made the object of special insult, intensified, perhaps, by disappointment. The harmless parchments were stripped of their trappings and thrown to the floor. One was pulled open, dragged into the street outside, and rolled about in the mire amid the jeers of the mob.

iii

At this stage (so legend reports) a most curious thing occurred. There happened to be in Sienna at that moment a *Shadar*, an "Emissary of the Merciful" from Palestine, collecting money on behalf of the Four Holy Communities of the Land of Promise. With him there was his daughter— a young girl of unusual beauty, brought up in the fullest traditions of a rabbinical house. When she saw the holy Scroll of the Law, given by God from Sinai, thrown to the ground and insulted, with the probability of even worse to come, she could contain herself no more. Disdaining all personal danger she determined to save the Word of God. All at once the barbaric invaders saw a beautiful and unfamiliar girl, clad in a strange Oriental robe, white and flowing, spring into their midst and gather up the yellow parchment from the ground. They were too much taken aback to move, and she disappeared as suddenly and as mysteriously as she had come. The superstitious mob could offer no explanation of the phenomenon but one: "Assuredly," they said, "It is the Madonna come down from Heaven to save the Bible."

*   *   *   *   *   *   *

Late that evening the Sabbath brought some measure of peace. Guards were stationed at the ghetto gates, and, though it was unsafe for the Jews to stir abroad for another week or ten days, the worst was over. Captain Karl Schneider, commandant of the counter-revolutionary forces in Tuscany and the Romagna, entered the city on June 30th. Besides retaining any of the property robbed from the ghetto which was brought to his headquarters, he imposed an extraordinary levy of 50,000 lire on the community, to be paid within two hours, under the penalty of setting fire to the ghetto. To meet this it was found necessary to sell the few objects of silver which had "miraculously" escaped the sack of a couple of days earlier. This did not, however, save them from another similar imposition a week later, payable within

one hour, and another eight days after. The once pros-
perous community was reduced to petition all of its neighbors for assistance in the maintenace of the widows and
orphans with whom it was now burdened. Only three weeks
after the event, having discovered where the miserable remains of the victims of the massacre had been dragged from
the Piazza and were still lying—the majority in a pit in the
Old Market, others hard by merely covered with a sprinkling
of earth—they obtained permission from the Government to
give them proper burial. On this same day they had to make
a special "honorific" contribution for the equipment of the
new Civic Guard, from which they were excluded. In the
next week provision was made for the repair of the doors
of the Ark. Rightly, they should have been replaced. But
the expense at such a moment would have been too great,
and they contented themselves with the crude repairing
which perpetuated rather than concealed the traces of the
outrage. In perennial recollection of that event the whole
congregation bound itself by solemn vow to celebrate a
general fast each year upon the anniversary of the massacre,
Sivan 25th. This every individual—man, woman, and child—
was to observe. The synagogue, scene of some of the worst
scenes, was to be kept open all night as well as by day, and
a special order of service was laid down for recital.

Human memory, however, is short. It was not long
before the French armies again swept Tuscany; and the
reaction which followed the downfall of Napoleon was mild
by comparison with the former. Events which had occurred
so long before lost their appeal. Their unhappy experience
had so terrified some of the wealthiest and most influential
members of the community that they had thought it prudent
to remove elsewhere, thus accelerating the natural flow to the
larger towns. Thus the community was sadly reduced in
numbers. Those left, however, were beginning to suffer

from nineteenth century apathy. Whatever the reason, no later than 1825 (barely a quarter of a century after the event) the community came to the conclusion that their vow had been "too great for the general observance." With the permission of the rabbi of the neighboring community of Florence (called in as a disinterested party) it was therefore abrogated, upon condition that ten poor men should make the fast and recite the statutory prayers each year in lieu of the whole congregation—naturally in return for some slight monetary consideration.

From that period the decadence of the community of Sienna continued apace. Today the ancient synagogue is opened for service only occasionally, and it is doubtful whether the statutory ten poor Hebrews can be mustered in the whole city. The observance of the Fast of Commemoration has fallen into complete desuetude. Nevertheless, the memory of the events of June 28, 1799, remains vivid among the Jews throughout Tuscany; and among the superstitious populace of Sienna one may still hear how, on the day of the incursion of the Aretines, the Madonna herself came down from Heaven to save the Bible.

23. THE LAST DAY OF THE GHETTO[1]

IN THE semi-darkness, Marco-Mordecai Aboaf watched his elder brother, Leone-Judah, huddle on his clothes and stumble out of the room after perfunctory ablutions. He heard the footsteps clang away up the Ghetto Vecchio in the direction of the Spanish synagogue, the *scuola spagnuola*. For Leone-Judah, in the first flush of adolescent religiosity, belonged to the society of Mourners for Zion, who gathered together, an hour or more before dawn, to recite dirges for the loss of Jerusalem. One day, Marco-Mordecai promised himself, he also would become a member of that pious *Hebra*, and have the privilege of joining in their eerie rites, sitting barefoot on the floor of the synagogue, in complete darkness save for the flickerings of the perpetual lamp. . . . The macabre thought lulled him again to sleep.

He awoke with a start. It was almost broad daylight, now. At the next house, he heard the long drawn-out cry of the beadle summoning the "Watchers for the Morning" to their special service: *"Shomerim laBoker! Shomerim laBoker!"* The footsteps next stopped outside his own house. He heard the beadle's staff beat on the door, once and twice, and waited with bated breath, for it was only when a death had occurred overnight that two knocks were given. The third came, accompanied by a wheezy cough and the hoarse cry. Marco-Mordecai breathed again. His father, in the adjoining room, climbed heavily out of bed. Within a few minutes, the ghetto was filled with the sound of footsteps hurrying synagoguewards, and cries of *Buon Giorno,* with

---

[1] Originally published in the *Jewish Chronicle*, January 1933, and in *Opinion*, October 1933.

comments upon the weather, echoed at increasingly frequent intervals across the narrow street.

Marco-Mordecai stayed in bed a little longer, for a boy of twelve was not expected to put in too early an appearance at service. The sun was already penetrating the rare interstices between the houses, promising a day of blazing July heat, before he reached the baroque *scuola,* which Longhena (in practice for the church of Maria della Salute) had built a century and a half before.

Within the building, there was an air of suppressed excitement. The *cantarino* seemed to be gabbling over the prayers more rapidly than usual. There was a continual undercurrent of conversation. Some even of the most pious interrupted their devotions to exchange words with their neighbors. The climax was reached when Isaac Grego, in the height of fashion from his powdered hair down to his silver shoe-buckles, and actually wearing a sword at his side, bustled into the building with a self-important air and strode up to the rabbi's seat. A whispered conversation took place between the two in front of the Holy Ark itself. Grego bustled out, looking even more self-important than before. The white-haired rabbi, Abraham Jonah, who had been imported from Spalato thirteen years before to administer to the community, took off his *tallith* and his phylacteries with unaccustomed haste.

"After service today," he announced, "there will be no *Limmud.*"

The congregation broke up in unaccustomed confusion. To suspend the daily course of study, regarded as being on an equal footing with the daily course of the prayers, was an almost unprecedented event. Marco-Mordecai was however becoming daily more and more accustomed to such phenomena. In the course of the last few months, a whole succession of them had taken place. Venice had not seemed the same city. The narrow *calli* were filled with soldiers, lounging at every corner and occupying half the seats in the wine-shops. Great ships of war had been anchored in the lagoon, as though prepared to fire at the slightest pretext on the Piazza S. Marco. There had been suspiciously inexhaustible conversations throughout the ghetto, which ceased suddenly as soon as any stranger approached.

Marco had caught talk of the French, and of a French general with an Italian name, Bonaparte (*Helek Tob,* or the Good Portion, his father once called him). One day in March, the silverware had been sent to the Mint from all the seven synagogues, in order to assist in carrying on the war. On the next Saturday, service had seemed very strange, without the perpetual lamp in front of the Ark or the jingling bells which were placed above the Scrolls of the Law. But the sacrifice had been useless. Before long, news had come through that Padua had fallen. The reverberations of the cannon could now be heard across the lagoon. "Tonight we are not safe even in our beds," the Doge was reported to have said. The gossips repeated this pusillanimity from mouth to mouth, with increased forebodings.

Indeed, they had some reason. During the course of the next week, a force of five hundred Slavonian mercenaries were billeted in the ghetto to maintain order. There were a couple of them in the Aboaf household—wild looking fellows with long moustachios and curved sabres, who played dice interminably on the door-step and could not say a sentence without *Per Dio Santo!* as a prefix. Everybody treated them with the utmost deference, and the community provided them with a few casks of the best wine; but all the same, there was a general fear that they would sack the whole place at the first chance. Fortunately, Rabbi Abraham Jonah was well-versed in the Holy Cabala. He had written a number of special amulets, and affixed one on each of the ghetto gates. So long as they remained there, the place was safe; and it was noteworthy that the Slavonians deported themselves from that moment like so many lambs.

Even this had not sufficed to check the terrifying activity of General Bonaparte. The next Saturday but one, when the time for reciting the prayer for the Doge and the Signoria arrived, the *cantarino* had gone over to consult the rabbi, and then had solemnly called down the divine benediction, according to a new formula, upon the Provisional Government of this exalted city. The rule of the Doge had come to an end, after so many centuries of pomp and glory, and Venice was now governed by a Revolutionary Council. A couple of days after, the French troops entered the city. They were to be seen everywhere, lolling luxuriously in the gondolas and ogling the girls. A number of them, Jews, had come to the ghetto, where admiring groups would surround them and listen to their tales of recent exploits and accounts of how freedom had been brought to their co-religionists in a dozen cities of the *terra ferma*. That was happening in Venice, too. Moses Luzzatto, Vita Vivante, and Isaac Grego had been elected members of the new municipality. One day, Marco-Mordecai's father came home bearing a musket, with a tricolor badge in his hat. He had enrolled himself in the new Civic Guard.

The revolutionary spirit penetrated the Ghetto, too. The day before—it was Sunday, July 9th—a fresh election had been held for new Deputies of the Jewish Nation, as they were now to be called, under the auspices of the Committee of Public Safety itself. For the first time, every adult had been allowed to vote, excepting strangers and (of course) paupers. A detachment of French troops had been placed on duty at the Spanish synagogue, to maintain order. Their presence had not indeed been necessary. The proceedings had been orderly, though highly enthusiastic.

At the close, Marco-Mordecai had heard tumultuous cheers for "Fraternity, Democracy, and the Italian Nation."

That night, at supper, his mother had mentioned the *Signor Rabbino*. His father had interrupted her with twinkling eyes.

"There are no *signori* now, my dear," he said. "We are all equal. We must speak of the Citizen Rabbi in the future.."

"In that case, anyone is our equal—the beadle, for example," said Leone-Judah, doubtfully; for he was proud of the position which the family had enjoyed in the community for the past two hundred years, and of their ultimate descent from Grandees of Spain.

"By all means," rejoined his father. "They called him *Cittadino Nonzolo* at the meeting just now."

ii

That had been yesterday. Since then, excitement had been steadily growing. When they came out of synagogue that morning, a semi-festive air reigned in the streets, although it was the eve of the Fast of Tammuz, anniversary of the breach of the walls of Jerusalem and of manifold other disasters in the history of the race. Half the shops were closed, and excited groups were gathered at every corner. There was no activity save in the Ghetto Nuovo, where the three pawnbroking establishments which the Jews were forced to maintain as the price of their toleration in Venice were open, and already surrounded (for times were hard) by eager clients.

After breakfast, Marco ran off to school, picking up one or two of his friends on the way. The red-headed *rubbi* chased them off with unwonted cordiality.

"No teaching today, you rascals," he said. "We all have better things to do."

Marco-Mordecai preferred not to return home, fearing that he might be set to occupy his leisure with private study or household chores. He spent the forenoon with his friends on the Fondamenta della Pescaria, playing a hazardous game of football among the barges and watching the gondolas as they passed backwards and forwards along the Canareggio canal, with their loads of laughing French officers.

Towards noon, there was an unwonted flow of people under the low archway which led back into the ghetto. They followed. Mealtime was approaching, but they were too excited to give it much thought. Marco-Mordecai, as he passed his home, ran in and begged a hunk of bread and onion which he munched as he ran—though with slight misgivings since he had not recited the prescribed grace.

In the Ghetto Nuovo, the only open space which the Jewish quarter could boast, there had been set up a tall pole gaudily decorated. It was the Tree of Liberty, Marco-Mordecai heard someone say. The workmen were putting the finishing touches on it. Around it, there had gathered a vast crowd of Jews and Gentiles, all with tricolor cockades in their hats, talking excitedly together and clapping one another on the back with needless and unaccustomed geniality. Among the crowd there were even several priests, who seemed to be setting the example in fraternization. Marco-Mordecai recognized the curates of the neighboring parishes of SS. Ermagora e Fortunato and of S. Geremia, who in the past had been anything but notorious for friendly feelings towards the Jews. That was all over now. A new era dawned.

The work on the Tree of Liberty was finished. A number of young Jews and Gentiles, linking hands, began to dance around it in a circle. Everybody laughed. An old ragged-bearded Jew disappeared into his house and returned bearing a couple of flasks of wine, which he offered to drink to all and sundry. A burly gondolier seized him in his arms, and kissed him on the cheeks. Marco-Mordecai caught a glimpse of his own father, arm-in-arm with a young priest fresh from the Seminary.

There was distant sound of drums and fifes approaching up the Ghetto Nuovo. The boys made a simultaneous dash to see what was happening. It was a detachment of the newly-enrolled Civic Guard, under the command of Citta-dino Ferrari. They marched, with military precision, to the Ghetto Nuovo, where they formed a hollow square round the Tree of Liberty. The French soldiers in the crowd eyed their movements superciliously.

Suddenly a cry arose from the crowd. *"Le Porte! Le Porte!"* A couple of days before, the Committee of Public Safety had given instructions for the removal of the gates of the Ghetto, which had hitherto been kept sedulously closed from sunset to sunrise, as well as on the major solem-nities of the Christian year, converting the Jewish quarter into something in the nature of a prison. It was today that this order was to be executed, though in the general excite-ment the main reason for the proceedings was almost in danger of being overlooked. There was a general surge of the mob headed by a blacksmith brandishing a hammer, towards the Rio di S. Girolamo, where the nearest of the three entrances was situated. Another detachment rushed down the Ghetto Vecchio, and another to the Ghetto Nuovis-simo. Marco could not get near enough to the front to see what was happening. He could hear, however, above the shouting of the mob, the sickening thud of hammers and axes against the woodwork. Suddenly, there was a crash, followed by a yell of triumph. The crowd surged back, drag-ging the gate behind them, into the middle of the square where, in a delirium of excitement, it was hacked into small fragments. The same was done to the other gates as they were added to the pile. Somebody produced a steel and flint. Before many minutes were passed, the symbols of centuries of degradation were being destroyed in a roaring bonfire.

In the crowd there was an old rabbi wearing, through sheer conservatism, the red hat formerly prescribed for all Jews by law, as their badge of shame. A member of the Civic Guard snatched it from his head, and threw it into the flames.

"We are all equal now," he called, jovially. "Away with these shameful relics of the past!"

His words evoked a general huzza. Another Civic Guard, seeing the look of discomfort on the old man's face, clapped his own hat, with its enormous tricolor cockade, upon his head.

"Take this, Citizen Rabbi," he said. "This is the right headgear for a good republican, in the first year of Italian Liberty."

The guffaw which followed his jest was drowned in a shout of triumph, as the flames suddenly leapt upwards. Somebody began to dance the Carmagnola. Everyone followed his example. Within a few moments, Jews and Christians, men and women, soldiers and civilians, were capering deliriously round the flames.

There was a call for silence. Marco-Mordecai saw Raphael Vivante, a member of one of the most prominent Jewish families and an active member of the Civic Guard, climb painfully on the parapet of one of the three wells from which the inhabitants of the Ghetto Nuovo drew their water. He began to speak impressively, accentuating every phrase with a gesture:

"Brothers! At length, there has arrived that happy day, in which prejudice and superstition have been cast down,

and the insults from which we have unjustly suffered for so
long are avenged!"

A burst of applause followed. The orator resumed:

"The light of philosophy has shone forth from the happy
shores of France to this country, where an arid aristocracy
aggravated our woes and our ignominious chains."

The applause this time merged into a general hum of
conversation which did not completely die away; and the up-
roar of the mob, combined with the crackling of the flames,
prevented Marco-Mordecai from hearing any more of the
speech consecutively. Nothing daunted, the cultured Isaac
Grego, the foremost among the Jewish members of the new
municipality, and who had recently been elected head of the
communal organization, next mounted the improvised plat-
form. Little could be heard of what he had to say, excepting
that the shameful word Ghetto was henceforth to be banished
from the Italian language, and that what had formerly been
the Jewish quarter was henceforth to be known by the auspi-
cious name of *Contrada della Riunione*. He was succeeded
in turn by the Abbate Staddita, a Dalmatian priest, whose
enthusiasm for the Revolutionary cause was notorious. His
speech was listened to with the silent respect due to his cloth;
for no Christian ecclesiastic had ever before honored the
Jews of Venice with a friendly address. He had little to say,
however, excepting to thank the Jewish community for its
generous gift of three hundred ducats to the Christian poor
of the neighboring parishes.

The crowd was by now beginning to thin out. Marco-
Mordecai discovered with a start that the time for evening
service was approaching. His father, he knew, was not likely
to excuse his attendance even on so memorable an occasion;
and, relucantly, he made his way towards the Spanish synagogue. As he approached, he saw a number of non-Jews
filing in, automatically fingering their hats, which they were

unaccustomed to leave on their heads in a place of worship. The building was uncomfortably crowded, but Marco-Mordecai was just able to squeeze in. To his surprise, he found that there was to be no service. Those who had just gone in were the members of the Society for Public Instruction, whose main function was the propagation of republican doctrine; and the object of their attendance was to hear a patriotic harangue from Citizen Massa, who was to celebrate before a mixed audience the dawn of equality between Jew and Gentile.

Twilight was drawing on before the meeting was concluded. The distinguished guests were subsequently entertained to a splendid refection in the Vivante household. Marco-Mordecai's father, as one of the more prominent members of the community, was among the notables invited to meet them. Late into the night, Marco-Mordecai could hear the burst of conviviality which filled the ghetto on all sides: but, tired out with the excitement of the day, he was already asleep before the party broke up.

Thus after an existence of two hundred and eighty-one years and three months almost to the day, the Ghetto of Venice—the prototype and namesake of all those of Italy—came to an end.

THE MONTAIGNE FAMILY TREE

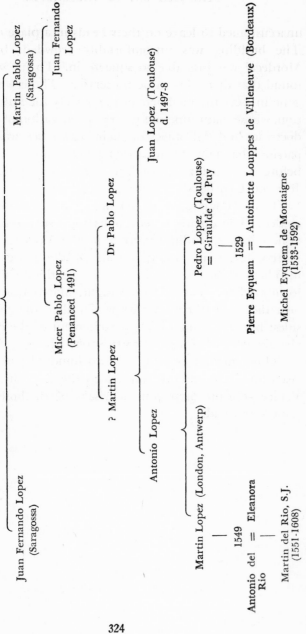

Mayer Paçagon (Calatayud)
Converted as Juan Lopez de Villanueva

Juan Fernando Lopez (Saragossa)

Martin Pablo Lopez (Saragossa)

Juan Fernando Lopez

Micer Pablo Lopez (Penanced 1491)

Dr Pablo Lopez

Juan Lopez (Toulouse) d. 1497-8

? Martin Lopez

Pedro Lopez (Toulouse) = Giraulde de Puy

Antonio Lopez

1529
Pierre Eyquem = Antoinette Louppes de Villeneuve (Bordeaux)

Martin Lopez (London, Antwerp)

Michel Eyquem de Montaigne (1533-1592)

1549
Antonio del = Eleanora
Rio

Martin del Rio, S.J. (1551-1608)